W9-BNJ-401

Making Names

Hands-On Spelling and Phonics Lessons

Patricia M. Cunningham

Carson-Dellosa Publishing Company, Inc.
Greensboro, NC

Credits

Editor
Joey Bland

Layout Design
Jon Nawrocik

Inside Illustrations
Mike Duggins

Cover Design
Matthew VanZomeren

© 2004, Carson-Dellosa Publishing Company, Inc., Greensboro, North Carolina 27425. Four-Blocks and associated logos are registered trademarks of Carson-Dellosa Publishing Co., Inc. The purchase of this material entitles the buyer to reproduce activities for classroom use only—not for commercial resale. Reproduction of these materials for an entire school or district is prohibited. No part of this book may be reproduced (except as noted above), stored in a retrieval system, or transmitted in any form or by any means (mechanically, electronically, recording, etc.) without the prior written consent of Carson-Dellosa Publishing Co., Inc.

Printed in the USA • All rights reserved.   ISBN 0-88724-212-X

Table of Contents

Table of Contents

Making Names • CD-2429 • © Carson-Dellosa

Table of Contents

Since the publication of *Making Words* which Dottie Hall and I wrote in 1994 (Good Apple), teachers and children have enjoyed this hands-on concrete way to learn how to decode and spell words. Children seem to particularly enjoy making those words which are their names and the names of their brothers, sisters, cousins, and friends. *Making Names* was written to capitalize on the delight most children show in names by providing 210 Making Words lessons in which each secret word is a person's name. In addition to the secret word, each lesson contains as many other names as possible so that children's names that don't have enough letters to be secret words are included.

While the *Making Names* lessons are fun, they also teach children important information about phonics and spelling. As children manipulate the letters to make the words, they learn how small changes, such as changing one letter or moving the letters around, result in completely new words. Children learn to stretch out words and listen for the sounds they hear and the order of those sounds. Children also learn that when you change the first letter, you also change the sound you hear at the beginning of the word. Likewise, when you change the last letter, you change the sound you hear at the end of the word. These ideas seem commonplace and obvious to those of us who have been reading and writing for almost as long as we can remember. But, they are a revelation to many beginners—a revelation that gives them tremendous independence in and power over the challenge of decoding and spelling words.

A *Making Names* lesson is an example of a type of instruction called "guided discovery." In order to truly learn and retain strategies, children must discover them. But some children do not seem to make discoveries about words very easily on their own. In a *Making Names* lesson, the teacher guides students toward those discoveries by carefully sequencing the words they will make and giving them explicit guidance about how much change is needed.

Step One: Making Words

Each *Making Names* lesson begins with some short, easy words and builds to longer, more complex words, including a secret word which can be made with all of the letters. As children make the words at their desks, a child who makes a word successfully goes up to the pocket chart or chalk ledge and makes the word with big letters. Children who didn't make the word correctly quickly fix the word to be ready for the next word. The small changes between most words in the lesson encourage even those children who do not make words perfectly to fix them. Children soon realize that spelling the current word correctly increases their chances of spelling the next word correctly. In each lesson, the teacher and students make 9-15 words including a secret word that can be made with all of the letters. When it is time to make the secret word, the teacher gives children one minute to try to come up with the word. After one minute, if no one has discovered the secret word, the teacher gives the children clues that allow them to figure it out. A few lessons have two or more secret words. Children enjoy moving the letters and seeing how the word changes as the positions of the letters change.

Step Two: Sorting the Words into Patterns

Many children discover some patterns just through making the words in the carefully sequenced order, but some children need more explicit guidance. This guidance happens when all of the words have been made and the teacher guides children to sort the words into patterns. Depending on the sophistication of the children and the words available in the lesson, words might be sorted according to their beginning letters or rime (all of the letters up to the vowel). Alternatively, to focus on just one sound/letter combination, teachers may ask children to sort all of the words that begin with **qu**, **br**, or **sh**. Once the words with these letters are sorted, the teacher and children pronounce the words and discover that most words that have the same letters also have the same sounds which is an important discovery for all emerging readers and writers.

Another pattern that children need to discover is that many words have the same root word. If children can pronounce and spell the root word and if they recognize root words with endings, prefixes, or suffixes added, then they are able to decode and spell many additional words. To some children, every new word they meet is a new experience! They fail to recognize how new words are related to already known words and thus are in the difficult—if not impossible—position of starting from "scratch" each time. These children just try to learn and remember every new word. To be fluent, fast, automatic decoders and spellers, children must learn that **play**, **playing**, **played**, **plays**, **player**, and **replay** all have **play** as their roots. Children must also use their knowledge of how to decode and spell **play** to quickly transfer to these related words. Whenever possible, *Making Names* lessons include related words that use the letters available. The teacher tells children that people are related by blood and words are related by meaning. The teacher asks children to find any related words and sort them, then she creates sentences to show how these words are related. For example: A person who **plays** ball is a **player**. We like to **play** soccer. We have been **playing** soccer since we were little. We **played** on Saturdays.

In each lesson, the teacher and students sort the rhyming words. There are several sets of rhyming words in each lesson. Children need to recognize that words that have the same spelling pattern from the vowels to the ends of the words usually rhyme. Unlike Spanish in which one letter has one sound, the sounds of many letters in English are determined by the letters that follow them. The vowel **a**, for example, has what are commonly called long and short sounds in words like **cake** and **can**. It has very different sounds in words such as **saw**, **park**, **all**, **talk**, **laugh**, **usual**, and **mama**. In other words, such as **fear**, **said**, and **coat**, the letter **a** has no sound at all. To add to the confusion, some words, such as **weight**, have the long sound of **a** but no letter **a**! English—and especially the vowels in English—simply cannot be explained based on individual letter sounds. But, if you look at the spelling patterns—the vowels and the letters that follow them—English makes sense. All of the words that end in **a-k-e**, including **make**, **flake**, **snake**, and **shake**, rhyme with **cake**. All of the words that end in **a-l-l**, including **tall**, **small**, and **squall**, rhyme with **all**. When we sort the words into rhyming words and notice that the words that rhyme have the same spelling pattern, children learn rhyming patterns and how to use words they know to decode and spell lots of other words.

Step Three: Transfer to Reading and Writing

All of the working and playing with words is worth nothing if children do not use what they know when they need to use it. Many children know letter sounds and patterns and do not apply these to decode unknown words encountered during reading or spell words they need while writing. All teachers know that it is much easier to teach children phonics than it is to actually get them to use it. This is the reason that each *Making Names* lesson ends with a transfer step. Once words are sorted according to rhyme, the teacher tells children to pretend they are reading and come to a new word. As the teacher says this, she writes a word that has the same spelling pattern and rhymes with one set of rhyming words. The teacher shows this word to a child and asks that child to come up and put the new word with the words it rhymes with. The teacher doesn't allow anyone to say the new word until it is lined up under the other rhyming words. She leads the children to pronounce the rhyming words they made and the new word. Then, the teacher shows them one more word and says to a child:

"Pretend you're reading and come to this new word. Put it with the words that would help you figure it out."

Once students have decoded two new words using the rhyming patterns from the words they made, the teacher helps children transfer their letter-sound knowledge to writing. To do this, the teacher asks children to pretend they are writing and need to spell a word:

"Pretend you're writing and you need to spell the word **stray**. You stretch out **stray** and hear the beginning letters **str**. If you can think of the words we made today that rhyme with **stray**, you will have the correct spelling of the word."

The children decide that **stray** rhymes with the **ay** words they made and that **stray** is spelled **s-t-r-a-y**. The teacher finishes the lesson by having children spell one more word by deciding which of the words they made it rhymes with.

A Sample *Making Names* Lesson

As the person who is teaching the lesson, you are always the best person to decide exactly what to say to your class and how to cue children about the different words. If you have a child in your class named **Ryan**, you will cue students differently than a teacher who does not have a **Ryan**. Your children will relate better to example sentences you come up with that relate to their communities and lives. With the caveat that you can do this much better for your children than I can (since I have never worked with your class), here is a sample lesson you can use to construct your own lesson cues.

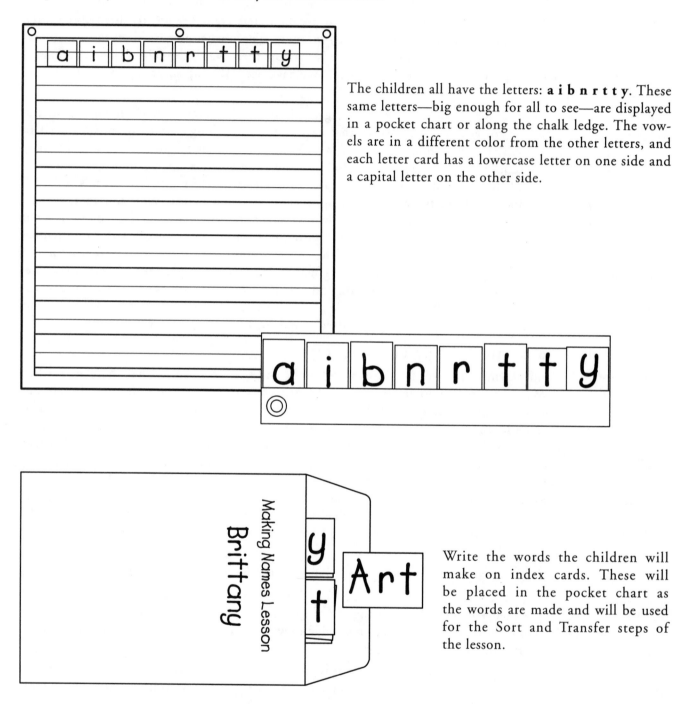

The children all have the letters: **a i b n r t t y**. These same letters—big enough for all to see—are displayed in a pocket chart or along the chalk ledge. The vowels are in a different color from the other letters, and each letter card has a lowercase letter on one side and a capital letter on the other side.

Write the words the children will make on index cards. These will be placed in the pocket chart as the words are made and will be used for the Sort and Transfer steps of the lesson.

Begin the lesson by having each child hold up and name each letter as she holds up the big letters from the pocket chart or chalk ledge.

"Hold up and name each letter as I hold up the big letter. Let's start with your vowels. Show me your **a** and your **i**. Now show me your **b**, **n**, **r**, two **t**'s, and **y**. You all have eight letters. In a few minutes, we will see if anyone can figure out the secret word which uses all eight letters.

Make sure all of your letters cards have their lowercase sides showing to start with. When we are making a name, I will cue you and look to see who remembers to turn the first letter in that name to the capital side. Let's get started making words."

Step One: Making Words

"Use three letters to spell the name **Art**. **Art** is sometimes not a name—like when we go to art. But **Art** is also a name sometimes. Spell **Art** the way you would if you have a friend named **Art**."

(Find a student with **Art** spelled correctly—including the capital letter—and send that child to spell **Art** with the big letters.)

"Good, now let's use three letters again to spell another name, **Ray**."

(Quickly send someone with the correct spelling to the big letters. Keep the pace brisk. Do not wait until everyone has **Ray** spelled with their little letters to send a student to the big letters. It is fine if some children are making **Ray** as **Ray** is being spelled with the big letters.)

"Make sure you have **Ray** spelled correctly. Turn the **R** to its lowercase side and add one letter to spell **tray**. You use a **tray** to carry your lunch."

(Continue sending children to make the words with the big letters. Remind children to use the big letters to check what they have made with their letters, and to fix each word, as needed, before going on to the next word. Move the lesson along at a fast pace.)

"Start over and use four letters to spell the name **Bart**. How many of you watch **Bart** Simpson on TV?"

"Turn the **B** in **Bart** to its lowercase side, change one letter, and you can spell **barn**. We put the horse in the **barn**."

"Change just one letter and you can spell **yarn**. My grandma knits scarves with **yarn**."

"Start over and use four letters to spell the name **Ryan**."

"Start over and use four letters to spell **tiny**. The premature baby was very **tiny**."

"Start over and use four letters to spell **rain**. You only hear three sounds but you need four letters to spell **rain**."

"Add one letter to **rain** and you can spell **train**."

"Change a letter in **train** to spell **brain**."

"Use the same letters you have in **brain**, but put them in a different order to spell the name **Brian**."

"Use five letters to spell the word **rainy**. Yesterday was a **rainy** day."

"Add one letter to rainy and you can spell **brainy**. When someone is very smart, we say he is **brainy**."

"I have just one word left. It is the secret word that you can make with all of your letters. See if you can figure it out."

(Give them one minute to figure out the secret word and then give clues, if needed.)

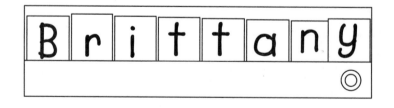

"Our secret word today is a name that begins with **Br** and ends in **y**."

Let someone go to the big letters and spell the secret word **Brittany**.

Let all of the children make the word **Brittany** and talk about anyone named **Brittany** that they know.

Step Two: Sorting the Words into Patterns

Have the children read aloud with you all of the words made in the lesson.

Sort Br Words (Optional)

If some of your children need a review of the **br** sound, have them pull out and sort the words that begin with **br**. Have students pronounce these words by emphasizing the sound of **b** and **r** heard at the beginnings.

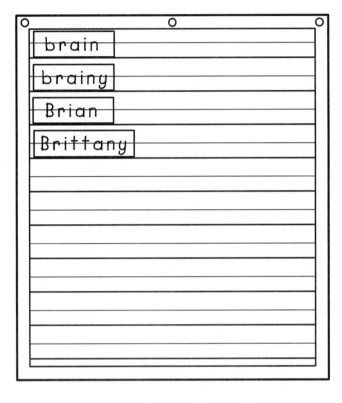

Sort Related Words: rain, rainy; brain, brainy

Remind children that some words are related because they share the same root word. Have children place **rain** and **rainy** in a column. Make up a sentence to show the related meaning.

"When the **rain** lasts all day, we say it is a **rainy** day."

Do the same thing with **brain** and **brainy**.

"Someone who really uses her **brain** is **brainy**."

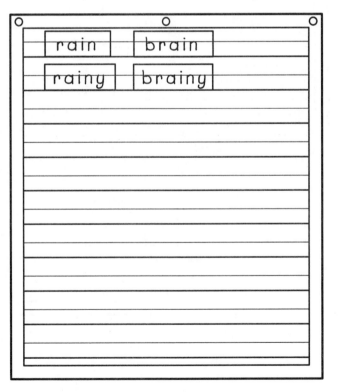

First pocket chart

| rainy | Art | tray |
| brainy | Bart | Ray |

| barn | train |
| yarn | rain |

Sort Rhymes

Send several children to the pocket chart to find rhyming words with the same pattern and place the rhymes in columns.

Second pocket chart

rainy	Art	tray
brainy	Bart	Ray
	chart	spray

barn	train
yarn	rain
	sprain
	chain

Reading Transfer

Tell children to pretend they are reading and come to a new word. Show one child the word **spray** written on an index card. Let that child put **spray** under **tray** and **Ray** and have all of the children pronounce all three words, using the rhyming words they made to decode the new word, **spray**. Do the same thing with **sprain**.

Writing Transfer:

Tell children to pretend they are writing and need to spell a word.

"Let's pretend Joey is writing and he is trying to spell the word **chart**."

Have children tell you that **chart** begins with **ch** and write **ch** on an index card. Then, have children pronounce the sets of rhyming words in the pocket chart and decide that **chart** rhymes with **Art** and **Bart**. Use the **a-r-t** pattern to finish spelling **chart** on the index card.

Do the same thing with **chain**.

When you finish the lesson, the rhyming words you made will be lined up in the pocket chart, along with two new words students helped you read and two new words they helped you spell.

12

Making Names Homework

Because students like to manipulate letters and come up with their own words, we usually give them take-home sheets with the same letters used in the lesson. (See page 239 for a reproducible *Making Names* Take-Home Sheet.) The sheet has spaces for the letters across the top and spaces for writing words at the bottom. Students write corresponding capital letters on the backs, and then cut the letters apart. They manipulate the letters to make words, and then write them in the spaces. This is a popular homework assignment with students and their parents. When you write the letters in the spaces at the top, write them in alphabetical order—vowels, then consonants—so as not to give away the secret word. Before children take the sheets home, have them turn them over and write the capital letters on the backs. Children love being the "smart" ones who "know the secret word," and they love watching parents and other relatives try to figure it out.

Making Names Take-Home Sheet											
a	i	b	n	r	t	t	y				

Making Names Lessons

There are 210 *Making Names* lessons in this book. The lessons use a variety of common names—including some multicultural names. Some of the names are simple, with only five or six letters. The lessons with the secret names **Brent**, **Grant**, **Ethan**, and **Janet** are some of the simplest lessons, and you may want to use these first so that your children experience immediate success with the activity. Other secret names (like **Christopher**, **Hermione**, **Josephine**, and **Francisco**) with more letters are also more complex lessons. You should pick and choose lessons that suit the needs and preferences of your particular class.

I have tried to include as many "short" names as I can in the lessons. These cannot be secret words because they don't yield enough other words, but children enjoy finding their names and the names of their friends and relatives in the lessons. On pages 225-236, you will find an index listing which lessons contain which names. Use this index to pick lessons that include names important to your class. You might also want to review the lessons to see where your students' names with unusual spellings might fit, then add these names to the appropriate lessons.

In choosing the words for each lesson, I have tried to include only words which most primary-aged children would have in their listening/meaning vocabularies, but children vary in their word familiarity. If a word that is totally unknown to your class occurs in one of the lessons, you might want to omit that word from the lesson.

It is fun to plan *Making Names* lessons. You may want to plan lessons for names of children or other important people at your school not included in this book. To do this, simply go to *www.wordplays.com*, click on "Words in a Word," and type in the name you want to use. Instantly, the computer will display all of the words (excluding some proper names) that you could use to plan a customized lesson for your class. Remember that you can use last names as well as first names, if these names are important to your class. I hope that you and the children will enjoy *Making Names* and that the decoding and spelling knowledge they gain will enable them all to be avid and successful readers and writers!

Making Words Lessons

For Making Words lessons by grade level, see *Making Words: Lessons for Home or School—Grade 1*, *Making Words: Lessons for Home or School—Grade 2*, *Making Words: Lessons for Home or School—Grade 3*, and *Making Words: Lessons for Home or School—Grade 4* (Carson-Dellosa, 2001).

Abigail

a a i i b g l

Make Words: Tell children how many letters to use to make each word. (A slash indicates words that can be made with the same letters.)

Emphasize how changing just one letter or rearranging letters makes a different word.

> "Add a letter to **Al** to spell **gal**."

> "Change 1 letter in **big** to spell **bag**."

When children are not just adding or changing one letter, cue them to start over.

> "Start over and use 4 new letters to spell **bail**."

Give a meaning or sentence clue, when needed, to clarify the word children are making.

> "Start over and use 5 new letters to spell **alibi**. The man was questioned about the crime but he was released because he had a good **alibi**."

Always alert children when they are making a name and expect them to use a capital letter.

> "Take 2 letters and spell the name **Al**."

> "Change 1 letter to spell the name **Gail**."

Give children one minute to figure out the secret word and then give clues, if needed.

> "Our secret word is a name that can be made by adding your letters to **Gail**."

Sort Beginning Letters (Optional)

Sort Rhymes

Reading Transfer: "Pretend you are reading and come to a new word." Have children put the transfer words under the appropriate rhymes and use the rhymes to decode them.

Spelling Transfer: "Pretend you are writing and need to spell these words." Have children tell you how the words begin. Then, have children find and use the appropriate rhymes to finish spelling the transfer words.

Step-by-step directions for a sample *Making Names* lesson are on pages 8-12.

MAKE WORDS

Al
gal/lag
lab
big
bag/gab
bail
Gail
alibi
Abigail

SORT WORDS

Beginning Letters (Optional)

Rhymes:

Al	lag	lab	bail
gal	bag	gab	Gail

TRANSFER WORDS

Reading:
flag trail

Spelling:
crab pal

Albert

a e b l r t

MAKE WORDS

Al
at
bat
rat
brat
bear
tear/rate
late
Bert
able
table
later
Albert

SORT WORDS

Beginning Letters (Optional)

Related Words:
late, later

Rhymes:

at	bear	rate	able
bat	tear	late	table
rat			
brat			

TRANSFER WORDS

Reading:
flat cable

Spelling:
clear crate

Make Words: Tell children how many letters to use to make each word. (A slash indicates words that can be made with the same letters.)

Emphasize how changing just one letter or rearranging letters makes a different word.

> "Add a letter to **rat** to spell **brat**."

> "Change 1 letter in **rate** to spell **late**."

When children are not just adding or changing one letter, cue them to start over.

> "Start over and use 5 new letters to spell **later**."

Give a meaning or sentence clue, when needed, to clarify the word children are making.

> "Start over and use 4 new letters to spell **bear**. We saw a black **bear** at the zoo."

> "Change 1 letter to spell **tear**. She tried not to **tear** the paper as she opened the gift."

Always alert children when they are making a name and expect them to use a capital letter.

> "Take 2 letters and spell the name **Al**."

> "Use 4 letters to spell the name **Bert**."

Give children one minute to figure out the secret word and then give clues, if needed.

> "Our secret word is a name that can be made by adding your letters to **Bert**."

Sort Beginning Letters (Optional)

Sort Related Words

Sort Rhymes

Reading Transfer: "Pretend you are reading and come to a new word." Have children put the transfer words under the appropriate rhymes and use the rhymes to decode them.

Spelling Transfer: "Pretend you are writing and need to spell these words." Have children tell you how the words begin. Then, have children find and use the appropriate rhymes to finish spelling the transfer words.

Step-by-step directions for a sample *Making Names* lesson are on pages 8-12.

Alexander

a a e e d l n r x

Make Words: Tell children how many letters to use to make each word. (A slash indicates words that can be made with the same letters.)

Emphasize how changing just one letter or rearranging letters makes a different word.

> "Add a letter to **and** to spell **land**."

> "Use the same letters in **lead** to spell **deal**."

When children are not just adding or changing one letter, cue them to start over.

> "Start over and use 5 new letters to spell **relax**."

Give a meaning or sentence clue, when needed, to clarify the word children are making.

> "Start over and use 7 new letters to spell **relaxed**. After the game, we watched a movie and **relaxed**."

Always alert children when they are making a name and expect them to use a capital letter.

> "Take 6 letters and spell the name **Andrea**."

> "Use 4 letters to spell the name **Alex**."

Give children one minute to figure out the secret word and then give clues, if needed.

> "Our secret word is a name that can be made by adding your letters to **Alex**."

Sort Related Words

Sort Rhymes

Reading Transfer: "Pretend you are reading and come to a new word." Have children put the transfer words under the appropriate rhymes and use the rhymes to decode them.

Spelling Transfer: "Pretend you are writing and need to spell these words." Have children tell you how the words begin. Then, have children find and use the appropriate rhymes to finish spelling the transfer words.

Step-by-step directions for a sample *Making Names* lesson are on pages 8-12.

MAKE WORDS

Ned
Rex
and
land
Alan
Alex
lead/deal
real
relax
Andrea
leader
dealer
relaxed
Alexander

SORT WORDS

Related Words:
lead, leader   deal, dealer
relax, relaxed

Rhymes:
and   deal
land   real

TRANSFER WORDS

Reading:
squeal stand

Spelling:
steal grand

Alexandra

MAKE WORDS

Ed
Ned
Rex
ear
dear
Dean
lean
Dale
Alan
Alex
earn
learn
relax
Andrea
Alexandra

SORT WORDS

Beginning Letters (Optional)

Rhymes:

Ed	ear	Dean	earn
Ned	dear	lean	learn

TRANSFER WORDS

Reading:
clean bled

Spelling:
spear fled

Make Words: Tell children how many letters to use to make each word. (A slash indicates words that can be made with the same letters.)

Emphasize how changing just one letter or rearranging letters makes a different word.

> "Add a letter to **ear** to spell **dear**."

When children are not just adding or changing one letter, cue them to start over.

> "Start over and use 5 new letters to spell **relax**."

Give a meaning or sentence clue, when needed, to clarify the word children are making.

> "Start over and use 4 new letters to spell **earn**. He wants to get a good job and **earn** lots of money."

Always alert children when they are making a name and expect them to use a capital letter.

> "Take 2 letters and spell the name **Ed**."

> "Use 4 letters to spell the name **Alan**."

Give children one minute to figure out the secret word and then give clues, if needed.

> "Our secret word is a name that can be made by adding your letters to **Alex**."

Sort Beginning Letters (Optional)

Sort Rhymes

Reading Transfer: "Pretend you are reading and come to a new word." Have children put the transfer words under the appropriate rhymes and use the rhymes to decode them.

Spelling Transfer: "Pretend you are writing and need to spell these words." Have children tell you how the words begin. Then, have children find and use the appropriate rhymes to finish spelling the transfer words.

Step-by-step directions for a sample *Making Names* lesson are on pages 8-12.

Alfred

Make Words: Tell children how many letters to use to make each word. (A slash indicates words that can be made with the same letters.)

Emphasize how changing just one letter or rearranging letters makes a different word.

"Add a letter to **red** to spell the name **Fred**."

"Use the same letters in **dare** to spell **read**."

When children are not just adding or changing one letter, cue them to start over.

"Start over and use 4 new letters to spell **fear**."

Give a meaning or sentence clue, when needed, to clarify the word children are making.

"Change 1 letter in **fear** to spell **dear**. We sometimes begin our letters with the greeting, **Dear** Jacob (or Sally, or whoever)."

Always alert children when they are making a name and expect them to use a capital letter.

"Take 2 letters and spell the name **Ed**."

"Use the same 4 letters in **deal** to spell the name **Dale**."

Give children one minute to figure out the secret word and then give clues, if needed.

"Our secret word is a name that can be made by adding your letters to **Fred**."

Sort Beginning Letters

Sort Rhymes

Reading Transfer: "Pretend you are reading and come to a new word." Have children put the transfer words under the appropriate rhymes and use the rhymes to decode them.

Spelling Transfer: "Pretend you are writing and need to spell these words." Have children tell you how the words begin. Then, have children find and use the appropriate rhymes to finish spelling the transfer words.

Step-by-step directions for a sample *Making Names* lesson are on pages 8-12.

MAKE WORDS

Al
Ed
red
Fred
fear
dear
deal/Dale
dare/read
real
lead
Alfred

SORT WORDS

Beginning Letters (Optional)

Rhymes:

Ed	fear	deal	read
red	dear	real	lead
Fred			

TRANSFER WORDS

Reading:
spear plead

Spelling:
fled meal

Alisha

a a i h l s

is
as
Al
Hal
Sal
has
his
Lisa/sail
hail
Asia
Alisha

Beginning Letters (Optional)

Rhymes:

Al	is	as	sail
Hal	his	has	hail
Sal			

Reading:
snail trail

Spelling:
pal quail

Make Words: Tell children how many letters to use to make each word. (A slash indicates words that can be made with the same letters.)

Emphasize how changing just one letter or rearranging letters makes a different word.

> "Change a letter in **has** to spell **his**."

> "Use the same letters in **Lisa** to spell **sail**."

When children are not just adding or changing one letter, cue them to start over.

> "Start over and use 3 new letters to spell **has**."

Give a meaning or sentence clue, when needed, to clarify the word children are making.

> "Change 1 letter in **sail** to spell **hail**. We had a big storm and the pieces of **hail** were as big as baseballs!"

Always alert children when they are making a name and expect them to use a capital letter.

> "Take 2 letters and spell the name **Al**."

> "Use 4 letters to spell the name **Lisa**."

Give children one minute to figure out the secret word and then give clues, if needed.

> "Our secret word is a name that can be made by adding your letters to **Al**."

Sort Beginning Letters (Optional)

Sort Rhymes

Reading Transfer: "Pretend you are reading and come to a new word." Have children put the transfer words under the appropriate rhymes and use the rhymes to decode them.

Spelling Transfer: "Pretend you are writing and need to spell these words." Have children tell you how the words begin. Then, have children find and use the appropriate rhymes to finish spelling the transfer words.

Step-by-step directions for a sample *Making Names* lesson are on pages 8-12.

Alison

a i o l n s

Make Words: Tell children how many letters to use to make each word. (A slash indicates words that can be made with the same letters.)

Emphasize how changing just one letter or rearranging letters makes a different word.

> "Add a letter to **nail** to spell **snail**."

> "Use the same letters in **Lisa** to spell **sail**."

When children are not just adding or changing one letter, cue them to start over.

> "Start over and use 5 new letters to spell **lions**."

Give a meaning or sentence clue, when needed, to clarify the word children are making.

> "Use the same letters in **soil** to spell **silo**. The grain was stored in a **silo**."

Always alert children when they are making a name and expect them to use a capital letter.

> "Use 4 new letters to spell the name **Lisa**."

Give children one minute to figure out the secret word and then give clues, if needed.

> "Our secret word is a name that begins with **A** and ends with **n**."

Sort Rhymes

Reading Transfer: "Pretend you are reading and come to a new word." Have children put the transfer words under the appropriate rhymes and use the rhymes to decode them.

Spelling Transfer: "Pretend you are writing and need to spell these words." Have children tell you how the words begin. Then, have children find and use the appropriate rhymes to finish spelling the transfer words.

Step-by-step directions for a sample *Making Names* lesson are on pages 8-12.

MAKE WORDS

Al
Sal
Ali/ail
oil
soil/silo
Lisa/sail
nail
snail
lions
Alison

SORT WORDS

Rhymes:

Al	ail	oil
Sal	sail	soil
	nail	
	snail	

TRANSFER WORDS

Reading:
spoil frail

Spelling:
broil pal

Andrew

MAKE WORDS

an
ran
raw/war
new
dew
Drew
draw
Dean
warn
Ward
warned/wander/warden/Andrew

SORT WORDS

W Words (Optional)

Related Words:
warn, warned

Rhymes:
an   new
ran   Drew
         dew

TRANSFER WORDS

Reading:
flew plan

Spelling:
span grew

Make Words: Tell children how many letters to use to make each word. (A slash indicates words that can be made with the same letters.)

Emphasize how changing just one letter or rearranging letters makes a different word.

"Change a letter in **Drew** to spell **draw**."

"Use the same letters in **raw** to spell **war**."

When children are not just adding or changing one letter, cue them to start over.

"Start over and use 4 new letters to spell the name **Dean**."

Give a meaning or sentence clue, when needed, to clarify the word children are making.

"Use 4 new letters to spell **warn**. The siren sounded to **warn** people of the approaching tornado."

Always alert children when they are making a name and expect them to use a capital letter.

"Take 4 new letters and spell the name **Dean**."

This lesson has 4 secret words! Give children one minute to figure out each secret word and then give clues, if needed.

"One secret word is **warn** with an ending added to it."

"Another secret word means when you go off on your own. It begins with **w** and ends with **r**."

"The next secret word is what we call the person who is in charge of a jail or prison. This words begins with **w** and ends with **n**."

"One more secret word can be made with all of these letters. It is a name that can be made by adding your letters to **Drew**."

Sort W Words (Optional)

Sort Related Words

Sort Rhymes

Reading Transfer: "Pretend you are reading and come to a new word." Have children put the transfer words under the appropriate rhymes and use the rhymes to decode them.

Spelling Transfer: "Pretend you are writing and need to spell these words." Have children tell you how the words begin. Then, have children find and use the appropriate rhymes to finish spelling the transfer words.

Step-by-step directions for a sample *Making Names* lesson are on pages 8-12.

Angelina

a a e i g l n n

Make Words: Tell children how many letters to use to make each word. (A slash indicates words that can be made with the same letters.)

Emphasize how changing just one letter or rearranging letters makes a different word.

> "Change a letter in **nine** to spell **line**."

> "Add a letter to **Al** to spell **gal**."

When children are not just adding or changing one letter, cue them to start over.

> "Start over and use 4 new letters to spell the name **Gina**."

Give a meaning or sentence clue, when needed, to clarify the word children are making.

> "Use 5 letters to spell **alien**. The movie was about an **alien** from outer space."

Always alert children when they are making a name and expect them to use a capital letter.

> "Take 5 letters and spell the name **Angel**."

> "Add 1 letter to **Angel** to spell the name **Angela**."

Give children one minute to figure out the secret word and then give clues, if needed.

> "Our secret word is a name that you can make by adding your letters to **Angel**."

Sort Rhymes

Reading Transfer: "Pretend you are reading and come to a new word." Have children put the transfer words under the appropriate rhymes and use the rhymes to decode them.

Spelling Transfer: "Pretend you are writing and need to spell these words." Have children tell you how the words begin. Then, have children find and use the appropriate rhymes to finish spelling the transfer words.

Step-by-step directions for a sample *Making Names* lesson are on pages 8-12.

MAKE WORDS

Al
gal
Ann
Anna
Gina
Nina
nine
line
alien
Angie
Angel
Angela
Angelina

SORT WORDS

Rhymes:

Al	nine	Gina
gal	line	Nina

TRANSFER WORDS

Reading:
pal spine

Spelling:
gal shrine

Anthony

MAKE WORDS

Ann
ant/Nat
not
hot
hat
any
toy
Tony
Noah
annoy
Anthony

SORT WORDS

Beginning Letters (Optional)

Rhymes:
not   Nat
hot   hat

TRANSFER WORDS

Reading:
slot flat

Spelling:
plot chat

Make Words: Tell children how many letters to use to make each word. (A slash indicates words that can be made with the same letters.)

Emphasize how changing just one letter or rearranging letters makes a different word.

> "Add a letter to **toy** to spell the name **Tony**."

> "Use the same letters in **tan** to spell **ant**."

When children are not just adding or changing one letter, cue them to start over.

> "Start over and use 5 new letters to spell **annoy**."

Give a meaning or sentence clue, when needed, to clarify the word they are making.

> "Start over and use 5 new letters to spell **annoy**. Sometimes my little brother can **annoy** me."

Always alert children when they are making a name and expect them to use a capital letter.

> "Take 3 letters and spell the name **Ann**."

Give children one minute to figure out the secret word and then give clues, if needed.

> "Our secret word is a name that begins with **A** and ends with **y**."

Sort Beginning Letters (Optional)

Sort Rhymes

Reading Transfer: "Pretend you are reading and come to a new word." Have children put the transfer words under the appropriate rhymes and use the rhymes to decode them.

Spelling Transfer: "Pretend you are writing and need to spell these words." Have children tell you how the words begin. Then, have children find and use the appropriate rhymes to finish spelling the transfer words.

Step-by-step directions for a sample *Making Names* lesson are on pages 8-12.

Ashley

a e h l s y

Make Words: Tell children how many letters to use to make each word. (A slash indicates words that can be made with the same letters.)

Emphasize how changing just one letter or rearranging letters makes a different word.

> "Change a letter in **say** to spell **sly**."

> "Use the same letters in **heal** to spell the name **Leah**."

When children are not just adding or changing one letter, cue them to start over.

> "Start over and use 4 new letters to spell **easy**."

Give a meaning or sentence clue, when needed, to clarify the word children are making.

> "Change a letter in **say** to spell **sly**. The magician was a **sly** and clever man."

Always alert children when they are making a name and expect them to use a capital letter.

> "Take 2 letters and spell the name **Al**."

Give children one minute to figure out the secret word and then give clues, if needed.

> "Our secret word is a name that can be made by adding your letters to **ash**."

Sort Sh Words (Optional)

Sort Rhymes

Reading Transfer: "Pretend you are reading and come to a new word." Have children put the transfer words under the appropriate rhymes and use the rhymes to decode them.

Spelling Transfer: "Pretend you are writing and need to spell these words." Have children tell you how the words begin. Then, have children find and use the appropriate rhymes to finish spelling the transfer words.

Step-by-step directions for a sample *Making Names* lesson are on pages 8-12.

MAKE WORDS

Al
Sal
Hal
ash/has
hay
say
sly
shy
yes
easy
heal/Leah
leash
Ashley

SORT WORDS

Sh Words (Optional):
ash, shy, leash, Ashley

Rhymes:

hay	sly	Al
say	shy	Hal
		Sal

TRANSFER WORDS

Reading:
sky stray

Spelling:
spray spy

Ashton

a o h n s t

MAKE WORDS

at
an
as
has/ash
ant/tan
sat
hat
not
hot
shot
Noah
than
Ashton

SORT WORDS

Sh Words (Optional):
ash, shot, Ashton

Rhymes:

as	an	at	hot
has	tan	hat	not
	than		shot

TRANSFER WORDS

Reading:
van flat

Spelling:
spot clot

Make Words: Tell children how many letters to use to make each word. (A slash indicates words that can be made with the same letters.)

Emphasize how changing just one letter or rearranging letters makes a different word.

> "Add a letter to **hot** to spell **shot**."

> "Use the same letters in **has** to spell **ash**."

When children are not just adding or changing one letter, cue them to start over.

> "Start over and use 4 new letters to spell **than**."

Give a meaning or sentence clue, when needed, to clarify the word children are making.

> "Use the same letters in **has** to spell **ash**. **Ash** is what is left when something burns."

Always alert children when they are making a name and expect them to use a capital letter.

> "Use 4 new letters to spell the name **Noah**."

Give children one minute to figure out the secret word and then give clues, if needed.

> "Our secret word is a name that can be made by adding your letters to **ash**."

Sort Sh Words (Optional)

Sort Rhymes

Reading Transfer: "Pretend you are reading and come to a new word." Have children put the transfer words under the appropriate rhymes and use the rhymes to decode them.

Spelling Transfer: "Pretend you are writing and need to spell these words." Have children tell you how the words begin. Then, have children find and use the appropriate rhymes to finish spelling the transfer words.

Step-by-step directions for a sample *Making Names* lesson are on pages 8-12.

Austin

Make Words: Tell children how many letters to use to make each word. (A slash indicates words that can be made with the same letters.)

Emphasize how changing just one letter or rearranging letters makes a different word.

"Add a letter to **ant** to spell **aunt**."

"Use the same letters in **aunt** to spell **tuna**."

When children are not just adding or changing one letter, cue them to start over.

"Start over and use 4 new letters to spell the name **Tina**."

Give a meaning or sentence clue, when needed, to clarify the word children are making.

"Start over and use 4 new letters to spell **suit**. The man wore a dark blue **suit**."

Always alert children when they are making a name and expect them to use a capital letter.

"Take 4 letters and spell the name **Stan**."

Give children one minute to figure out the secret word and then give clues, if needed.

"Our secret word is a name that can be made by adding your letters to **tin**."

Sort Beginning Letters (Optional)

Sort Rhymes

Reading Transfer: "Pretend you are reading and come to a new word." Have children put the transfer words under the appropriate rhymes and use the rhymes to decode them.

Spelling Transfer: "Pretend you are writing and need to spell these words." Have children tell you how the words begin. Then, have children find and use the appropriate rhymes to finish spelling the transfer words.

Step-by-step directions for a sample *Making Names* lesson are on pages 8-12.

MAKE WORDS

an
in
it
at
sat
sit
tin
tan/ant
aunt/tuna
suit
Stan
Tina
Austin

SORT WORDS

Beginning Letters (Optional)

Rhymes:

an	in	it	at
tan	tin	sit	sat
Stan			

TRANSFER WORDS

Reading:
clan spit

Spelling:
twin flat

Barney

MAKE WORDS

ear
Ray
bay
ban
ran
bran/barn
yarn
year
near/earn
yearn
Barney

SORT WORDS

Beginning Letters (Optional)

Rhymes:

Ray	ban	barn	year	earn
bay	ran	yarn	near	yearn
		bran		

TRANSFER WORDS

Reading:
van flat

Spelling:
stray clan

Make Words: Tell children how many letters to use to make each word. (A slash indicates words that can be made with the same letters.)

Emphasize how changing just one letter or rearranging letters makes a different word.

"Add a letter to **ran** to spell **bran**."

"Use the same letters in **bran** to spell **barn**."

When children are not just adding or changing one letter, cue them to start over.

"Start over and use 3 new letters to spell the name **Ray**."

Give a meaning or sentence clue, when needed, to clarify the word children are making.

"Add 1 letter to **earn** to spell **yearn**. When you are away for a long time, you **yearn** to go home."

Always alert children when they are making a name and expect them to use a capital letter.

"Take 3 letters and spell the name **Ray**."

Give children one minute to figure out the secret word and then give clues, if needed.

"Our secret word is a name that begins with **B** and ends with **y**."

Sort Beginning Letters (Optional)

Sort Rhymes

Reading Transfer: "Pretend you are reading and come to a new word." Have children put the transfer words under the appropriate rhymes and use the rhymes to decode them.

Spelling Transfer: "Pretend you are writing and need to spell these words." Have children tell you how the words begin. Then, have children find and use the appropriate rhymes to finish spelling the transfer words.

Step-by-step directions for a sample *Making Names* lesson are on pages 8-12.

Belinda

a e i b d l n

Make Words: Tell children how many letters to use to make each word. (A slash indicates words that can be made with the same letters.)

Emphasize how changing just one letter or rearranging letters makes a different word.

> "Add a letter to **Len** to spell **lend**."

> "Use the same letters in **line** to spell the name **Neil**."

When children are not just adding or changing one letter, cue them to start over.

> "Start over and use 5 new letters to spell the name **Diane**."

Give a meaning or sentence clue, when needed, to clarify the word children are making.

> "Use 4 letters to spell **bind**. We will **bind** the books we publish."

Always alert children when they are making a name and expect them to use a capital letter.

> "Take 3 letters and spell the name **Abe**."

Give children one minute to figure out the secret word and then give clues, if needed.

> "Our secret word is a name that can be made by adding your letters to **Linda**."

Sort Rhymes

Reading Transfer: "Pretend you are reading and come to a new word." Have children put the transfer words under the appropriate rhymes and use the rhymes to decode them.

Spelling Transfer: "Pretend you are writing and need to spell these words." Have children tell you how the words begin. Then, have children find and use the appropriate rhymes to finish spelling the transfer words.

Step-by-step directions for a sample *Making Names* lesson are on pages 8-12.

MAKE WORDS

Abe/Bea
Ben
Len
lend
bend
dine
line/Neil
Edna
bind
blind
Diane
Linda
Belinda

SORT WORDS

Rhymes:

Ben	lend	dine	bind
Len	bend	line	blind

TRANSFER WORDS

Reading:
kind blend

Spelling:
spend twine

Benjamin

MAKE WORDS

Ian
man
Jan
Jen
men
Ben
bean
Jean/Jane
mane/mean/name
Benji
Benjamin

SORT WORDS

Beginning Letters (Optional)

Rhymes:

Jan	Jen	bean	mane
man	men	Jean	Jane
	Ben	mean	

TRANSFER WORDS

Reading:
clean crane

Spelling:
plane plan

Make Words: Tell children how many letters to use to make each word. (A slash indicates words that can be made with the same letters.)

Emphasize how changing just one letter or rearranging letters makes a different word.

> "Add a letter to **Ben** to spell **bean**."

> "Use the same letters in **mane** to spell **mean**."

When children are not just adding or changing one letter, cue them to start over.

> "Start over and use 5 new letters to spell the name **Benji**."

Give a meaning or sentence clue, when needed, to clarify the word children are making.

> "Change 1 letter in **Jane** to spell **mane**. The hair on a horse's head and neck is called a **mane**."

Always alert children when they are making a name and expect them to use a capital letter.

> "Take 3 letters and spell the name **Jan**."

> "Use the same letters in the name **Jean** to spell the name **Jane**."

Give children one minute to figure out the secret word and then give clues, if needed.

> "Our secret word is a name that can be made by adding your letters to **Ben**."

Sort Beginning Letters (Optional)

Sort Rhymes

Reading Transfer: "Pretend you are reading and come to a new word." Have children put the transfer words under the appropriate rhymes and use the rhymes to decode them.

Spelling Transfer: "Pretend you are writing and need to spell these words." Have children tell you how the words begin. Then, have children find and use the appropriate rhymes to finish spelling the transfer words.

Step-by-step directions for a sample *Making Names* lesson are on pages 8-12.

Bernard

a e b d n r r

Make Words: Tell children how many letters to use to make each word. (A slash indicates words that can be made with the same letters.)

Emphasize how changing just one letter or rearranging letters makes a different word.

> "Change a letter in **Ned** to spell **bed**."

> "Use the same letters in **dear** to spell **dare**."

When children are not just adding or changing one letter, cue them to start over.

> "Start over and use 4 new letters to spell **dear**."

Give a meaning or sentence clue, when needed, to clarify the word children are making.

> "Start over and use 6 new letters to spell **errand**. Sometimes we have to stop and do an **errand** on the way home from school."

Always alert children when they are making a name and expect them to use a capital letter.

> "Take 2 letters and spell the name **Ed**."

> "Use 6 letters to spell the name **Brenda**."

Give children one minute to figure out the secret word and then give clues, if needed.

> "Our secret word is a name that begins with **B** and ends with **d**."

Sort Rhymes

Reading Transfer: "Pretend you are reading and come to a new word." Have children put the transfer words under the appropriate rhymes and use the rhymes to decode them.

Spelling Transfer: "Pretend you are writing and need to spell these words." Have children tell you how the words begin. Then, have children find and use the appropriate rhymes to finish spelling the transfer words.

Step-by-step directions for a sample *Making Names* lesson are on pages 8-12.

MAKE WORDS

Ed
red
Ned
bed
Bea/Abe
bad
Brad
dear/dare
rare/rear
errand
Brenda
Bernard

SORT WORDS

Rhymes:

Ed	bad	dare	dear
Ned	Brad	rare	rear
red			
bed			

TRANSFER WORDS

Reading:
fear fled

Spelling:
spear spare

Bertha

a e b h r t

MAKE WORDS

Art
Abe/Bea
bet
beat
heat/hate
rate
Beth
bath
Bart
Bert
breath/Bertha

SORT WORDS

Beginning Letters (Optional)

Rhymes:
Art   heat   hate
Bart   beat   rate

TRANSFER WORDS

Reading:
start state

Spelling:
plate pleat

Make Words: Tell children how many letters to use to make each word. (A slash indicates words that can be made with the same letters.)

Emphasize how changing just one letter or rearranging letters makes a different word.

> "Use the same letters in **heat** to spell **hate**."

> "Change a letter in **hate** to spell **rate**."

When children are not just adding or changing one letter, cue them to start over.

> "Start over and use 4 new letters to spell the name **Beth**."

Give a meaning or sentence clue, when needed, to clarify the word children are making.

> "Change a letter in **hate** to spell **rate**. We refinanced our house because we got a lower interest **rate**."

Always alert children when they are making a name and expect them to use a capital letter.

> "Take 3 letters and spell the name **Art**."

> "Use 4 letters to spell the name **Beth**."

This lesson has two secret words. Give children one minute to figure out each secret word and then give clues, if needed.

> "Today, there are two secret words. One secret word begins with **br** and ends with **th**."

> "The other secret word is a name that begins with **B** and ends with **a**."

Sort Beginning Letters (Optional)

Sort Rhymes

Reading Transfer: "Pretend you are reading and come to a new word." Have children put the transfer words under the appropriate rhymes and use the rhymes to decode them.

Spelling Transfer: "Pretend you are writing and need to spell these words." Have children tell you how the words begin. Then, have children find and use the appropriate rhymes to finish spelling the transfer words.

Step-by-step directions for a sample *Making Names* lesson are on pages 8-12.

B e t h a n y

a e b h n t y

Make Words: Tell children how many letters to use to make each word. (A slash indicates words that can be made with the same letters.)

Emphasize how changing just one letter or rearranging letters makes a different word.

> "Add a letter to **bat** to spell **bath**."

> "Change a letter in **bath** to spell the name **Beth**."

When children are not just adding or changing one letter, cue them to start over.

> "Start over and use 5 new letters to spell **hyena**."

Give a meaning or sentence clue, when needed, to clarify the word children are making.

> "Start over and use 5 new letters to spell **hyena**. A **hyena** is an animal in the cat family."

Always alert children when they are making a name and expect them to use a capital letter.

> "Change a letter in **bath** to spell the name **Beth**."

Give children one minute to figure out the secret word and then give clues, if needed.

> "Our secret word is a name that can be made by adding your letters to **Beth**."

Sort Beginning Letters (Optional)

Sort Rhymes

Reading Transfer: "Pretend you are reading and come to a new word." Have children put the transfer words under the appropriate rhymes and use the rhymes to decode them.

Spelling Transfer: "Pretend you are writing and need to spell these words." Have children tell you how the words begin. Then, have children find and use the appropriate rhymes to finish spelling the transfer words.

Step-by-step directions for a sample *Making Names* lesson are on pages 8-12.

MAKE WORDS

Abe/Bea
ten
hen
yet
bet
bat
bath
Beth
bean
beat
neat
heat
hyena
Bethany

SORT WORDS

Beginning Letters (Optional)

Rhymes:

ten	yet	beat
hen	bet	heat
		neat

TRANSFER WORDS

Reading:
cheat then

Spelling:
vet treat

Blanche

MAKE WORDS

can
ban
Ben
Bea
bean
lean/Lane
cane
each
able
cable
clean
beach
bleach
Blanche

SORT WORDS

Beginning Letters (Optional)

Rhymes:

can	bean	Lane	able	beach
ban	lean	cane	cable	bleach
	clean			each

TRANSFER WORDS

Reading:
table peach

Spelling:
sable mean

Make Words: Tell children how many letters to use to make each word. (A slash indicates words that can be made with the same letters.)

Emphasize how changing just one letter or rearranging letters makes a different word.

"Add a letter to **able** to spell **cable**."

"Change a letter in **Lane** to spell **cane**."

When children are not just adding or changing one letter, cue them to start over.

"Start over and use 5 new letters to spell **beach**."

Give a meaning or sentence clue, when needed, to clarify the word children are making.

"Start over and use 6 new letters to spell **bleach**. I put **bleach** in the wash to get things clean and white."

Always alert children when they are making a name and expect them to use a capital letter.

"Change 1 letter in **ban** to spell the name **Ben**."

Give children one minute to figure out the secret word and then give clues, if needed.

"Our secret word is a name that begins with **Bl** and ends with **e**."

Sort Beginning Letters (Optional)

Sort Rhymes

Reading Transfer: "Pretend you are reading and come to a new word." Have children put the transfer words under the appropriate rhymes and use the rhymes to decode them.

Spelling Transfer: "Pretend you are writing and need to spell these words." Have children tell you how the words begin. Then, have children find and use the appropriate rhymes to finish spelling the transfer words.

Step-by-step directions for a sample *Making Names* lesson are on pages 8-12.

Bradley

a e b d l r y

Make Words: Tell children how many letters to use to make each word. (A slash indicates words that can be made with the same letters.)

Emphasize how changing just one letter or rearranging letters makes a different word.

> "Add a letter to **Brad** to spell **bread**."

> "Change 1 letter in **relay** to spell **delay**."

When children are not just adding or changing one letter, cue them to start over.

> "Start over and use 5 new letters to spell **badly**."

Give a meaning or sentence clue, when needed, to clarify the word children are making.

> "Use the same letters in **early** to spell **relay**. Our team won the **relay** race."

Always alert children when they are making a name and expect them to use a capital letter.

> "Change 1 letter in **day** and spell the name **Ray**."

> "Add a letter to **bad** to spell the name **Brad**."

Give children one minute to figure out the secret word and then give clues, if needed.

> "Our secret word is a name that can be made by adding your letters to **Brad**."

Sort Br Words (Optional)

Sort Related Words

Sort Rhymes

Reading Transfer: "Pretend you are reading and come to a new word." Have children put the transfer words under the appropriate rhymes and use the rhymes to decode them.

Spelling Transfer: "Pretend you are writing and need to spell these words." Have children tell you how the words begin. Then, have children find and use the appropriate rhymes to finish spelling the transfer words.

Step-by-step directions for a sample *Making Names* lesson are on pages 8-12.

MAKE WORDS

Bea/Abe
ear
day
Ray
bay
bad
Brad
bread
ready
badly
early/relay
delay
Bradley

SORT WORDS

Br Words (Optional):
Brad, bread, Bradley

Related Words:
bad, badly

Rhymes:
Ray   bad
relay   Brad
bay
delay
day

TRANSFER WORDS

Reading:
tray   pad

Spelling:
pray   stray

Brandon

a o b d n n r

MAKE WORDS

an
on
Don/nod
bad
Rob
Rod
and
band
Brad
brand
Donna
Brandon

SORT WORDS

Br Words (Optional):
Brad, brand, Brandon

Rhymes:
on	nod	and	bad
Don	Rod	band	Brad
		brand	

TRANSFER WORDS

Reading:
con prod

Spelling:
grand grad

Make Words: Tell children how many letters to use to make each word. (A slash indicates words that can be made with the same letters.)

Emphasize how changing just one letter or rearranging letters makes a different word.

"Add a letter to **Brad** to spell **brand**."

"Change 1 letter in **Rob** to spell the name **Rod**."

When children are not just adding or changing one letter, cue them to start over.

"Start over and use 5 new letters to spell the name **Donna**."

Give a meaning or sentence clue, when needed, to clarify the word children are making.

"Use the same letters in **Don** to spell **nod**. I can **nod** my head."

Always alert children when they are making a name and expect them to use a capital letter.

"Take 3 new letters and spell the name **Rob**."

"Use 4 letters to spell the name **Brad**."

Give children one minute to figure out the secret word and then give clues, if needed.

"Our secret word is a name that can be made by adding your letters to **Don**."

Sort Br Words (Optional)

Sort Rhymes

Reading Transfer: "Pretend you are reading and come to a new word." Have children put the transfer words under the appropriate rhymes and use the rhymes to decode them.

Spelling Transfer: "Pretend you are writing and need to spell these words." Have children tell you how the words begin. Then, have children find and use the appropriate rhymes to finish spelling the transfer words.

Step-by-step directions for a sample *Making Names* lesson are on pages 8-12.

Brandy

a b d n r y

Make Words: Tell children how many letters to use to make each word. (A slash indicates words that can be made with the same letters.)

Emphasize how changing just one letter or rearranging letters makes a different word.

> "Add a letter to **Andy** to spell the name **Randy**."

> "Use the same letters in **bran** to spell **barn**."

When children are not just adding or changing one letter, cue them to start over.

> "Start over and use 4 new letters to spell the name **Brad**."

Give a meaning or sentence clue, when needed, to clarify the word children are making.

> "Start over and use 5 new letters to spell **brand**. What **brand** of toothpaste do you use?"

Always alert children when they are making a name and expect them to use a capital letter.

> "Take 4 letters and spell the name **Andy**."

Give children one minute to figure out the secret word and then give clues, if needed.

> "Our secret word is a name that can be made by adding your letters to **brand**."

Sort Br Words (Optional)

Sort Rhymes

Reading Transfer: "Pretend you are reading and come to a new word." Have children put the transfer words under the appropriate rhymes and use the rhymes to decode them.

Spelling Transfer: "Pretend you are writing and need to spell these words." Have children tell you how the words begin. Then, have children find and use the appropriate rhymes to finish spelling the transfer words.

Step-by-step directions for a sample *Making Names* lesson are on pages 8-12.

MAKE WORDS

and/Dan
ban
bad
Ray
ran
bran/barn
yarn
Brad
band
Andy
Randy
brand
Brandy

SORT WORDS

Br Words (Optional):
bran, Brad, brand, Brandy

Rhymes:

Dan	barn	and	bad	Andy
ban	yarn	band	Brad	Randy
ran		brand		Brandy

TRANSFER WORDS

Reading:
candy Chad

Spelling:
sandy handy

Brenda

a e b d n r

MAKE WORDS

an
Dan
den/Ned
Ben
bad
band
bear
bean
Dean
Brad
bread/beard
brand
Brenda

SORT WORDS

Br Words (Optional):
Brad, bread, brand, Brenda

Rhymes:
an	bean	bad	den
Dan	Dean	Brad	Ben

TRANSFER WORDS

Reading:
glad tan

Spelling:
when mean

Make Words: Tell children how many letters to use to make each word. (A slash indicates words that can be made with the same letters.)

Emphasize how changing just one letter or rearranging letters makes a different word.

> "Change a letter in **Dan** to spell **den**."

> "Use the same letters in **bread** to spell **beard**."

When children are not just adding or changing one letter, cue them to start over.

> "Start over and use 5 new letters to spell **brand**."

Give a meaning or sentence clue, when needed, to clarify the word children are making.

> "Start over and use 4 new letters to spell **bear**. The mother **bear** has two cubs."

Always alert children when they are making a name and expect them to use a capital letter.

> "Add a letter to **an** to spell the name **Dan**."

> "Change 1 letter in **bean** to spell the name **Dean**."

Give children one minute to figure out the secret word and then give clues, if needed.

> "Our secret word is a name that begins with **Br** and ends with **a**."

Sort Br Words (Optional)

Sort Rhymes

Reading Transfer: "Pretend you are reading and come to a new word." Have children put the transfer words under the appropriate rhymes and use the rhymes to decode them.

Spelling Transfer: "Pretend you are writing and need to spell these words." Have children tell you how the words begin. Then, have children find and use the appropriate rhymes to finish spelling the transfer words.

Step-by-step directions for a sample *Making Names* lesson are on pages 8-12.

Brent

Make Words: Tell children how many letters to use to make each word. (A slash indicates words that can be made with the same letters.)

Emphasize how changing just one letter or rearranging letters makes a different word.

> "Add a letter to **be** to spell the name **Ben**."

> "Use the same letters in **ten** to spell **net**."

Give a meaning or sentence clue, when needed, to clarify the word children are making.

> "Change 1 letter to spell **bent**. The bicycle wheel was **bent**."

Always alert children when they are making a name and expect them to use a capital letter.

> "Add a letter to **be** to spell the name **Ben**."

> "Add 1 letter to **bet** to spell the name **Bert**."

Give children one minute to figure out the secret word and then give clues, if needed.

> "Our secret word is a name that begins with **Br** and ends with **t**."

Sort Beginning Letters (Optional)

Sort Rhymes

Reading Transfer: "Pretend you are reading and come to a new word." Have children put the transfer words under the appropriate rhymes and use the rhymes to decode them.

Spelling Transfer: "Pretend you are writing and need to spell these words." Have children tell you how the words begin. Then, have children find and use the appropriate rhymes to finish spelling the transfer words.

Step-by-step directions for a sample *Making Names* lesson are on pages 8-12.

MAKE WORDS

be
Ben
ten/net
bet
Bert
bent
rent
Brent

SORT WORDS

Beginning Letters (Optional)

Rhymes:

Ben	net	bent
ten	bet	rent
		Brent

TRANSFER WORDS

Reading:
spent wet

Spelling:
vent dent

Brianna

a a i b n n r

MAKE WORDS

in
an
Ian
ran
ban
Nan
Anna
rain
barn/bran
brain/Brian
Brianna

SORT WORDS

Br Words (Optional):
bran, brain, Brian, Brianna

Rhymes:
an	rain
ran	brain
ban	
bran	
Nan	

TRANSFER WORDS

Reading:
Spain span

Spelling:
clan chain

Make Words: Tell children how many letters to use to make each word. (A slash indicates words that can be made with the same letters.)

Emphasize how changing just one letter or rearranging letters makes a different word.

"Add a letter to **bran** to spell **brain**."

"Use the same letters in **brain** to spell the name **Brian**."

When children are not just adding or changing one letter, cue them to start over.

"Start over and use 4 new letters to spell **barn**."

Give a meaning or sentence clue, when needed, to clarify the word children are making.

"Change 1 letter in **ran** to spell **ban**. Because of the drought, there was a **ban** on all outdoor watering and car washing."

Always alert children when they are making a name and expect them to use a capital letter.

"Take 4 letters and spell the name **Anna**."

"Change a letter in **ban** to spell the name **Nan**."

Give children one minute to figure out the secret word and then give clues, if needed.

"Our secret word is a name that can be made by adding your letters to **Anna**."

Sort Br Words (Optional)

Sort Rhymes

Reading Transfer: "Pretend you are reading and come to a new word." Have children put the transfer words under the appropriate rhymes and use the rhymes to decode them.

Spelling Transfer: "Pretend you are writing and need to spell these words." Have children tell you how the words begin. Then, have children find and use the appropriate rhymes to finish spelling the transfer words.

Step-by-step directions for a sample *Making Names* lesson are on pages 8-12.

Bridget

eibdgrt

Make Words: Tell children how many letters to use to make each word. (A slash indicates words that can be made with the same letters.)

Emphasize how changing just one letter or rearranging letters makes a different word.

> "Add a letter to **bid** to spell **bird**."

> "Change a letter in **tide** to spell **ride**."

When children are not just adding or changing one letter, cue them to start over.

> "Start over and use 5 new letters to spell **tribe**."

Give a meaning or sentence clue, when needed, to clarify the word children are making.

> "Start over and use 5 new letters to spell **ridge**. We stood on the **ridge** of the mountain and looked down into the valley."

Always alert children when they are making a name and expect them to use a capital letter.

> "Use 2 letters to spell the name **Ed**."

Give children one minute to figure out the secret word and then give clues, if needed.

> "Our secret word is a name that can be made by adding a letter to **bridge**."

Sort Br Words (Optional)

Sort Rhymes

Reading Transfer: "Pretend you are reading and come to a new word." Have children put the transfer words under the appropriate rhymes and use the rhymes to decode them.

Spelling Transfer: "Pretend you are writing and need to spell these words." Have children tell you how the words begin. Then, have children find and use the appropriate rhymes to finish spelling the transfer words.

Step-by-step directions for a sample *Making Names* lesson are on pages 8-12.

MAKE WORDS

Ed
Ted
bed
bid
bird
tide
ride
bride
tiger
tired
ridge
bridge
Bridget

SORT WORDS

Br Words (Optional):
bride, bridge, Bridget

Rhymes:
Ed	tide	ridge
Ted	ride	bridge
bed	bride	

TRANSFER WORDS

Reading:
sled slide

Spelling:
glide fled

Brittany

a i b n r t t y

MAKE WORDS

Art
Ray
tray
Bart
barn
yarn
Ryan
tiny
rain
train
brain/Brian
rainy
brainy
Brittany

SORT WORDS

Br Words (Optional):
brain, Brian, brainy, Brittany

Related Words:
rain, rainy; brain, brainy

Rhymes:
Art   tray   barn   train   rainy
Bart   Ray   yarn   rain   brainy
brain

TRANSFER WORDS

Reading:
spray   sprain

Spelling:
chart   chain

Make Words: Tell children how many letters to use to make each word. (A slash indicates words that can be made with the same letters.)

Emphasize how changing just one letter or rearranging letters makes a different word.

> "Add a letter to **Ray** to spell **tray**."

> "Change a letter in **train** to spell **brain**."

When children are not just adding or changing one letter, cue them to start over.

> "Start over and use 5 new letters to spell **rainy**."

Give a meaning or sentence clue, when needed, to clarify the word children are making.

> "Start over and use 4 new letters to spell **tiny**. The premature baby was very **tiny**."

Always alert children when they are making a name and expect them to use a capital letter.

> "Use 4 letters to spell the name **Bart**."

Give children one minute to figure out the secret word and then give clues, if needed.

> "Our secret word is a name that begins with **Br** and ends with **y**."

Sort Br Words (Optional)

Sort Related Words

Sort Rhymes

Reading Transfer: "Pretend you are reading and come to a new word." Have children put the transfer words under the appropriate rhymes and use the rhymes to decode them.

Spelling Transfer: "Pretend you are writing and need to spell these words." Have children tell you how the words begin. Then, have children find and use the appropriate rhymes to finish spelling the transfer words.

Step-by-step directions for a sample *Making Names* lesson are on pages 8-12.

Making Names • CD-2429 • © Carson-Dellosa

Bryant

a b n r t y

Make Words: Tell children how many letters to use to make each word. (A slash indicates words that can be made with the same letters.)

Emphasize how changing just one letter or rearranging letters makes a different word.

> "Add a letter to **Art** to spell the name **Bart**."

> "Use the same letters in **rat** to spell **tar**."

When children are not just adding or changing one letter, cue them to start over.

> "Start over and use 4 new letters to spell **tray**."

Give a meaning or sentence clue, when needed, to clarify the word children are making.

> "Use the same letters in **Bart** to spell **brat**. Sometimes my little brother is a **brat**."

Always alert children when they are making a name and expect them to use a capital letter.

> "Change 1 letter in **bay** to spell the name **Ray**."

> "Add 1 letter to **Art** to spell the name **Bart**."

Give children one minute to figure out the secret word and then give clues, if needed.

> "Our secret word is a name that begins with **Br** and ends with **t**."

Sort Beginning Letters (Optional)

Sort Rhymes

Reading Transfer: "Pretend you are reading and come to a new word." Have children put the transfer words under the appropriate rhymes and use the rhymes to decode them.

Spelling Transfer: "Pretend you are writing and need to spell these words." Have children tell you how the words begin. Then, have children find and use the appropriate rhymes to finish spelling the transfer words.

Step-by-step directions for a sample *Making Names* lesson are on pages 8-12.

MAKE WORDS

at
bat
bar
bay
Ray
rat/tar/Art
Bart/brat
barn
yarn
tray
Ryan
Bryant

SORT WORDS

Beginning Letters (Optional)

Rhymes:

at	bar	Art	yarn	Ray
bat	tar	Bart	barn	tray
rat				bay

TRANSFER WORDS

Reading:
chart flat

Spelling:
spray stray

Cameron

MAKE WORDS

on
Ron
ran
can
cane
came
name
Nora
come
corn
acorn
crane
ocean
romance/Cameron

SORT WORDS

Beginning Letters (Optional)

Rhymes:

on	ran	corn	came
Ron	can	acorn	name

TRANSFER WORDS

Reading:
squeal stand

Spelling:
steal sled

Make Words: Tell children how many letters to use to make each word. (A slash indicates words that can be made with the same letters.)

Emphasize how changing just one letter or rearranging letters makes a different word.

"Add a letter to **corn** to spell **acorn**."

"Change 1 letter in **cane** to spell **came**."

When children are not just adding or changing one letter, cue them to start over.

"Start over and use 5 new letters to spell **ocean**."

Give a meaning or sentence clue, when needed, to clarify the word children are making.

"Start over and use 5 new letters to spell **crane**. They used a **crane** to lift the truck out of the ditch."

Always alert children when they are making a name and expect them to use a capital letter.

"Add a letter to **on** to spell the name **Ron**."

This lesson has two secret words. Give children one minute to figure out each secret word and then give clues, if needed.

"Today, we have 2 secret words. One secret word begins with **ro** and ends with **ce**."

"The other secret word is a name that can be made by adding your letters to **Ron**."

Sort Beginning Letters (Optional)

Sort Rhymes

Reading Transfer: "Pretend you are reading and come to a new word." Have children put the transfer words under the appropriate rhymes and use the rhymes to decode them.

Spelling Transfer: "Pretend you are writing and need to spell these words." Have children tell you how the words begin. Then, have children find and use the appropriate rhymes to finish spelling the transfer words.

Step-by-step directions for a sample *Making Names* lesson are on pages 8-12.

Carlos

Make Words: Tell children how many letters to use to make each word. (A slash indicates words that can be made with the same letters.)

Emphasize how changing just one letter or rearranging letters makes a different word.

> "Add a letter to **car** to spell **cars**."

> "Use the same letters in **Carol** to spell **coral**."

When children are not just adding or changing one letter, cue them to start over.

> "Start over and use 4 new letters to spell **also**."

Give a meaning or sentence clue, when needed, to clarify the word children are making.

> "Start over and use 5 new letters to spell **solar**. Energy we get from the sun is called **solar** energy."

Always alert children when they are making a name and expect them to use a capital letter.

> "Add a letter to **Al** to spell the name **Sal**."

Give children one minute to figure out the secret word and then give clues, if needed.

> "Our secret word is a name that can be made by adding your letters to **Carl**."

Sort Beginning Letters (Optional)

Sort Rhymes

Reading Transfer: "Pretend you are reading and come to a new word." Have children put the transfer words under the appropriate rhymes and use the rhymes to decode them.

Spelling Transfer: "Pretend you are writing and need to spell these words." Have children tell you how the words begin. Then, have children find and use the appropriate rhymes to finish spelling the transfer words.

Step-by-step directions for a sample *Making Names* lesson are on pages 8-12.

MAKE WORDS

Al
Sal
car
cars/scar
also
Arlo
Cora
Carl
Carol/coral
solar
Oscar
Carlos

SORT WORDS

Beginning Letters (Optional)

Rhymes:
Al   car
Sal   scar

TRANSFER WORDS

Reading:
gal star

Spelling:
pal par

Carlotta

a a o c l r t t

MAKE WORDS

Art
act/cat
rat
rot
cot
coat/taco
Cora
Arlo
trot
cart
Carl
Carol
actor
Carlotta

SORT WORDS

Related Words:
act, actor

Rhymes:

art	rot	cat
cart	cot	rat
	trot	

TRANSFER WORDS

Reading:
chart chat

Spelling:
slot spot

Make Words: Tell children how many letters to use to make each word. (A slash indicates words that can be made with the same letters.)

Emphasize how changing just one letter or rearranging letters makes a different word.

"Change a letter in **rat** to spell **rot**."

"Use the same letters in **act** to spell **cat**."

When children are not just adding or changing one letter, cue them to start over.

"Start over and use 4 new letters to spell **cart**."

Give a meaning or sentence clue, when needed, to clarify the word children are making.

"Start over and use 4 letters to spell **trot**. I watched the horse **trot** around the track."

Always alert children when they are making a name and expect them to use a capital letter.

"Take 3 letters and spell the name **Art**."

"Change 1 letter to spell the name **Carl**."

Give children one minute to figure out the secret word and then give clues if needed.

"Our secret word is a name and can be made by adding your letters to **Carl**."

Sort Related Words

Sort Rhymes

Reading Transfer: "Pretend you are reading and come to a new word." Have children put the transfer words under the appropriate rhymes and use the rhymes to decode them.

Spelling Transfer: "Pretend you are writing and need to spell these words." Have children tell you how the words begin. Then, have children find and use the appropriate rhymes to finish spelling the transfer words.

Step-by-step directions for a sample *Making Names* lesson are on pages 8-12.

Carlton

a o c l n r t

Make Words: Tell children how many letters to use to make each word. (A slash indicates words that can be made with the same letters.)

Emphasize how changing just one letter or rearranging letters makes a different word.

> "Change a letter in **Carl** to spell **cart**."

> "Use the same letters in **coat** to spell **taco**."

When children are not just adding or changing one letter, cue them to start over.

> "Start over and use 5 new letters to spell **actor**."

Give a meaning or sentence clue, when needed, to clarify the word children are making.

> "Start over and use 6 new letters to spell **carton**. We packed the books in a **carton** and shipped them to my brother."

Always alert children when they are making a name and expect them to use a capital letter.

> "Take 4 new letters and spell the name **Carl**."

> "Use 5 new letters to spell the name **Carol**."

Give children one minute to figure out the secret word and then give clues, if needed.

> "Our secret word is a name that can be made by adding your letters to **Carl**."

Sort Related Words

Sort Rhymes

Reading Transfer: "Pretend you are reading and come to a new word." Have children put the transfer words under the appropriate rhymes and use the rhymes to decode them.

Spelling Transfer: "Pretend you are writing and need to spell these words." Have children tell you how the words begin. Then, have children find and use the appropriate rhymes to finish spelling the transfer words.

Step-by-step directions for a sample *Making Names* lesson are on pages 8-12.

MAKE WORDS

Art
act
lot
cot
coat/taco
Carl
cart
torn
corn
acorn
actor
Carol
carton
Carlton

SORT WORDS

Related Words:
act, actor

Rhymes:

art	lot	torn
cart	cot	corn
		acorn

TRANSFER WORDS

Reading:
start shot

Spelling:
born thorn

Carolyn

a o c l n r y

can
ran
Ray
lay
clay
Cary
Cora
corn
acorn
Carol/coral
royal
rayon
crayon
Carolyn

SORT WORDS

Beginning Letters (Optional)

Rhymes:

can	Ray	rayon
ran	lay	crayon
	clay	

TRANSFER WORDS

Reading:
clan stay

Spelling:
gray pray

Make Words: Tell children how many letters to use to make each word. (A slash indicates words that can be made with the same letters.)

Emphasize how changing just one letter or rearranging letters makes a different word.

> "Add a letter to **corn** to spell **acorn**."

> "Use the same letters in **Carol** to spell **coral**."

When children are not just adding or changing one letter, cue them to start over.

> "Start over and use 5 new letters to spell **royal**."

Give a meaning or sentence clue, when needed, to clarify the word children are making.

> "Start over and use 5 new letters to spell **rayon**. The jacket was made of **rayon**."

Always alert children when they are making a name and expect them to use a capital letter.

> "Change 1 letter in **Roy** to spell the name **Ray**."

> "Use 4 letters to spell the name **Cary**."

Give children one minute to figure out the secret word and then give clues, if needed.

> "Our secret word is a name that can be made by adding your letters to **Carol**."

Sort Beginning Letters (Optional)

Sort Rhymes

Reading Transfer: "Pretend you are reading and come to a new word." Have children put the transfer words under the appropriate rhymes and use the rhymes to decode them.

Spelling Transfer: "Pretend you are writing and need to spell these words." Have children tell you how the words begin. Then, have children find and use the appropriate rhymes to finish spelling the transfer words.

Step-by-step directions for a sample *Making Names* lesson are on pages 8-12.

Carter

Make Words: Tell children how many letters to use to make each word. (A slash indicates words that can be made with the same letters.)

Emphasize how changing just one letter or rearranging letters makes a different word.

> "Add a letter to **race** to spell **trace**."

> "Use the same letters in **trace** to spell **react**."

When children are not just adding or changing one letter, cue them to start over.

> "Start over and use 4 new letters to spell **race**."

Give a meaning or sentence clue, when needed, to clarify the word children are making.

> "Use the same letters in **trace** to spell **react**. When the siren sounds, the firefighters have to **react** quickly."

Always alert children when they are making a name and expect them to use a capital letter.

> "Use the same letters in **rat** to spell the name **Art**."

This lesson has two secret words. Give children one minute to figure out each secret word and then give clues, if needed.

> "Today, we have 2 secret words. One secret word is the big hole at the top of a volcano."

> "The other secret word is a name that you can make by adding your letters to **cart**."

Sort Related Words

Sort Rhymes

Reading Transfer: "Pretend you are reading and come to a new word." Have children put the transfer words under the appropriate rhymes and use the rhymes to decode them.

Spelling Transfer: "Pretend you are writing and need to spell these words." Have children tell you how the words begin. Then, have children find and use the appropriate rhymes to finish spelling the transfer words.

Step-by-step directions for a sample *Making Names* lesson are on pages 8-12.

MAKE WORDS

act/cat
rat/Art
cart
care
rare/rear
tear
race
trace/react/crate
crater/Carter

SORT WORDS

Related Words:
act, react

Rhymes:

cat	art	care	rear	race
rat	cart	rare	tear	trace

TRANSFER WORDS

Reading:
start stare

Spelling:
Grace Bart

Casper

a e c p r s

ape
ace
cap
car
par/rap
race
pace
care
scare
scrap
scrape/Casper

Scr Words (Optional):
scrap, scrape

Rhymes:

ape	ace	car	care	rap
scrape	pace	par	scare	scrap
		race		cap

Reading:
space grape

Spelling:
share scar

Make Words: Tell children how many letters to use to make each word. (A slash indicates words that can be made with the same letters.)

Emphasize how changing just one letter or rearranging letters makes a different word.

> "Add a letter to **care** to spell **scare**."

> "Use the same letters in **par** to spell **rap**."

When children are not just adding or changing one letter, cue them to start over.

> "Start over and use 4 new letters to spell **care**."

Give a meaning or sentence clue, when needed, to clarify the word children are making.

> "Start over and use 5 letters to spell **scrap**. We cleaned up the mess and not a **scrap** was left on the floor."

This lesson has two secret words. Give children one minute to figure out each secret word and then give clues, if needed. Always alert children when they are making a name and expect them to use a capital letter.

> "Today, we have two secret words. One secret word can be made by adding a letter to **scrap**."

> "The other secret word is a name that begins with **C** and ends with **r**."

Sort Scr Words (Optional)

Sort Rhymes

Reading Transfer: "Pretend you are reading and come to a new word." Have children put the transfer words under the appropriate rhymes and use the rhymes to decode them.

Spelling Transfer: "Pretend you are writing and need to spell these words." Have children tell you how the words begin. Then, have children find and use the appropriate rhymes to finish spelling the transfer words.

Step-by-step directions for a sample *Making Names* lesson are on pages 8-12.

Cassandra

MAKE WORDS

an
can
Dan
ran
and
sand
card
cars
scars
Canada
Sandra
Cassandra

Make Words: Tell children how many letters to use to make each word. (A slash indicates words that can be made with the same letters.)

Emphasize how changing just one letter or rearranging letters makes a different word.

"Add a letter to **cars** to spell **scars**."

"Change 1 letter in **Dan** to spell **ran**."

When children are not just adding or changing one letter, cue them to start over.

"Start over and use 6 new letters to spell the name **Sandra**."

Give a meaning or sentence clue, when needed, to clarify the word children are making.

"Start over and use 6 new letters to spell the country of **Canada**. **Canada** is a huge country to the north of the United States."

Always alert children when they are making a name and expect them to use a capital letter.

"Change one letter in **can** to spell the name **Dan**."

Give children one minute to figure out the secret word and then give clues, if needed.

"One secret word is a name that can be made by adding your letters to **Sandra**."

Sort Beginning Letters (Optional)

Sort Rhymes

Reading Transfer: "Pretend you are reading and come to a new word." Have children put the transfer words under the appropriate rhymes and use the rhymes to decode them.

Spelling Transfer: "Pretend you are writing and need to spell these words." Have children tell you how the words begin. Then, have children find and use the appropriate rhymes to finish spelling the transfer words.

Step-by-step directions for a sample *Making Names* lesson are on pages 8-12.

SORT WORDS

Beginning Letters (Optional)

Rhymes:
an	and	cars
can	sand	scars
Dan		
ran		

TRANSFER WORDS

Reading:
brand bran

Spelling:
stars stand

Catherine

MAKE WORDS

ice
rice
Rita
Tina
each
rain
chain/China
cheer
chant
chart
cheat/teach
teacher
Catherine

SORT WORDS

Ch Words (Optional):
chain, China, cheer, chant, chart, cheat, each, teach, teacher

Related Words:
teach, teacher

Rhymes:
ice   rain   each
rice   chain   teach

TRANSFER WORDS

Reading:
beach   stain

Spelling:
spice   peach

Make Words: Tell children how many letters to use to make each word. (A slash indicates words that can be made with the same letters.)

Emphasize how changing just one letter or rearranging letters makes a different word.

"Add a letter to **ice** to spell **rice**."

"Use the same letters in **chain** to spell **China**."

When children are not just adding or changing one letter, cue them to start over.

"Start over and use 5 new letters to spell **cheer**."

Give a meaning or sentence clue, when needed, to clarify the word children are making.

"Start over and use 5 new letters to spell **cheer**. We always **cheer** for our team."

Always alert children when they are making a name and expect them to use a capital letter.

"Take 4 new letters and spell the name **Rita**."

"Use the same letters in **chain** to spell the country **China**."

Give children one minute to figure out the secret word and then give clues, if needed.

"Our secret word is a name that begins with **C** and ends with **e**."

Sort Ch Words (Optional)

Sort Related Words

Sort Rhymes

Reading Transfer: "Pretend you are reading and come to a new word." Have children put the transfer words under the appropriate rhymes and use the rhymes to decode them.

Spelling Transfer: "Pretend you are writing and need to spell these words." Have children tell you how the words begin. Then, have children find and use the appropriate rhymes to finish spelling the transfer words.

Step-by-step directions for a sample *Making Names* lesson are on pages 8-12.

Charisse

a e i c h r s s

Make Words: Tell children how many letters to use to make each word. (A slash indicates words that can be made with the same letters.)

Emphasize how changing just one letter or rearranging letters makes a different word.

> "Add a letter to **ice** to spell **rice**."

> "Use the same letters in **rice** to spell the name **Eric**."

When children are not just adding or changing one letter, cue them to start over.

> "Start over and use 4 new letters to spell **each**."

Give a meaning or sentence clue, when needed, to clarify the word children are making.

> "Start over and use 7 new letters to spell **cashier**. The **cashier** took the money and gave me back change."

Always alert children when they are making a name and expect them to use a capital letter.

> "Take 5 new letters and spell the name **Erica**."

Give children one minute to figure out the secret word and then give clues, if needed.

> "Our secret word is a name that begins with **Ch** and ends with **e**."

Sort Related Words

Sort Rhymes

Reading Transfer: "Pretend you are reading and come to a new word." Have children put the transfer words under the appropriate rhymes and use the rhymes to decode them.

Spelling Transfer: "Pretend you are writing and need to spell these words." Have children tell you how the words begin. Then, have children find and use the appropriate rhymes to finish spelling the transfer words.

Step-by-step directions for a sample *Making Names* lesson are on pages 8-12.

MAKE WORDS

ice
rice/Eric
each
cash
crash
reach
Erica
Chris
search
cashes
cashier
crashes
Charisse

SORT WORDS

Related Words:
cash, cashes, cashier;
crash, crashes

Rhymes:
ice   each   cash   cashes
rice   reach   crash   crashes

TRANSFER WORDS

Reading:
twice   smash

Spelling:
smashes   peach

Charlene

MAKE WORDS

ear
hear
heal
real
lean/Lane
Earl
earn
learn
crane
clear
clean
cereal
cleaner
Charlene

SORT WORDS

Cl Words (Optional):
clean, cleaner, clear

Related Words:
clean, cleaner

Rhymes:
ear   earn   heal   lean   Lane
hear   learn   real   clean   crane

TRANSFER WORDS

Reading:
mean   meal

Spelling:
clear   plane

Make Words: Tell children how many letters to use to make each word. (A slash indicates words that can be made with the same letters.)

Emphasize how changing just one letter or rearranging letters makes a different word.

> "Add a letter to **ear** to spell **hear**."

> "Use the same letters in **lean** to spell the name **Lane**."

When children are not just adding or changing one letter, cue them to start over.

> "Start over and use 6 new letters to spell **cereal**."

Give a meaning or sentence clue, when needed, to clarify the word children are making.

> "Start over and use 5 new letters to spell **crane**. A **crane** was at the construction site for the new building."

Always alert children when they are making a name and expect them to use a capital letter.

> "Take 4 new letters and spell the name **Earl**."

Give children one minute to figure out the secret word and then give clues, if needed.

> "Our secret word is a name that begins with **Ch** and ends with **e**."

Sort Cl Words (Optional)

Sort Related Words

Sort Rhymes

Reading Transfer: "Pretend you are reading and come to a new word." Have children put the transfer words under the appropriate rhymes and use the rhymes to decode them.

Spelling Transfer: "Pretend you are writing and need to spell these words." Have children tell you how the words begin. Then, have children find and use the appropriate rhymes to finish spelling the transfer words.

Step-by-step directions for a sample *Making Names* lesson are on pages 8-12.

Charles

MAKE WORDS

car
Carl
case
cash
rash
each
reach
chase
crash
search
Charles

Make Words: Tell children how many letters to use to make each word. (A slash indicates words that can be made with the same letters.)

Emphasize how changing just one letter or rearranging letters makes a different word.

"Add a letter to **each** to spell **reach**."

"Change 1 letter in **cash** to spell **rash**."

When children are not just adding or changing one letter, cue them to start over.

"Start over and use 4 new letters to spell **case**."

Give a meaning or sentence clue, when needed, to clarify the word children are making.

"Change 1 letter in **cash** to spell **rash**. I had an itchy **rash** after touching the poison ivy."

Always alert children when they are making a name and expect them to use a capital letter.

"Add 1 letter to **car** to spell the name **Carl**."

Give children one minute to figure out the secret word and then give clues, if needed.

"Our secret word is a name that begins with **Ch** and ends with **s**."

Sort Ch Words (Optional)

Sort Rhymes

SORT WORDS

Ch Words (Optional):
chase, Charles, each, reach, search

Rhymes:
case	crash	each
chase	cash	reach
	rash	

Reading Transfer: "Pretend you are reading and come to a new word." Have children put the transfer words under the appropriate rhymes and use the rhymes to decode them.

Spelling Transfer: "Pretend you are writing and need to spell these words." Have children tell you how the words begin. Then, have children find and use the appropriate rhymes to finish spelling the transfer words.

Step-by-step directions for a sample *Making Names* lesson are on pages 8-12.

TRANSFER WORDS

Reading:
base splash

Spelling:
vase bleach

Charlotte

a e o c h l r t t

MAKE WORDS

heat
coat
chat
Chet
Cora
Earl
each
reach
teach/cheat
treat
Carol
throat
chatter
Charlotte

SORT WORDS

Related Words:
chat, chatter

Rhymes:
treat	coat	each
heat	throat	reach
cheat		teach

TRANSFER WORDS

Reading:
wheat goat

Spelling:
float beach

Make Words: Tell children how many letters to use to make each word. (A slash indicates words that can be made with the same letters.)

Emphasize how changing just one letter or rearranging letters makes a different word.

"Add a letter to **each** to spell **reach**."

"Use the same letters in **teach** to spell **cheat**."

When children are not just adding or changing one letter, cue them to start over.

"Start over and use 6 new letters to spell **throat**."

Give a meaning or sentence clue, when needed, to clarify the word children are making.

"Start over and use 7 new letters to spell **chatter**. Sometimes the teacher says there is too much **chatter** in this room."

Always alert children when they are making a name and expect them to use a capital letter.

"Take 4 new letters and spell the name **Cora**."

Give children one minute to figure out the secret word and then give clues, if needed.

"Our secret word is a name that begins with **Ch** and ends with **e**."

Sort Related Words

Sort Rhymes

Reading Transfer: "Pretend you are reading and come to a new word." Have children put the transfer words under the appropriate rhymes and use the rhymes to decode them.

Spelling Transfer: "Pretend you are writing and need to spell these words." Have children tell you how the words begin. Then, have children find and use the appropriate rhymes to finish spelling the transfer words.

Step-by-step directions for a sample *Making Names* lesson are on pages 8-12.

Chester

eechrst

Make Words: Tell children how many letters to use to make each word. (A slash indicates words that can be made with the same letters.)

Emphasize how changing just one letter or rearranging letters makes a different word.

> "Change a letter in **cheer** to spell **sheer**."

> "Add a letter to **Chet** to spell **chest**."

When children are not just adding or changing one letter, cue them to start over.

> "Start over and use 6 new letters to spell **secret**."

Give a meaning or sentence clue, when needed, to clarify the word children are making.

> "Use the same letters in **three** to spell **there**. I left my hat and coat over **there** by the door."

Always alert children when they are making a name and expect them to use a capital letter.

> "Take 4 new letters and spell the name **Chet**."

Give children one minute to figure out the secret word and then give clues, if needed.

> "Our secret word is a name that can be made by adding your letters to **chest**."

Sort Ch Words (Optional)

Sort Sh Words (Optional)

Sort Rhymes

Reading Transfer: "Pretend you are reading and come to a new word." Have children put the transfer words under the appropriate rhymes and use the rhymes to decode them.

Spelling Transfer: "Pretend you are writing and need to spell these words." Have children tell you how the words begin. Then, have children find and use the appropriate rhymes to finish spelling the transfer words.

Step-by-step directions for a sample *Making Names* lesson are on pages 8-12.

MAKE WORDS

set
rest
tree
Chet
chest
cheer
sheer
sheet
three/there
these
secret
Chester

SORT WORDS

Ch Words (Optional):
Chet, chest, cheer, Chester

Sh Words (Optional):
sheer, sheet

Rhymes:

sheer	three	rest	set
cheer	tree	chest	Chet

TRANSFER WORDS

Reading:
steer free

Spelling:
vest spree

Christian/Christina

a i i c h n r s t

MAKE WORDS

Rita
Tina
hair
chair
chain/China
Chris
train
strain
snatch
raisin
Trisha
Christian/Christina

SORT WORDS

Ch Words—both sounds
(Optional):
chair, chain, China, snatch;
Chris, Christian, Christina

Rhymes:
strain   hair
chain   chair
train

TRANSFER WORDS

Reading:
brain Blair

Spelling:
drain pair

Make Words: Tell children how many letters to use to make each word. (A slash indicates words that can be made with the same letters.)

Emphasize how changing just one letter or rearranging letters makes a different word.

> "Add a letter to **hair** to spell **chair**."

When children are not just adding or changing one letter, cue them to start over.

> "Start over and use 5 new letters to spell the word **train**."

Give a meaning or sentence clue, when needed, to clarify the word children are making:

> "Use the same letters in **chain** to spell **China**. My grandma was born in **China**."

Always alert children when they are making a name and expect them to use a capital letter.

> "Take 4 new letters and spell the name **Tina**."

This lesson has two secret words. Give children one minute to figure out each secret word and then give clues, if needed.

> "Today we have two secret words, and they are both names. Both secret words can be made by adding your letters to **Chris**."

Sort Ch Words—both sounds (Optional)

Sort Rhymes

Reading Transfer: "Pretend you are reading and come to a new word." Have children put the transfer words under the appropriate rhymes and use the rhymes to decode them.

Spelling Transfer: "Pretend you are writing and need to spell these words." Have children tell you how the words begin. Then, have children find and use the appropriate rhymes to finish spelling the transfer words.

Step-by-step directions for a sample *Making Names* lesson are on pages 8-12.

Christopher

eiochhprrst

Make Words: Tell children how many letters to use to make each word. (A slash indicates words that can be made with the same letters.)

Emphasize how changing just one letter or rearranging letters makes a different word.

> "Add a letter to **itch** to spell **pitch**."

> "Change one letter in **short** to spell **sport**."

When children are not just adding or changing one letter, cue them to start over.

> "Start over and use 5 new letters to spell **short**."

Give a meaning or sentence clue, when needed, to clarify the word children are making.

> "Change one letter in **porches** to spell **torches**. We used **torches** to light our way in the dark cave."

Always alert children when they are making a name and expect them to use a capital letter.

> "Use 4 new letters to spell the name **Chris**."

Give children one minute to figure out the secret word and then give clues, if needed.

> "Our secret word is a name that can be made by adding your letters to **Chris**."

Sort Related Words

Sort Rhymes

Reading Transfer: "Pretend you are reading and come to a new word." Have children put the transfer words under the appropriate rhymes and use the rhymes to decode them.

Spelling Transfer: "Pretend you are writing and need to spell these words." Have children tell you how the words begin. Then, have children find and use the appropriate rhymes to finish spelling the transfer words.

Step-by-step directions for a sample *Making Names* lesson are on pages 8-12.

MAKE WORDS

ripe
itch
pitch
short
sport
porch
torch
Chris
riper
ripest
porches
torches
pitches
pitcher
Christopher

SORT WORDS

Related Words:
ripe, riper, ripest; torch, torches; porch, porches; pitch, pitches, pitcher

Rhymes:
itch torch torches sport
pitch porch porches short

TRANSFER WORDS

Reading:
stitch scorch

Spelling:
hitch scorches

Christy

ichrsty

MAKE WORDS

is
his
hit
sir
sit
cry
try
shy
this
city
Rich
shirt
Chris
Christy

SORT WORDS

Rhymes:
cry	sit	is
try	hit	his
shy		

TRANSFER WORDS

Reading:
sky skit

Spelling:
spy spit

Make Words: Tell children how many letters to use to make each word. (A slash indicates words that can be made with the same letters.)

Emphasize how changing just one letter or rearranging letters makes a different word.

> "Change a letter in **sir** to spell **sit**."

> "Change 1 letter in **cry** to spell **try**."

When children are not just adding or changing one letter, cue them to start over.

> "Start over and use 3 new letters to spell **cry**."

Give a meaning or sentence clue, when needed, to clarify the word they are making.

> "Start over and use 3 new letters to spell **shy**. The little boy was very **shy** and didn't talk very much."

Always alert children when they are making a name and expect them to use a capital letter.

> "Take 5 new letters and spell the name **Chris**."

Give children one minute to figure out the secret word and then give clues, if needed.

> "Our secret word is a name that can be made by adding your letters to **Chris**."

Sort Rhymes

Reading Transfer: "Pretend you are reading and come to a new word." Have children put the transfer words under the appropriate rhymes and use the rhymes to decode them.

Spelling Transfer: "Pretend you are writing and need to spell these words." Have children tell you how the words begin. Then, have children find and use the appropriate rhymes to finish spelling the transfer words.

Step-by-step directions for a sample *Making Names* lesson are on pages 8-12.

Clarence

a e e c c l n r

Make Words: Tell children how many letters to use to make each word. (A slash indicates words that can be made with the same letters.)

Emphasize how changing just one letter or rearranging letters makes a different word.

> "Add a letter to **earn** to spell **learn**."

> "Change 1 letter in **race** to spell **lace**."

When children are not just adding or changing one letter, cue them to start over.

> "Start over and use 6 new letters to spell **cereal**."

Give a meaning or sentence clue, when needed, to clarify the word children are making.

> "Start over and use 4 new letters to spell **lean**. We trimmed all of the fat so that the steak was as **lean** as possible."

Always alert children when they are making a name and expect them to use a capital letter.

> "Take 4 new letters and spell the name **Carl**."

Give children one minute to figure out the secret word and then give clues, if needed.

> "Our secret word is a name that begins with **Cl** and ends with **e**."

Sort Cl Words (Optional)

Sort Related Words

Sort Rhymes

Reading Transfer: "Pretend you are reading and come to a new word." Have children put the transfer words under the appropriate rhymes and use the rhymes to decode them.

Spelling Transfer: "Pretend you are writing and need to spell these words." Have children tell you how the words begin. Then, have children find and use the appropriate rhymes to finish spelling the transfer words.

Step-by-step directions for a sample *Making Names* lesson are on pages 8-12.

MAKE WORDS

can
ran
race
lace
lean
Carl
earn
learn
clean
cereal
cancer
cancel
leaner
cleaner
Clarence

SORT WORDS

Cl Words (Optional):
clean, cleaner, Clarence

Related Words:
lean, leaner; clean, cleaner

Rhymes:
can   race   lean   leaner   earn
ran   lace   clean   cleaner   learn

TRANSFER WORDS

Reading:
bean   brace

Spelling:
trace   yearn

Clifford

MAKE WORDS

of
off
for
old
oil
coil
foil
Lori
cold
fold
Ford®
cord
Cliff
Clifford

SORT WORDS

Beginning Letters (Optional)

Rhymes:

old	Ford®	oil
cold	cord	coil
fold		foil

TRANSFER WORDS

Reading:
told boil

Spelling:
broil scold

Make Words: Tell children how many letters to use to make each word. (A slash indicates words that can be made with the same letters.)

Emphasize how changing just one letter or rearranging letters makes a different word.

> "Add a letter to **oil** to spell **coil**."

> "Change 1 letter in **Ford®** to spell **cord**."

When children are not just adding or changing one letter, cue them to start over.

> "Start over and use 5 new letters to spell the name **Cliff**."

Give a meaning or sentence clue, when needed, to clarify the word children are making.

> "Change 1 letter in **coil** to spell **foil**. We wrapped the leftovers in aluminum **foil**."

Always alert children when they are making a name and expect them to use a capital letter.

> "Take 4 new letters and spell the name **Lori**."

Give children one minute to figure out the secret word and then give clues, if needed.

> "Our secret word is a name that can be made by adding your letters to **Cliff**."

Sort Beginning Letters (Optional)

Sort Rhymes

Reading Transfer: "Pretend you are reading and come to a new word." Have children put the transfer words under the appropriate rhymes and use the rhymes to decode them.

Spelling Transfer: "Pretend you are writing and need to spell these words." Have children tell you how the words begin. Then, have children find and use the appropriate rhymes to finish spelling the transfer words.

Step-by-step directions for a sample *Making Names* lesson are on pages 8-12.

C l i n t o n

Make Words: Tell children how many letters to use to make each word. (A slash indicates words that can be made with the same letters.)

Emphasize how changing just one letter or rearranging letters makes a different word.

"Add a letter to **oil** to spell **coil**."

When children are not just adding or changing one letter, cue them to start over.

"Start over and use 4 new letters to spell **lint**."

Give a meaning or sentence clue, when needed, to clarify the word children are making.

"Start over and use 4 letters to spell **colt**. The **colt** was sleeping next to the mother horse."

Always alert children when they are making a name and expect them to use a capital letter.

"Add 1 letter to **lint** to spell the name **Clint**."

Give children one minute to figure out the secret word and then give clues, if needed.

"Our secret word is a name that can be made by adding your letters to **Clint**."

Sort Cl Words (Optional)

Sort Rhymes

Reading Transfer: "Pretend you are reading and come to a new word." Have children put the transfer words under the appropriate rhymes and use the rhymes to decode them.

Spelling Transfer: "Pretend you are writing and need to spell these words." Have children tell you how the words begin. Then, have children find and use the appropriate rhymes to finish spelling the transfer words.

Step-by-step directions for a sample *Making Names* lesson are on pages 8-12.

MAKE WORDS

on/no
not
cot
lot
oil
coil
coin
lion
into
colt/clot
lint
Clint
Clinton

SORT WORDS

Cl Words (Optional):
clot, Clint, Clinton

Rhymes:
not	oil	lint
cot	coil	Clint
lot		
clot		

TRANSFER WORDS

Reading:
foil squint

Spelling:
spot hint

Courtney

eoucnrty

MAKE WORDS

Roy
nut
cut
cute
cure
core
tore
tone
cone
Tony
Troy
count
county
country
Courtney

SORT WORDS

Beginning Letters (Optional)

Rhymes:

nut	core	tone	Roy
cut	tore	cone	Troy

TRANSFER WORDS

Reading:
bone score

Spelling:
shut bore

Make Words: Tell children how many letters to use to make each word. (A slash indicates words that can be made with the same letters.)

Emphasize how changing just one letter or rearranging letters makes a different word.

"Add a letter to **cut** to spell **cute**."

"Change a letter in **tore** to spell **tone**."

When children are not just adding or changing one letter, cue them to start over.

"Start over and use 3 new letters to spell **nut**."

Give a meaning or sentence clue, when needed, to clarify the word children are making.

"Add 1 letter to **count** to spell **county**. What **county** do you live in?"

Always alert children when they are making a name and expect them to use a capital letter.

"Take 4 new letters and spell the name **Tony**."

Give children one minute to figure out the secret word and then give clues, if needed.

"Our secret word is a name that begins with **C** and ends with **y**."

Sort Beginning Letters (Optional)

Sort Rhymes

Reading Transfer: "Pretend you are reading and come to a new word." Have children put the transfer words under the appropriate rhymes and use the rhymes to decode them.

Spelling Transfer: "Pretend you are writing and need to spell these words." Have children tell you how the words begin. Then, have children find and use the appropriate rhymes to finish spelling the transfer words.

Step-by-step directions for a sample *Making Names* lesson are on pages 8-12.

64

Making Names • CD-2429 • © Carson-Dellosa

C r y s t a l

a c l r s t y

Make Words: Tell children how many letters to use to make each word. (A slash indicates words that can be made with the same letters.)

Emphasize how changing just one letter or rearranging letters makes a different word.

"Change a letter in **cast** to spell **last**."

"Use the same letters in **last** to spell **salt**."

When children are not just adding or changing one letter, cue them to start over.

"Start over and use 5 new letters to spell **stray**."

Give a meaning or sentence clue, when needed, to clarify the word children are making.

"Start over and use 4 new letters to spell **cast**. He had a **cast** on his broken left arm."

Always alert children when they are making a name and expect them to use a capital letter.

"Take 5 new letters and spell the name **Stacy**."

Give children one minute to figure out the secret word and then give clues, if needed.

"Our secret word is a name that can be made by adding your letters to **cry**."

Sort Cr Words (Optional)

Sort Tr Words (Optional)

Sort Related Words

Sort Rhymes

Reading Transfer: "Pretend you are reading and come to a new word." Have children put the transfer words under the appropriate rhymes and use the rhymes to decode them.

Spelling Transfer: "Pretend you are writing and need to spell these words." Have children tell you how the words begin. Then, have children find and use the appropriate rhymes to finish spelling the transfer words.

Step-by-step directions for a sample *Making Names* lesson are on pages 8-12.

MAKE WORDS

cry
try
Art
cart
Cary
tray
stay
cast
last/salt
salty
stray
Stacy
Tracy
Crystal

SORT WORDS

Cr Words (Optional):
cry, Crystal

Tr Words (Optional):
try, tray, Tracy

Related Words:
salt, salty

Rhymes:

cry	Art	tray	cast	Tracy
try	cart	stray	last	Stacy
		stay		

TRANSFER WORDS

Reading:
blast shy

Spelling:
sway fast

Cynthia

MAKE WORDS

ant/Nat
cat
hat
chat
city
chin/inch
itch
itchy
Cathy
chant
chain/China
Cynthia

SORT WORDS

Ch Words (Optional):
chat, chin, chant, chain,
China, inch, itch, itchy

C Words—both sounds
(Optional):
cat, Cathy; city, Cynthia

Related Words:
itch, itchy

Rhymes:
Nat   ant
cat   chant
hat
chat

TRANSFER WORDS

Reading:
pant flat

Spelling:
slant slat

Make Words: Tell children how many letters to use to make each word. (A slash indicates words that can be made with the same letters.)

Emphasize how changing just one letter or rearranging letters makes a different word.

"Change a letter in **inch** to spell **itch**."

"Use the same letters in **chain** to spell the country of **China**."

When children are not just adding or changing one letter, cue them to start over.

"Start over and use 4 new letters to spell **city**."

Give a meaning or sentence clue, when needed, to clarify the word children are making.

"Use 5 new letters to spell **chant**. We always **chant** the spelling of each new Word Wall word."

Always alert children when they are making a name and expect them to use a capital letter.

"Take 5 new letters and spell the name **Cathy**."

Give children one minute to figure out the secret word and then give clues, if needed.

"One secret word is a name that begins with **C** and ends with **a**."

Sort Ch Words (Optional)

Sort C Words—both sounds (Optional)

Sort Related Words

Sort Rhymes

Reading Transfer: "Pretend you are reading and come to a new word." Have children put the transfer words under the appropriate rhymes and use the rhymes to decode them.

Spelling Transfer: "Pretend you are writing and need to spell these words." Have children tell you how the words begin. Then, have children find and use the appropriate rhymes to finish spelling the transfer words.

Step-by-step directions for a sample *Making Names* lesson are on pages 8-12.

Dameon

a e o d m n

Make Words: Tell children how many letters to use to make each word. (A slash indicates words that can be made with the same letters.)

Emphasize how changing just one letter or rearranging letters makes a different word.

> "Change a letter in **mean** to spell **moan**."

> "Add a letter to **ad** to spell **mad**."

When children are not just adding or changing one letter, cue them to start over.

> "Start over and use 4 new letters to spell the name **Dean**."

Give a meaning or sentence clue, when needed, to clarify the word children are making.

> "Add a letter to **name** to spell **named**. They **named** the baby Alexis."

Always alert children when they are making a name and expect them to use a capital letter.

> "Change 1 letter in **man** to spell the name **Dan**."

This lesson has two secret words. Give children one minute to figure out each secret word and then give clues, if needed.

> "One secret word has **moan** as the root word."

> "The other secret word is a name that begins with **D** and ends with **n**."

Sort Beginning Letters (Optional)

Sort Related Words

Sort Rhymes

Reading Transfer: "Pretend you are reading and come to a new word." Have children put the transfer words under the appropriate rhymes and use the rhymes to decode them.

Spelling Transfer: "Pretend you are writing and need to spell these words." Have children tell you how the words begin. Then, have children find and use the appropriate rhymes to finish spelling the transfer words.

Step-by-step directions for a sample *Making Names* lesson are on pages 8-12.

MAKE WORDS

Ed
ad
mad
man
Dan
Don
end
mend
Dean
mean
moan
name
named
moaned/Dameon

SORT WORDS

Beginning Letters (Optional)

Related Words:
name, named; moan, moaned

Rhymes:

ad	man	end	Dean
mad	Dan	mend	mean

TRANSFER WORDS

Reading:
spend   clean

Spelling:
blend   pad

Daniel

a e i d l n

▶ MAKE WORDS

Dan/and
end
die
lie
lied
dine
line
Lane
land
lend
nail
Linda
nailed/Daniel

▶ SORT WORDS

Related Words:
lie, lied; nail, nailed

Rhymes:
and   end   dine   die
land   lend   line   lie

▶ TRANSFER WORDS

Reading:
spend spine

Spelling:
grand blend

Make Words: Tell children how many letters to use to make each word. (A slash indicates words that can be made with the same letters.)

Emphasize how changing just one letter or rearranging letters makes a different word.

"Add a letter to **lie** to spell **lied**."

"Use the same letters in **Dan** to spell **and**."

When children are not just adding or changing one letter, cue them to start over.

"Start over and use 4 new letters to spell **nail**."

Give a meaning or sentence clue, when needed, to clarify the word children are making.

"Change 1 letter in **land** to spell **lend**. I asked my friend to **lend** me a dollar."

Always alert children when they are making a name and expect them to use a capital letter.

"Change 1 letter in **line** to spell the name **Lane**."

This lesson has two secret words. Give children one minute to figure out each secret word and then give clues, if needed.

"You can spell one secret word by adding your letters to **nail**."

"The other secret word is a name that can be made by adding your letters to **Dan**."

Sort Related Words

Sort Rhymes

Reading Transfer: "Pretend you are reading and come to a new word." Have children put the transfer words under the appropriate rhymes and use the rhymes to decode them.

Spelling Transfer: "Pretend you are writing and need to spell these words." Have children tell you how the words begin. Then, have children find and use the appropriate rhymes to finish spelling the transfer words.

Step-by-step directions for a sample *Making Names* lesson are on pages 8-12.

Danielle

a e e i d l l n

Make Words: Tell children how many letters to use to make each word. (A slash indicates words that can be made with the same letters.)

Emphasize how changing just one letter or rearranging letters makes a different word.

"Use the same letters in **Dan** to spell **and**."

"Add a letter to **and** to spell **land**."

When children are not just adding or changing one letter, cue them to start over.

"Start over and use 6 new letters to spell **nailed**."

Give a meaning or sentence clue, when needed, to clarify the word children are making.

"Start over and use 4 new letters to spell **nail**. He hit the **nail** with the hammer."

Always alert children when they are making a name and expect them to use a capital letter.

"Use the same letters in **Dean** to spell the name **Edna**."

Give children one minute to figure out the secret word and then give clues, if needed.

"Our secret word is a name that you can make it be adding your letters to **Daniel**."

Sort Beginning Letters (Optional)

Sort Related Words

Sort Rhymes

Reading Transfer: "Pretend you are reading and come to a new word." Have children put the transfer words under the appropriate rhymes and use the rhymes to decode them.

Spelling Transfer: "Pretend you are writing and need to spell these words." Have children tell you how the words begin. Then, have children find and use the appropriate rhymes to finish spelling the transfer words.

Step-by-step directions for a sample *Making Names* lesson are on pages 8-12.

MAKE WORDS

Dan/and
land
Dean/Edna
lean
nail
Neil
Delia
Linda
Diane
nailed
Nellie
Daniel
Danielle

SORT WORDS

Beginning Letters (Optional)

Related Words:
nail, nailed

Rhymes:
and   Dean
land   lean

TRANSFER WORDS

Reading:
stand Jean

Spelling:
grand strand

Daphne

a e d h n p

MAKE WORDS

an
and/Dan
den
hen
pen
pan
pad
had
head
hand
Dean/Edna
Daphne

SORT WORDS

Beginning Letters (Optional)

Rhymes:

an	den	had	and
Dan	hen	pad	hand
pan	pen		

TRANSFER WORDS

Reading:
when bad

Spelling:
mad sand

Make Words: Tell children how many letters to use to make each word. (A slash indicates words that can be made with the same letters.)

Emphasize how changing just one letter or rearranging letters makes a different word.

"Add a letter to **had** to spell **head**."

"Use the same letters in **and** to spell the name **Dan**."

When children are not just adding or changing one letter, cue them to start over.

"Start over and use 4 new letters to spell **hand**."

Give a meaning or sentence clue, when needed, to clarify the word children are making.

"Change 1 letter in **pan** to spell **pad**. The frog sat on the lily **pad**."

Always alert children when they are making a name and expect them to use a capital letter.

"Take 4 new letters and spell the name **Dean**."

Give children one minute to figure out the secret word and then give clues, if needed.

"Our secret word is a name that begins with **D** and ends with **e**."

Sort Beginning Letters (Optional)

Sort Rhymes

Reading Transfer: "Pretend you are reading and come to a new word." Have children put the transfer words under the appropriate rhymes and use the rhymes to decode them.

Spelling Transfer: "Pretend you are writing and need to spell these words." Have children tell you how the words begin. Then, have children find and use the appropriate rhymes to finish spelling the transfer words.

Step-by-step directions for a sample *Making Names* lesson are on pages 8-12.

Darlene

a e e d l n r

Make Words: Tell children how many letters to use to make each word. (A slash indicates words that can be made with the same letters.)

Emphasize how changing just one letter or rearranging letters makes a different word.

"Add a letter to **earn** to spell **learn**."

"Change 1 letter in **lend** to spell **land**."

When children are not just adding or changing one letter, cue them to start over.

"Start over and use 6 new letters to spell **leader**."

Give a meaning or sentence clue, when needed, to clarify the word children are making.

"Add 1 letter to **end** to spell **lend**. My brother is going to **lend** me ten dollars."

Always alert children when they are making a name and expect them to use a capital letter.

"Use 4 new letters to spell the name **Dale**."

This lesson has two secret words. Give children one minute to figure out each secret word and then give clues, if needed.

"One secret word can be made by adding your letters to **learn**."

"The other secret word is a name that begins with **D** and ends with **e**."

Sort Related Words

Sort Rhymes

Reading Transfer: "Pretend you are reading and come to a new word." Have children put the transfer words under the appropriate rhymes and use the rhymes to decode them.

Spelling Transfer: "Pretend you are writing and need to spell these words." Have children tell you how the words begin. Then, have children find and use the appropriate rhymes to finish spelling the transfer words.

Step-by-step directions for a sample *Making Names* lesson are on pages 8-12.

MAKE WORDS

Dan/and
end
lend
land
Dale/deal/lead
earn
learn
leader
earned
learned/Darlene

SORT WORDS

Related Words:
lead, leader; earn, earned; learn, learned

Rhymes:

and	end	earn	earned
land	lend	learn	learned

TRANSFER WORDS

Reading:
trend brand

Spelling:
yearn yearned

Darrell

a e d l l r r

72

MAKE WORDS

Del
deal/Dale/lead
read/dear/dare
rare/rear
real/Earl
Ella
Darrell

SORT WORDS

Beginning Letters (Optional)
Rhymes:

deal	lead	dear	dare
real	read	rear	rare

TRANSFER WORDS

Reading:
fear plead

Spelling:
steal clear

Make Words: Tell children how many letters to use to make each word. (A slash indicates words that can be made with the same letters.)

Emphasize how changing just one letter or rearranging letters makes a different word.

"Change a letter in **lead** to spell **read**."

"Use the same letters in **real** to spell the name **Earl**."

When children are not just adding or changing one letter, cue them to start over.

"Start over and use 4 new letters to spell the name **Ella**."

Give a meaning or sentence clue, when needed, to clarify the word children are making.

"Change 1 letter in **dare** to spell **rare**. Some people like their steaks cooked **rare**."

Always alert children when they are making a name and expect them to use a capital letter.

"Take 3 letters and spell the name **Del**."

Give children one minute to figure out the secret word and then give clues, if needed.

"Our secret word is a name that begins with **D** and ends with **l**."

Sort Beginning Letters (Optional)

Sort Rhymes

Reading Transfer: "Pretend you are reading and come to a new word." Have children put the transfer words under the appropriate rhymes and use the rhymes to decode them.

Spelling Transfer: "Pretend you are writing and need to spell these words." Have children tell you how the words begin. Then, have children find and use the appropriate rhymes to finish spelling the transfer words.

Step-by-step directions for a sample *Making Names* lesson are on pages 8-12.

Deborah

a e o b d h r

Make Words: Tell children how many letters to use to make each word. (A slash indicates words that can be made with the same letters.)

Emphasize how changing just one letter or rearranging letters makes a different word.

> "Add a letter to **Bo** to spell **boa**."

> "Change a letter in **Rob** to spell the name **Rod**."

When children are not just adding or changing one letter, cue them to start over.

> "Start over and use 4 new letters to spell the name **Brad**."

Give a meaning or sentence clue, when needed, to clarify the word children are making.

> "Start over and use 5 new letters to spell **adore**. The children all **adore** their grandmother."

Always alert children when they are making a name and expect them to use a capital letter.

> "Use 2 new letters to spell the name **Bo**."

Give children one minute to figure out the secret word and then give clues, if needed.

> "Our secret word is a name and you can make it by adding your letters to **Deb**."

Sort Beginning Letters (Optional)

Sort Rhymes

Reading Transfer: "Pretend you are reading and come to a new word." Have children put the transfer words under the appropriate rhymes and use the rhymes to decode them.

Spelling Transfer: "Pretend you are writing and need to spell these words." Have children tell you how the words begin. Then, have children find and use the appropriate rhymes to finish spelling the transfer words.

Step-by-step directions for a sample *Making Names* lesson are on pages 8-12.

MAKE WORDS

Bo
boa
bad
bed/Deb
Rob
Rod
ear
hear
dear/read
Brad
adore
Deborah

SORT WORDS

Beginning Letters (Optional)

Rhymes:
ear	bad
hear	Brad
dear	

TRANSFER WORDS

Reading:
mad gear

Spelling:
fear fad

Delores

e e o d l r s

MAKE WORDS

Ed
led
red
Rod
old
sold
sled
rode
role
sole/lose
loser
older
Delores

SORT WORDS

Related Words:
lose, loser; old, older

Rhymes:
Ed   old
led   sold
red
sled

TRANSFER WORDS

Reading:
Fred gold

Spelling:
Ted fold

Make Words: Tell children how many letters to use to make each word. (A slash indicates words that can be made with the same letters.)

Emphasize how changing just one letter or rearranging letters makes a different word.

> "Change a letter in **red** to spell the name **Rod**."

> "Use the same letters in **sole** to spell **lose**."

When children are not just adding or changing one letter, cue them to start over.

> "Start over and use 5 new letters to spell **older**."

Give a meaning or sentence clue, when needed, to clarify the word children are making.

> "Change 1 letter in **role** to spell **sole**. **Sole** is a type of fish, and some people call it flounder."

Always alert children when they are making a name and expect them to use a capital letter.

> "Take 2 letters and spell the name **Ed**."

Give children one minute to figure out the secret word and then give clues, if needed.

> "Our secret word is a name that begins with **D** and ends with **s**."

Sort Related Words

Sort Rhymes

Reading Transfer: "Pretend you are reading and come to a new word." Have children put the transfer words under the appropriate rhymes and use the rhymes to decode them.

Spelling Transfer: "Pretend you are writing and need to spell these words." Have children tell you how the words begin. Then, have children find and use the appropriate rhymes to finish spelling the transfer words.

Step-by-step directions for a sample *Making Names* lesson are on pages 8-12.

Derrick

Make Words: Tell children how many letters to use to make each word. (A slash indicates words that can be made with the same letters.)

Emphasize how changing just one letter or rearranging letters makes a different word.

> "Add a letter to **ice** to spell **dice**."

> "Use the same letters in **cried** to spell **cider**."

When children are not just adding or changing one letter, cue them to start over.

> "Start over and use 3 new letters to spell **ice**."

Give a meaning or sentence clue, when needed, to clarify the word children are making.

> "Start over and use 4 new letters to spell **cried**. The baby **cried** when he was hungry."

Always alert children when they are making a name and expect them to use a capital letter.

> "Change 1 letter in **Rick** to spell the name **Dick**."

> "Use 4 new letters to spell the name **Keri**."

Give children one minute to figure out the secret word and then give clues, if needed.

> "Our secret word is a name that you can spell by adding your letters to **Rick**."

Sort C Words—s sound (Optional)

Sort Related Words

Sort Rhymes

Reading Transfer: "Pretend you are reading and come to a new word." Have children put the transfer words under the appropriate rhymes and use the rhymes to decode them.

Spelling Transfer: "Pretend you are writing and need to spell these words." Have children tell you how the words begin. Then, have children find and use the appropriate rhymes to finish spelling the transfer words.

Step-by-step directions for a sample *Making Names* lesson are on pages 8-12.

MAKE WORDS

kid
ice
dice
rice
ride
Eric
Rick
Dick
Keri
cried/cider
rider
Derrick

SORT WORDS

C Words—s sound
(Optional):
cider, ice, dice, rice

Related Words:
ride, rider

Rhymes:

ice	Rick	cider
dice	Dick	rider
rice		

TRANSFER WORDS

Reading:
spice trick

Spelling:
spider slice

Deshawn

a e d h n s w

MAKE WORDS

and/Dan
den
hen
new
news
when
Dean
hand
wash
Dawn
Shawn
Shane
washed
Deshawn

SORT WORDS

Sh Words (Optional):
Shawn, Shane, Deshawn,
wash, washed

Related Words:
wash, washed; new, news

Rhymes:
den	and	Dawn
hen	hand	Shawn
when		Deshawn

TRANSFER WORDS

Reading:
lawn then

Spelling:
pawn brand

Make Words: Tell children how many letters to use to make each word. (A slash indicates words that can be made with the same letters.)

Emphasize how changing just one letter or rearranging letters makes a different word.

> "Add a letter to **new** to spell **news**."

> "Use the same letters in **and** to spell the name **Dan**."

When children are not just adding or changing one letter, cue them to start over.

> "Start over and use 4 new letters to spell the name **Dawn**."

Give a meaning or sentence clue, when needed, to clarify the word children are making.

> "Start over and use 6 new letters to spell **washed**. We **washed** clothes at the laundromat."

Always alert children when they are making a name and expect them to use a capital letter.

> "Use 4 new letters to spell the name **Dean**."

Give children one minute to figure out the secret word and then give clues, if needed.

> "Our secret word is a name that you can spell by adding your letters to **Shawn**."**Sort Rhymes**

Sort Sh Words (Optional)

Sort Related Words

Sort Rhymes

Reading Transfer: "Pretend you are reading and come to a new word." Have children put the transfer words under the appropriate rhymes and use the rhymes to decode them.

Spelling Transfer: "Pretend you are writing and need to spell these words." Have children tell you how the words begin. Then, have children find and use the appropriate rhymes to finish spelling the transfer words.

Step-by-step directions for a sample *Making Names* lesson are on pages 8-12.

Destiny

Make Words: Tell children how many letters to use to make each word. (A slash indicates words that can be made with the same letters.)

Emphasize how changing just one letter or rearranging letters makes a different word.

> "Add a letter to **end** to spell **send**."

> "Use the same letters in **tide** to spell **edit**."

When children are not just adding or changing one letter, cue them to start over.

> "Start over and use 4 new letters to spell **side**."

Give a meaning or sentence clue, when needed, to clarify the word children are making.

> "Use 4 new letters to spell **tiny**. The **tiny** kittens were born yesterday."

Always alert children when they are making a name and expect them to use a capital letter.

> "Change one letter in **Ned** to spell the name **Ted**."

Give children one minute to figure out the secret word and then give clues, if needed.

> "The secret word is a name and you can make it by adding your letters to **tiny**."

Sort Beginning Letters (Optional)

Sort Rhymes

Reading Transfer: "Pretend you are reading and come to a new word." Have children put the transfer words under the appropriate rhymes and use the rhymes to decode them.

Spelling Transfer: "Pretend you are writing and need to spell these words." Have children tell you how the words begin. Then, have children find and use the appropriate rhymes to finish spelling the transfer words.

Step-by-step directions for a sample *Making Names* lesson are on pages 8-12.

MAKE WORDS

Ed
Ned
Ted
ten
den/end
send
sent
dent
side
tide/edit
tiny
Destiny

SORT WORDS

Beginning Letters (Optional)

Rhymes:

Ed	ten	end	sent	tide
Ted	den	send	dent	side
Ned				

TRANSFER WORDS

Reading:
bent hide

Spelling:
glide bend

Dominique

e i i o u d m n q

MAKE WORDS

Ed
end/den
Don
done
dune
dine
dime
dome
mine
mind
mend
menu
Monique
Dominique

SORT WORDS

Beginning Letters (Optional)

Rhymes:
dine   end
mine   mend

TRANSFER WORDS

Reading:
shine tend

Spelling:
trend nine

Make Words: Tell children how many letters to use to make each word. (A slash indicates words that can be made with the same letters.)

Emphasize how changing just one letter or rearranging letters makes a different word.

> "Add a letter to **Ed** to spell **end**."

> "Use the same letters in **end** to spell **den**."

When children are not just adding or changing one letter, cue them to start over.

> "Start over and use 4 new letters to spell the word **mine**."

Give a meaning or sentence clue, when needed, to clarify the word children are making.

> "Change 1 letter in **mend** to spell **menu**. We ordered food from the **menu**."

Always alert students when they are making a name and expect them to use a capital letter.

> "Use 7 new letters to spell the name **Monique**."

Give children one minute to figure out the secret word and then give clues, if needed.

> "The secret word is a name that begins with **D** and ends with **e**."

Sort Beginning Letters (Optional)

Sort Rhymes

Reading Transfer: "Pretend you are reading and come to a new word." Have children put the transfer words under the appropriate rhymes and use the rhymes to decode them.

Spelling Transfer: "Pretend you are writing and need to spell these words." Have children tell you how the words begin. Then, have children find and use the appropriate rhymes to finish spelling the transfer words.

Step-by-step directions for a sample *Making Names* lesson are on pages 8-12.

78

Dorothy

oodhrty

Make Words: Tell children how many letters to use to make each word. (A slash indicates words that can be made with the same letters.)

Emphasize how changing just one letter or rearranging letters makes a different word.

"Use the same letters in **door** to spell **odor**."

"Change 1 letter in **hood** to spell **hoot**."

When children are not just adding or changing one letter, cue them to start over.

"Start over and use 3 new letters to spell **try**."

Give a meaning or sentence clue, when needed, to clarify the word children are making.

"Change 1 letter in **hoot** to spell **root**. Water comes into a plant through a **root**."

Always alert children when they are making a name and expect them to use a capital letter.

"Change 1 letter in **Rod** to spell the name **Roy**."

Give children one minute to figure out the secret word and then give clues, if needed.

"Our secret word is a name that begins with **D** and ends with **y**."

Sort Beginning Letters (Optional)

Sort Rhymes

Reading Transfer: "Pretend you are reading and come to a new word." Have children put the transfer words under the appropriate rhymes and use the rhymes to decode them.

Spelling Transfer: "Pretend you are writing and need to spell these words." Have children tell you how the words begin. Then, have children find and use the appropriate rhymes to finish spelling the transfer words.

Step-by-step directions for a sample *Making Names* lesson are on pages 8-12.

MAKE WORDS

hot
rot
Rod
Roy
try
dry
toy
hood
hoot
root
Troy
door/odor
Dorothy

SORT WORDS

Beginning Letters (Optional)

Rhymes:

hot	Roy	hoot	try
rot	Troy	root	dry

TRANSFER WORDS

Reading:
boot sky

Spelling:
shoot shot

Douglas

a o u d g l s

sad
old
Ola
dog
Doug
sold
gold
glad
soda
loud
aloud
Douglas

SORT WORDS

Related Words:
loud, aloud

Rhymes:
sad   old
glad   sold
         gold

TRANSFER WORDS

Reading:
Brad   cold

Spelling:
Chad   hold

Make Words: Tell children how many letters to use to make each word. (A slash indicates words that can be made with the same letters.)

Emphasize how changing just one letter or rearranging letters makes a different word.

> "Add a letter to **dog** to spell the name **Doug**."

> "Change a letter in **sold** to spell **gold**."

When children are not just adding or changing one letter, cue them to start over.

> "Start over and use 4 new letters to spell **loud**."

Give a meaning or sentence clue, when needed, to clarify the word children are making.

> "Add a letter to **loud** to spell **aloud**. We love it when our teacher reads **aloud** to us."

Always alert children when they are making a name and expect them to use a capital letter.

> "Change 1 letter in **old** to spell the name **Ola**."

Give children one minute to figure out the secret word and then give clues, if needed.

> "Our secret word is a name that you can make by adding your letters to **Doug**."

Sort Related Words

Sort Rhymes

Reading Transfer: "Pretend you are reading and come to a new word." Have children put the transfer words under the appropriate rhymes and use the rhymes to decode them.

Spelling Transfer: "Pretend you are writing and need to spell these words." Have children tell you how the words begin. Then, have children find and use the appropriate rhymes to finish spelling the transfer words.

Step-by-step directions for a sample *Making Names* lesson are on pages 8-12.

Eleanor

a e e o l n r

Make Words: Tell children how many letters to use to make each word. (A slash indicates words that can be made with the same letters.)

Emphasize how changing just one letter or rearranging letters makes a different word.

> "Add a letter to **ear** to spell **near**."

> "Use the same letters in **lean** to spell the name **Lena**."

When children are not just adding or changing one letter, cue them to start over.

> "Start over and use 3 new letters to spell **are**."

Give a meaning or sentence clue, when needed, to clarify the word children are making.

> "Use the same letters in **near** to spell **earn**. He delivers papers to **earn** money to buy a surfboard."

Always alert children when they are making a name and expect them to use a capital letter.

> "Take 4 new letters and spell the name **Nora**."

Give children one minute to figure out the secret word and then give clues, if needed.

> "Our secret word is a name that you can make by adding your letters to **nor**."

Sort Related Words

Sort Rhymes

Reading Transfer: "Pretend you are reading and come to a new word." Have children put the transfer words under the appropriate rhymes and use the rhymes to decode them.

Spelling Transfer: "Pretend you are writing and need to spell these words." Have children tell you how the words begin. Then, have children find and use the appropriate rhymes to finish spelling the transfer words.

Step-by-step directions for a sample *Making Names* lesson are on pages 8-12.

MAKE WORDS

on
or
nor/Ron
are/ear
near/earn
lean/Lena
Nora
lone
alone
learn
Eleanor

SORT WORDS

Related Words:
lone, alone

Rhymes:

or	on	ear	ear
nor	Ron	near	learn

TRANSFER WORDS

Reading:
clear Jon

Spelling:
for year

Elizabeth

a e e i b h l t z

▶ MAKE WORDS

Zeb
Liz
lit
hit
bit
bite
Beth
bath
late
hate
able
table
Eliza
Hazel
Elizabeth

▶ SORT WORDS

Z Words (Optional):
Zeb, Eliza, Hazel, Elizabeth

Rhymes:
lit	late	able
hit	hate	table
bit		

▶ TRANSFER WORDS

Reading:
cable quit

Spelling:
stable state

Make Words: Tell children how many letters to use to make each word. (A slash indicates words that can be made with the same letters.)

Emphasize how changing just one letter or rearranging letters makes a different word.

> "Add a letter to **bit** to spell **bite**."

> "Change a letter in **late** to spell **hate**."

When children are not just adding or changing one letter, cue them to start over.

> "Start over and use 4 new letters to spell **able**."

Give a meaning or sentence clue, when needed, to clarify the word children are making.

> "Add a letter to **able** to spell **table**. We put the books on the **table**."

Always alert children when they are making a name and expect them to use a capital letter.

> "Take 4 new letters and spell the name **Hazel**."

Give children one minute to figure out the secret word and then give clues, if needed.

> "Our secret word is a name that you can spell by adding your letters to **Eliza**."

Sort Z Words (Optional)

Sort Rhymes

Reading Transfer: "Pretend you are reading and come to a new word." Have children put the transfer words under the appropriate rhymes and use the rhymes to decode them.

Spelling Transfer: "Pretend you are writing and need to spell these words." Have children tell you how the words begin. Then, have children find and use the appropriate rhymes to finish spelling the transfer words.

Step-by-step directions for a sample *Making Names* lesson are on pages 8-12.

82

Ernest

e e n r s t

Make Words: Tell children how many letters to use to make each word. (A slash indicates words that can be made with the same letters.)

Emphasize how changing just one letter or rearranging letters makes a different word.

> "Add a letter to **see** to spell **seen**."

> "Use the same letters in **net** to spell **ten**."

When children are not just adding or changing one letter, cue them to start over.

> "Start over and use 5 new letters to spell **enter**."

Give a meaning or sentence clue, when needed, to clarify the word children are making.

> "Add a letter to **rest** to spell **reset**. You can fix that by pushing the **reset** button."

This lesson has two secret words. Give children one minute to figure out each secret word and then gives clues, if needed. Always alert children when they are making a name and expect them to use a capital letter.

> "One secret word can be made by adding a letter to **enter**."

> "The other secret word is a name that you can spell by adding your letters to **nest**."

Sort Related Words

Sort Rhymes

Reading Transfer: "Pretend you are reading and come to a new word." Have children put the transfer words under the appropriate rhymes and use the rhymes to decode them.

Spelling Transfer: "Pretend you are writing and need to spell these words." Have children tell you how the words begin. Then, have children find and use the appropriate rhymes to finish spelling the transfer words.

Step-by-step directions for a sample *Making Names* lesson are on pages 8-12.

MAKE WORDS

set
net/ten
tee
see
seen
teen
nest/sent
rent
rest
reset
enter
enters/Ernest

SORT WORDS

Related Words:
set, reset; enter, enters

Rhymes:

tee	seen	sent	set	nest
see	teen	rent	net	rest

TRANSFER WORDS

Reading:
quest green

Spelling:
pest queen

Ethan

a e h n t

MAKE WORDS

at
an
ant/tan/Nat
hat
net/ten
then
than
neat
heat/hate
Nate
Ethan

SORT WORDS

Th Words (Optional):
than, then, Ethan

Rhymes:
at   an   ten   neat hate
Nat   tan   then   heat Nate
hat   than

TRANSFER WORDS

Reading:
beat skate

Spelling:
treat gate

Make Words: Tell children how many letters to use to make each word. (A slash indicates words that can be made with the same letters.)

Emphasize how changing just one letter or rearranging letters makes a different word.

"Add a letter to **an** to spell **ant**."

"Change 1 letter in **then** to spell **than**."

When children are not just adding or changing one letter, cue them to start over.

"Start over and use 4 new letters to spell **neat**."

Give a meaning or sentence clue, when needed, to clarify the word children are making.

"Add a letter to **ten** to spell **then**. **Then**, the dog was found at the school."

Always alert children when they are making a name and expect them to use a capital letter.

"Use the same letters in **tan** to spell the name **Nat**."

Give children one minute to figure out the secret word and then give clues, if needed.

"Our secret word is a name that begins with **E** and ends with **n**."

Sort Th Words (Optional)

Sort Rhymes

Reading Transfer: "Pretend you are reading and come to a new word." Have children put the transfer words under the appropriate rhymes and use the rhymes to decode them.

Spelling Transfer: "Pretend you are writing and need to spell these words." Have children tell you how the words begin. Then, have children find and use the appropriate rhymes to finish spelling the transfer words.

Step-by-step directions for a sample *Making Names* lesson are on pages 8-12.

Fernando

a e o d f n n r

Make Words: Tell children how many letters to use to make each word. (A slash indicates words that can be made with the same letters.)

Emphasize how changing just one letter or rearranging letters makes a different word.

"Add a letter to **Ed** to spell the name **Ned**."

"Use the same letters in **nod** to spell the name **Don**."

When children are not just adding or changing one letter, cue them to start over.

"Start over and use 5 new letters to spell the name **Donna**."

Give a meaning or sentence clue, when needed, to clarify the word children are making.

"Change 1 letter in **Ned** to spell **nod**. **Nod** your head if you agree."

Always alert children when they are making a name and expect them to use a capital letter.

"Use 4 new letters and spell the name **Fred**."

Give children one minute to figure out the secret word and then give clues, if needed.

"Our secret word is a name that begins with **F** and ends with **o**."

Sort Rhymes

Reading Transfer: "Pretend you are reading and come to a new word." Have children put the transfer words under the appropriate rhymes and use the rhymes to decode them.

Spelling Transfer: "Pretend you are writing and need to spell these words." Have children tell you how the words begin. Then, have children find and use the appropriate rhymes to finish spelling the transfer words.

Step-by-step directions for a sample *Making Names* lesson are on pages 8-12.

MAKE WORDS

Ed
Ned
nod/Don
Ron
Rod
Ann
Anne
Dean
dear
fear
near
Fred
Donna
Fernando

SORT WORDS

Rhymes:

Ed	Don	dear
Ned	Ron	fear
Fred		near

TRANSFER WORDS

Reading:
shed hear

Spelling:
sled spear

Frances

a e c f n r s

MAKE WORDS

an
ran
can
ace
face
race/care
fare/fear
near
Fran
scare
France
Frances

SORT WORDS

Fr Words (Optional):
Fran, France, Frances

Rhymes:

an	ace	care	fear
ran	face	scare	near
can	race	fare	
Fran			

TRANSFER WORDS

Reading:
square trace

Spelling:
spare space

Make Words: Tell children how many letters to use to make each word. (A slash indicates words that can be made with the same letters.)

Emphasize how changing just one letter or rearranging letters makes a different word.

> "Add a letter to **ace** to spell **face**."

> "Use the same letters in **race** to spell **care**."

When children are not just adding or changing one letter, cue them to start over.

> "Start over and use 5 new letters to spell **scare**."

Give a meaning or sentence clue, when needed, to clarify the word children are making.

> "Change 1 letter in **care** to spell **fare**. The bus **fare** was one dollar."

Always alert children when they are making a name and expect them to use a capital letter.

> "Use 6 new letters to spell the country of **France**."

Give children one minute to figure out the secret word and then give clues, if needed.

> "Our secret word is a name that you can spell by adding a letter to **France**."

Sort Fr Words (Optional)

Sort Rhymes

Reading Transfer: "Pretend you are reading and come to a new word." Have children put the transfer words under the appropriate rhymes and use the rhymes to decode them.

Spelling Transfer: "Pretend you are writing and need to spell these words." Have children tell you how the words begin. Then, have children find and use the appropriate rhymes to finish spelling the transfer words.

Step-by-step directions for a sample *Making Names* lesson are on pages 8-12.

Francisco

a i o c c f n r s

Make Words: Tell children how many letters to use to make each word. (A slash indicates words that can be made with the same letters.)

Emphasize how changing just one letter or rearranging letters makes a different word.

"Change a letter in **scan** to spell **scar**."

"Add one letter to **fan** to spell the name **Fran**."

When children are not just adding or changing one letter, cue them to start over.

"Start over and use 3 new letters to spell **fin**."

Give a meaning or sentence clue, when needed, to clarify the word children are making.

"Change a letter in **far** to spell **fir**. The **fir** tree was covered in snow."

Always alert children when they are making a name and expect them to use a capital letter.

"Take 7 new letters and spell the name **Francis**."

Give children one minute to figure out the secret word and then give clues, if needed.

"Our secret word is a name that can be made by adding your letters to **Francis**."

Sort Fr Words (Optional)

Sort Rhymes

Reading Transfer: "Pretend you are reading and come to a new word." Have children put the transfer words under the appropriate rhymes and use the rhymes to decode them.

Spelling Transfer: "Pretend you are writing and need to spell these words." Have children tell you how the words begin. Then, have children find and use the appropriate rhymes to finish spelling the transfer words.

Step-by-step directions for a sample *Making Names* lesson are on pages 8-12.

MAKE WORDS

Ian
Ira
ran
can
car
far
fir
sir
fin
fan
Fran
scan
scar
Francis
Francisco

SORT WORDS

Fr Words (Optional):
Fran, Francis, Francisco

Rhymes:

ran	car	fir
can	far	sir
fan	scar	
Fran		

TRANSFER WORDS

Reading:
star stir

Spelling:
plan jar

Franklin

a i f k l n n r

MAKE WORDS

ink
air
fair
fail
nail
rail
rain
link
rink
rank
Nina
Fran
Frank
final
Franklin

SORT WORDS

Fr Words (Optional):
Fran, Frank, Franklin

Rhymes:

ink	rail	rank	air
link	fail	Frank	fair
rink	nail		

TRANSFER WORDS

Reading:
thank think

Spelling:
clink clank

Make Words: Tell children how many letters to use to make each word. (A slash indicates words that can be made with the same letters.)

Emphasize how changing just one letter or rearranging letters makes a different word.

> "Change a letter in **link** to spell **rink**."

> "Add a letter to **Fran** to spell the name **Frank**."

When children are not just adding or changing one letter, cue them to start over.

> "Start over and use 3 new letters to spell **air**."

Give a meaning or sentence clue, when needed, to clarify the word children are making.

> "Start over and use 5 letters to spell the word **final**. We arrived just as the **final** act of the play was beginning."

Always alert children when they are making a name and expect them to use a capital letter.

> "Use 4 new letters to spell the name **Nina**."

Give children one minute to figure out the secret word and then give clues, if needed.

> "Our secret word is a name that you can spell by adding your letters to **Frank**."

Sort Fr Words (Optional)

Sort Rhymes

Reading Transfer: "Pretend you are reading and come to a new word." Have children put the transfer words under the appropriate rhymes and use the rhymes to decode them.

Spelling Transfer: "Pretend you are writing and need to spell these words." Have children tell you how the words begin. Then, have children find and use the appropriate rhymes to finish spelling the transfer words.

Step-by-step directions for a sample *Making Names* lesson are on pages 8-12.

Frederick

e e i c d f k r r

Make Words: Tell children how many letters to use to make each word. (A slash indicates words that can be made with the same letters.)

Emphasize how changing just one letter or rearranging letters makes a different word.

> "Change a letter in **cider** to spell **rider**."

> "Add a letter to **fire** to spell **fired**."

When children are not just adding or changing one letter, cue them to start over.

> "Start over and use 7 new letters to spell the name **Derrick**."

Give a meaning or sentence clue, when needed, to clarify the word children are making.

> "Change 1 letter in **fried** to spell **cried**. The baby **cried** all night."

Always alert children when they are making a name and expect them to use a capital letter.

> "Use 4 letters to spell the name **Eric**."

Give children one minute to figure out the secret word and then give clues, if needed.

> "Our secret word is a name that you can spell by adding your letters to **Fred**."

Sort Fr Words (Optional)

Sort Related Words

Sort Rhymes

Reading Transfer: "Pretend you are reading and come to a new word." Have children put the transfer words under the appropriate rhymes and use the rhymes to decode them.

Spelling Transfer: "Pretend you are writing and need to spell these words." Have children tell you how the words begin. Then, have children find and use the appropriate rhymes to finish spelling the transfer words.

Step-by-step directions for a sample *Making Names* lesson are on pages 8-12.

MAKE WORDS

kid
rid
Eric
Fred
Rick
Dick
fire
fired/fried
cried/cider
rider
Derrick
Frederick

SORT WORDS

Fr Words (Optional):
Fred, fried, Frederick

Related Words:
fire, fired

Rhymes:

kid	fried	rider
rid	cried	cider

TRANSFER WORDS

Reading:
tried spider

Spelling:
slid spied

Gabriel

a e i b g l r

MAKE WORDS

big
rig
age
Abe
Gabe
rail
Gail
girl
rage
large
barge
bagel
gerbil
Gabriel

SORT WORDS

G Words—both sounds
(Optional):
Gabe, Gail, Gabriel, girl, big,
rig, bagel; gerbil, large, barge,
rage, age

Rhymes:
big   age   Abe   rail   large
rig   rage   Gabe   Gail   barge

TRANSFER WORDS

Reading:
Marge   cage

Spelling:
stage   quail

Make Words: Tell children how many letters to use to make each word. (A slash indicates words that can be made with the same letters.)

Emphasize how changing just one letter or rearranging letters makes a different word.

"Add a letter to **Abe** to spell the name **Gabe**."

"Change one letter in **rail** and spell the name **Gail**."

When children are not just adding or changing one letter, cue them to start over.

"Start over and use 6 new letters to spell **gerbil**."

Give a meaning or sentence clue, when needed, to clarify the word children are making.

"Start over and use 5 new letters to spell **bagel**. I put cream cheese on my **bagel**."

Always alert children when they are making a name and expect them to use a capital letter.

"Take 3 new letters and spell the name **Abe**."

Give children one minute to figure out the secret word and then give clues, if needed.

"Our secret word is a name that begins with **G** and ends with **l**."

Sort G Words—both sounds (Optional)

Sort Rhymes

Reading Transfer: "Pretend you are reading and come to a new word." Have children put the transfer words under the appropriate rhymes and use the rhymes to decode them.

Spelling Transfer: "Pretend you are writing and need to spell these words." Have children tell you how the words begin. Then, have children find and use the appropriate rhymes to finish spelling the transfer words.

Step-by-step directions for a sample *Making Names* lesson are on pages 8-12.

Making Names • CD-2429 • © Carson-Dellosa

Gabriella

a a e i b g l l r

Make Words: Tell children how many letters to use to make each word. (A slash indicates words that can be made with the same letters.)

Emphasize how changing just one letter or rearranging letters makes a different word.

"Change a letter in **Bill** to spell **gill**."

"Use the same letters in **Bea** to spell the name **Abe**."

When children are not just adding or changing one letter, cue them to start over.

"Start over and use 5 new letters to spell **bagel**."

Give a meaning or sentence clue, when needed, to clarify the word children are making.

"Add a letter to **gill** to spell **grill**. We cooked chicken on the **grill**."

Always alert children when they are making a name and expect them to use a capital letter.

"Use 5 new letters to spell the name **Bella**."

Give children one minute to figure out the secret word and then give clues, if needed.

"Our secret word is a name that you can spell by adding your letters to **Gabriel**."

Sort Rhymes

Reading Transfer: "Pretend you are reading and come to a new word." Have children put the transfer words under the appropriate rhymes and use the rhymes to decode them.

Spelling Transfer: "Pretend you are writing and need to spell these words." Have children tell you how the words begin. Then, have children find and use the appropriate rhymes to finish spelling the transfer words.

Step-by-step directions for a sample *Making Names* lesson are on pages 8-12.

MAKE WORDS

Al
all
Bea/Abe
Gabe
Ella
ball
Bill
gill
grill
Bella
bagel
gerbil
Gabriel
Gabriella

SORT WORDS

Rhymes:

all	Abe	Bill
ball	Gabe	gill
		grill

TRANSFER WORDS

Reading:
still stall

Spelling:
spill mall

Garfield

a e i d f g l r

MAKE WORDS

die
lie
age
rage
Earl
lied
fail
Gail
fire
fired/fried
grade/raged
field
Garfield

SORT WORDS

Related Words:
rage, raged; lie, lied;
fire, fired

Rhymes:
| die | age | fail |
| lie | rage | Gail |

TRANSFER WORDS

Reading:
wage pail

Spelling:
tie cage

Make Words: Tell children how many letters to use to make each word. (A slash indicates words that can be made with the same letters.)

Emphasize how changing just one letter or rearranging letters makes a different word.

> "Change a letter in **fail** to spell the name **Gail**."

> "Use the same letters in **fired** to spell **fried**."

When children are not just adding or changing one letter, cue them to start over.

> "Start over and use 4 new letters to spell the name **Earl**."

Give a meaning or sentence clue, when needed, to clarify the word children are making.

> "Use 5 new letters to spell **field**. We drove by a huge wheat **field**."

Always alert children when they are making a name and expect them to use a capital letter.

> "Change 1 letter in **fail** to spell the name **Gail**."

Give children one minute to figure out the secret word and then give clues, if needed.

> "Our secret word is a name you can make it by adding your letters to **field**."

Sort Related Words

Sort Rhymes

Reading Transfer: "Pretend you are reading and come to a new word." Have children put the transfer words under the appropriate rhymes and use the rhymes to decode them.

Spelling Transfer: "Pretend you are writing and need to spell these words." Have children tell you how the words begin. Then, have children find and use the appropriate rhymes to finish spelling the transfer words.

Step-by-step directions for a sample *Making Names* lesson are on pages 8-12.

Georgia

Make Words: Tell children how many letters to use to make each word. (A slash indicates words that can be made with the same letters.)

Emphasize how changing just one letter or rearranging letters makes a different word.

> "Add a letter to **go** to spell **ago**."

> "Use the same letters in **gear** to spell **rage**."

When children are not just adding or changing one letter, cue them to start over.

> "Start over and use 3 new letters to spell **egg**."

Give a meaning or sentence clue, when needed, to clarify the word children are making.

> "Use the same letters in **gear** to spell **rage**. When the pirate discovered his treasure was gone, he flew into a **rage**."

Always alert children when they are making a name and expect them to use a capital letter.

> "Use 4 new letters to spell the name **Greg**."

Give children one minute to figure out the secret word and then give clues, if needed.

> "Our secret word is a name that begins with **G** and ends with **a**."

Sort G Words—both sounds (Optional)

Sort Rhymes

Reading Transfer: "Pretend you are reading and come to a new word." Have children put the transfer words under the appropriate rhymes and use the rhymes to decode them.

Spelling Transfer: "Pretend you are writing and need to spell these words." Have children tell you how the words begin. Then, have children find and use the appropriate rhymes to finish spelling the transfer words.

Step-by-step directions for a sample *Making Names* lesson are on pages 8-12.

MAKE WORDS

or
go
ago
age
are/ear
egg
Ira
gear/rage
Greg
Georgia

SORT WORDS

G Words—both sounds (Optional):
go, gear, Greg, ago, egg;
Georgia, rage, age

Rhymes:
age   ear
rage   gear

TRANSFER WORDS

Reading:
page cage

Spelling:
year stage

Geraldine

MAKE WORDS

rain
gain
Gail
Edna
Erin
need
greed
green
Ernie
Diane
rained
gained
Daniel
Gerald
Geraldine

SORT WORDS

Gr Words (Optional):
greed, green

Rhymes:
rain   rained   need
gain   gained   greed

TRANSFER WORDS

Reading:
strain strained

Spelling:
bleed speed

Make Words: Tell children how many letters to use to make each word. (A slash indicates words that can be made with the same letters.)

Emphasize how changing just one letter or rearranging letters makes a different word.

"Change a letter in **greed** to spell **green**."

When children are not just adding or changing one letter, cue them to start over.

"Start over and use 6 new letters to spell **rained**."

Give a meaning or sentence clue, when needed, to clarify the word children are making.

"Change 1 letter in **rained** to spell **gained**. When my sister was pregnant, she **gained** 20 pounds."

Always alert children when they are making a name and expect them to use a capital letter.

"Use 6 new letters to spell the name **Daniel**."

Give children one minute to figure out the secret word and then give clues, if needed.

"Our secret word is a name that you can make by adding your letters to **Gerald**."

Sort Gr Words (Optional)

Sort Rhymes

Reading Transfer: "Pretend you are reading and come to a new word." Have children put the transfer words under the appropriate rhymes and use the rhymes to decode them.

Spelling Transfer: "Pretend you are writing and need to spell these words." Have children tell you how the words begin. Then, have children find and use the appropriate rhymes to finish spelling the transfer words.

Step-by-step directions for a sample *Making Names* lesson are on pages 8-12.

Gordon

o o d g n r

Make Words: Tell children how many letters to use to make each word. (A slash indicates words that can be made with the same letters.)

Emphasize how changing just one letter or rearranging letters makes a different word.

> "Add a letter to **on** to spell the name **Don**."

> "Use the same letters in **door** to spell **odor**."

When children are not just adding or changing one letter, cue them to start over.

> "Start over and use 3 new letters to spell **dog**."

Give a meaning or sentence clue, when needed, to clarify the word children are making.

> "Use 5 new letters to spell **donor**. An organ **donor** is someone who donates his organs to save the lives of others."

Always alert children when they are making a name and expect them to use a capital letter.

> "Change 1 letter in **Ron** to spell the name **Rod**."

Give children one minute to figure out the secret word and then give clues, if needed.

> "You can make the secret word by adding your letters to **Don**."

Sort Beginning Letters (Optional)

Sort Rhymes

Reading Transfer: "Pretend you are reading and come to a new word." Have children put the transfer words under the appropriate rhymes and use the rhymes to decode them.

Spelling Transfer: "Pretend you are writing and need to spell these words." Have children tell you how the words begin. Then, have children find and use the appropriate rhymes to finish spelling the transfer words.

Step-by-step directions for a sample *Making Names* lesson are on pages 8-12.

MAKE WORDS

go
no
on
Don
Ron
Rod
nod
dog
door/odor
donor
Gordon

SORT WORDS

Beginning Letters (Optional)

Rhymes:

on	go	Rod
Don	no	nod
Ron		

TRANSFER WORDS

Reading:
plod con

Spelling:
clod pod

Grace

MAKE WORDS

car
ear
ace
age
rag
rage
cage
care/race
gear
Grace

SORT WORDS

Beginning Letters (Optional)

Rhymes:

ear	ace	rage
gear	race	cage
	Grace	age

TRANSFER WORDS

Reading:
brace spear

Spelling:
stage trace

Make Words: Tell children how many letters to use to make each word. (A slash indicates words that can be made with the same letters.)

Emphasize how changing just one letter or rearranging letters makes a different word.

> "Change a letter in **ace** to spell **age**."

> "Use the same letters in **care** to spell **race**."

When children are not just adding or changing one letter, cue them to start over.

> "Start over and use 4 new letters to spell **gear**."

Give a meaning or sentence clue, when needed, to clarify the word children are making.

> "Add 1 letter to **rag** to spell **rage**. When the man realized he had been tricked, he flew into a **rage**."

Give children one minute to figure out the secret word and then give clues, if needed. Always alert children when they are making a name and expect them to use a capital letter.

> "Our secret word is a name that you can spell by adding a letter to **race**."

Sort Beginning Letters (Optional)

Sort Rhymes

Reading Transfer: "Pretend you are reading and come to a new word." Have children put the transfer words under the appropriate rhymes and use the rhymes to decode them.

Spelling Transfer: "Pretend you are writing and need to spell these words." Have children tell you how the words begin. Then, have children find and use the appropriate rhymes to finish spelling the transfer words.

Step-by-step directions for a sample *Making Names* lesson are on pages 8-12.

Grant

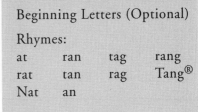

a g n r t

Make Words: Tell children how many letters to use to make each word. (A slash indicates words that can be made with the same letters.)

Emphasize how changing just one letter or rearranging letters makes a different word.

"Add a letter to **rag** to spell **rang**."

"Change 1 letter in **tar** to spell **tag**."

Give a meaning or sentence clue, when needed, to clarify the word children are making.

"Change 1 letter in **rang** to spell **Tang**®. **Tang**® is an orange-flavored drink."

Always alert children when they are making a name and expect them to use a capital letter.

"Use the same letters in **rat** to spell the name **Art**."

Give children one minute to figure out the secret word and then give clues, if needed.

"Our secret word is a name that you can make by adding your letters to **ant**."

Sort Beginning Letters (Optional)

Sort Rhymes

Reading Transfer: "Pretend you are reading and come to a new word." Have children put the transfer words under the appropriate rhymes and use the rhymes to decode them.

Spelling Transfer: "Pretend you are writing and need to spell these words." Have children tell you how the words begin. Then, have children find and use the appropriate rhymes to finish spelling the transfer words.

Step-by-step directions for a sample *Making Names* lesson are on pages 8-12.

MAKE WORDS

at
an
ran
tan/ant/Nat
rat/Art/tar
tag
rag
rang
Tang®
Grant

SORT WORDS

Beginning Letters (Optional)
Rhymes:

at	ran	tag	rang
rat	tan	rag	Tang®
Nat	an		

TRANSFER WORDS

Reading:
gang clan

Spelling:
fang flag

Gretchen

e e c g h n r t

MAKE WORDS

ten
hen
then
Chet
teen
tree
three
green
enter
center/recent
Gretchen

SORT WORDS

Gr Words (Optional):
green, Gretchen

Rhymes:

ten	teen	enter	tree
hen	green	center	three
then			

TRANSFER WORDS

Reading:
queen spree

Spelling:
screen free

Make Words: Tell children how many letters to use to make each word. (A slash indicates words that can be made with the same letters.)

Emphasize how changing just one letter or rearranging letters makes a different word.

"Add a letter to **tree** to spell **three**."

When children are not just adding or changing one letter, cue them to start over.

"Start over and use 5 new letters to spell **enter**."

Give a meaning or sentence clue, when needed, to clarify the word children are making.

"Use the same letters in center to spell **recent**. *Michael Jordan: Basketball Superstar* is the most **recent** addition to my collection of biographies."

Always alert children when they are making a name and expect them to use a capital letter.

"Use 4 new letters to spell the name **Chet**."

Sort Gr Words (Optional)

Sort Rhymes

Give children one minute to figure out the secret word and then give clues, if needed.

"Our secret word is a name that begins with **Gr** and ends with **n**."

Reading Transfer: "Pretend you are reading and come to a new word." Have children put the transfer words under the appropriate rhymes and use the rhymes to decode them.

Spelling Transfer: "Pretend you are writing and need to spell these words." Have children tell you how the words begin. Then, have children find and use the appropriate rhymes to finish spelling the transfer words.

Step-by-step directions for a sample *Making Names* lesson are on pages 8-12.

Making Names • CD-2429 • © Carson-Dellosa

Harold

a o d h l r

Make Words: Tell children how many letters to use to make each word. (A slash indicates words that can be made with the same letters.)

Emphasize how changing just one letter or rearranging letters makes a different word.

> "Add a letter to **old** to spell **hold**."

> "Change 1 letter in **road** to spell **load**."

When children are not just adding or changing one letter, cue them to start over.

> "Start over and use 3 new letters to spell **had**."

Give a meaning or sentence clue, when needed, to clarify the word children are making.

> "Change a letter in **hard** to spell **lard**. My grandma uses **lard** to make pie crust."

Always alert children when they are making a name and expect them to use a capital letter.

> "Take 3 new letters and spell the name **Ola**."

Sort Beginning Letters (Optional)

Sort Rhymes

Give children one minute to figure out the secret word and then give clues, if needed.

> "Our secret word is a name that you can make by adding your letters to **old**."

Reading Transfer: "Pretend you are reading and come to a new word." Have children put the transfer words under the appropriate rhymes and use the rhymes to decode them.

Spelling Transfer: "Pretend you are writing and need to spell these words." Have children tell you how the words begin. Then, have children find and use the appropriate rhymes to finish spelling the transfer words.

Step-by-step directions for a sample *Making Names* lesson are on pages 8-12.

MAKE WORDS

oh
or
do
had
Rod
Ola
old
hold
hard
lard
road
load
Harold

SORT WORDS

Beginning Letters (Optional)

Rhymes:
old	hard	road
hold	lard	load

TRANSFER WORDS

Reading:
toad   card

Spelling:
mold   yard

Harriet

a e i h r r t

► MAKE WORDS

eat
ear
air
hair
hear
rear
hire
tire
Rita
their
Earth/heart
rather
Harriet

► SORT WORDS

Beginning Letters (Optional)

Rhymes:

air	ear	hire
hair	rear	tire
	hear	

► TRANSFER WORDS

Reading:
chair wire

Spelling:
pair fear

Make Words: Tell children how many letters to use to make each word. (A slash indicates words that can be made with the same letters.)

Emphasize how changing just one letter or rearranging letters makes a different word.

"Add a letter to **air** to spell **hair**."

"Use the same letters in **Earth** to spell **heart**."

When children are not just adding or changing one letter, cue them to start over.

"Start over and use 4 new letters to spell **hire**."

Give a meaning or sentence clue, when needed, to clarify the word children are making.

"Use 6 new letters to spell **rather**. I like plain pizza, but my brother would **rather** have pepperoni pizza."

Always alert children when they are making a name and expect them to use a capital letter.

"Start over and use 4 new letters to spell the name **Rita**."

Give children one minute to figure out the secret word and then give clues, if needed.

"Our secret word is a name that begins with **H** and ends with **t**."

Sort Beginning Letters (Optional)

Sort Rhymes

Reading Transfer: "Pretend you are reading and come to a new word." Have children put the transfer words under the appropriate rhymes and use the rhymes to decode them.

Spelling Transfer: "Pretend you are writing and need to spell these words." Have children tell you how the words begin. Then, have children find and use the appropriate rhymes to finish spelling the transfer words.

Step-by-step directions for a sample *Making Names* lesson are on pages 8-12.

Heather

Make Words: Tell children how many letters to use to make each word. (A slash indicates words that can be made with the same letters.)

Emphasize how changing just one letter or rearranging letters makes a different word.

> "Add a letter to **at** to spell **ate**."

> "Use the same letters in **Earth** to spell **heart**."

When children are not just adding or changing one letter, cue them to start over.

> "Start over and use 4 new letters to spell **tree**."

Give a meaning or sentence clue, when needed, to clarify the word children are making.

> "Use the same letters in **three** to spell **there**. Our car is parked over **there**."

Give children one minute to figure out the secret word and then give clues, if needed. Always alert children when they are making a name and expect them to use a capital letter.

> "Our secret word is a name that you can spell by adding your letters to **heat**."

Sort Related Words

Sort Rhymes

Reading Transfer: "Pretend you are reading and come to a new word." Have children put the transfer words under the appropriate rhymes and use the rhymes to decode them.

Spelling Transfer: "Pretend you are writing and need to spell these words." Have children tell you how the words begin. Then, have children find and use the appropriate rhymes to finish spelling the transfer words.

Step-by-step directions for a sample *Making Names* lesson are on pages 8-12.

MAKE WORDS

at
ate/eat
hat
rat
rate
hate/heat
tree
three/there
reheat
heart/Earth
Heather

SORT WORDS

Related Words:
heat, reheat

Rhymes:

at	rate	heat	tree
hat	hate	eat	three
rat			

TRANSFER WORDS

Reading:
treat free

Spelling:
spree state

Henrietta

MAKE WORDS

hit
hen
ten
then
tree
Rita
Tina
Ernie
tenth
teeth
three
threat
hitter
threaten
Henrietta

SORT WORDS

Th Words (Optional):
then, three, threat, threaten, tenth, teeth

Related Words:
hit, hitter; threat, threaten; ten, tenth

Rhymes:
hen   tree
ten   three
then

TRANSFER WORDS

Reading:
when bee

Spelling:
flee den

Make Words: Tell children how many letters to use to make each word. (A slash indicates words that can be made with the same letters.)

Emphasize how changing just one letter or rearranging letters makes a different word.

> "Add 1 letter to **ten** to spell **then**."

> "Change a letter in **tenth** to spell **teeth**."

When children are not just adding or changing one letter, cue them to start over.

> "Start over and use 4 new letters to spell **tree**."

Give a meaning or sentence clue, when needed, to clarify the word children are making.

> "Use 6 new letters to spell **threat**. They arrested the man for making a **threat** to kidnap her."

Always alert children when they are making a name and expect them to use a capital letter.

> "Use 4 new letters to spell the name **Rita**."

Give children one minute to figure out the secret word and then give clues, if needed.

> "Our secret word is a name that you can make by adding your letters to **hen**."

Sort Th Words (Optional)

Sort Related Words

Sort Rhymes

Reading Transfer: "Pretend you are reading and come to a new word." Have children put the transfer words under the appropriate rhymes and use the rhymes to decode them.

Spelling Transfer: "Pretend you are writing and need to spell these words." Have children tell you how the words begin. Then, have children find and use the appropriate rhymes to finish spelling the transfer words.

Step-by-step directions for a sample *Making Names* lesson are on pages 8-12.

Hermione

eeiohmnr

Make Words: Tell children how many letters to use to make each word. (A slash indicates words that can be made with the same letters.)

Emphasize how changing just one letter or rearranging letters makes a different word.

> "Add a letter to **on** to spell the name **Ron**."

> "Change 1 letter in **here** to spell **hero**."

When children are not just adding or changing one letter, cue them to start over.

> "Start over and use 4 new letters to spell **mine**."

Give a meaning or sentence clue, when needed, to clarify the word children are making.

> "Add 1 letter to **mine** to spell **miner**. My uncle is a coal **miner**."

Always alert children when they are making a name and expect them to use a capital letter.

> "Take 4 new letters and spell the name **Erin**."

Give children one minute to figure out the secret word and then give clues, if needed.

> "Our secret word is a name that you can make by adding your letters to **her**."

Sort Related Words

Sort Rhymes

Reading Transfer: "Pretend you are reading and come to a new word." Have children put the transfer words under the appropriate rhymes and use the rhymes to decode them.

Spelling Transfer: "Pretend you are writing and need to spell these words." Have children tell you how the words begin. Then, have children find and use the appropriate rhymes to finish spelling the transfer words.

Step-by-step directions for a sample *Making Names* lesson are on pages 8-12.

MAKE WORDS

Ron
her
hen
men
Erin
here
hero
home
Rome
mine
miner
Homer
Ernie
Hermione

SORT WORDS

Related Words:
mine, miner

Rhymes:
| hen | home |
| men | Rome |

TRANSFER WORDS

Reading:
chrome pen

Spelling:
dome Jen

Hernando

a e o d h n n r

do
Don
Dan
Nan
ran
Ron
Edna/Dean
dear
near
hear
rode/redo
Donna
Hernando

SORT WORDS

Related Words:
do, redo

Rhymes:
Ron	Dan	dear
Don	Nan	near
	ran	hear

TRANSFER WORDS

Reading:
scan   gear

Spelling:
clear   smear

Make Words: Tell children how many letters to use to make each word. (A slash indicates words that can be made with the same letters.)

Emphasize how changing just one letter or rearranging letters makes a different word.

> "Use the same letters in **rode** to spell **redo**."

> "Change 1 letter in **near** to spell **hear**."

When children are not just adding or changing one letter, cue them to start over.

> "Start over and use 4 new letters to spell **rode**."

Give a meaning or sentence clue, when needed, to clarify the word children are making.

> "Change 1 letter in **Dean** to spell **dear**. My grandma is always saying that I am a **dear** boy!"

Always alert children when they are making a name and expect them to use a capital letter.

> "Use 4 new letters to make the name **Edna**."

Give children one minute to figure out the secret word and then give clues, if needed.

> "Our secret word is a name that you can make by adding your letters to **Nan**."

Sort Related Words

Sort Rhymes

Reading Transfer: "Pretend you are reading and come to a new word." Have children put the transfer words under the appropriate rhymes and use the rhymes to decode them.

Spelling Transfer: "Pretend you are writing and need to spell these words." Have children tell you how the words begin. Then, have children find and use the appropriate rhymes to finish spelling the transfer words.

Step-by-step directions for a sample *Making Names* lesson are on pages 8-12.

Hildaberry

a e i b d h l r r y

Make Words: Tell children how many letters to use to make each word. (A slash indicates words that can be made with the same letters.)

Emphasize how changing just one letter or rearranging letters makes a different word.

"Change a letter in **dare** to spell **rare**."

"Add a letter to **bad** to spell the name **Brad**."

When children are not just adding or changing one letter, cue them to start over.

"Start over and use 4 new letters to spell **dare**."

Give a meaning or sentence clue, when needed, to clarify the word children are making.

"Start over and use 6 new letters to spell **rarely**. My brother lives in France and I **rarely** see him."

Always alert children when they are making a name and expect them to use a capital letter.

"Take 5 new letters and spell the name **Hilda**."

Give children one minute to figure out the secret word and then give clues, if needed.

"Our secret word is a name that you can make by adding your letters to **Hilda**."

Sort Related Words

Sort Rhymes

Reading Transfer: "Pretend you are reading and come to a new word." Have children put the transfer words under the appropriate rhymes and use the rhymes to decode them.

Spelling Transfer: "Pretend you are writing and need to spell these words." Have children tell you how the words begin. Then, have children find and use the appropriate rhymes to finish spelling the transfer words.

Step-by-step directions for a sample *Making Names* lesson are on pages 8-12.

MAKE WORDS

Hal
bad
Brad
dare
rare
Hilda
Barry
Larry
Harry
badly
rarely
Hilary
library
Hildaberry

SORT WORDS

Related Words:
bad, badly; rare, rarely

Rhymes:

bad	dare	Barry
Brad	rare	Larry
		Harry

TRANSFER WORDS

Reading:
carry stare

Spelling:
marry scare

Hunter

euhnrt

her
hen
ten/net
nut
rut
hut
hurt
turn/runt
rent
true
hunt
Hunter

SORT WORDS

Beginning Letters (Optional)

Rhymes:

hen	nut	runt
ten	rut	hunt
	hut	

TRANSFER WORDS

Reading:
shut stunt

Spelling:
grunt strut

Make Words: Tell children how many letters to use to make each word. (A slash indicates words that can be made with the same letters.)

Emphasize how changing just one letter or rearranging letters makes a different word.

"Add a letter to **hut** to spell **hurt**."

"Use the same letters in **turn** to spell **runt**."

When children are not just adding or changing one letter, cue them to start over.

"Start over and use 4 new letters to spell **true**."

Give a meaning or sentence clue, when needed, to clarify the word children are making.

"Change 1 letter in **nut** to spell **rut**. After the storm, there was a big **rut** in the road."

Give children one minute to figure out the secret word and then give clues, if needed. Always alert children when they are making a name and expect them to use a capital letter.

"Our secret word is a name that you can make by adding your letters to **hunt**."

Sort Beginning Letters (Optional)

Sort Rhymes

Reading Transfer: "Pretend you are reading and come to a new word." Have children put the transfer words under the appropriate rhymes and use the rhymes to decode them.

Spelling Transfer: "Pretend you are writing and need to spell these words." Have children tell you how the words begin. Then, have children find and use the appropriate rhymes to finish spelling the transfer words.

Step-by-step directions for a sample *Making Names* lesson are on pages 8-12.

Making Names • CD-2429 • © Carson-Dellosa

Isabella

a a e i b l l s

Make Words: Tell children how many letters to use to make each word. (A slash indicates words that can be made with the same letters.)

Emphasize how changing just one letter or rearranging letters makes a different word.

> "Change a letter in the name **Bill** to spell **ball**."

> "Use the same letters in **label** to spell the name **Bella**."

When children are not just adding or changing one letter, cue them to start over.

> "Start over and use 4 new letters to spell **base**."

Give a meaning or sentence clue, when needed to clarify the word children are making.

> "Start over and use 5 letters to spell **label**. The ingredients are listed on the **label**."

Always alert children when they are making a name and expect them to use a capital letter.

> "Take 4 new letters and spell the name **Lisa**."

Give children one minute to figure out the secret word and then give clues, if needed.

> "Our secret word is a name that you can make by adding your letters to **Bella**."

Sort Rhymes

Reading Transfer: "Pretend you are reading and come to a new word." Have children put the transfer words under the appropriate rhymes and use the rhymes to decode them.

Spelling Transfer: "Pretend you are writing and need to spell these words." Have children tell you how the words begin. Then, have children find and use the appropriate rhymes to finish spelling the transfer words.

Step-by-step directions for a sample *Making Names* lesson are on pages 8-12.

MAKE WORDS

Al
Sal
Abe/Bea
all
ill
Bill
ball
bell
sell
base
Lisa
label/Bella
Isabella

SORT WORDS

Rhymes:

Al	all	bell	ill
Sal	ball	sell	Bill

TRANSFER WORDS

Reading:
shell chill

Spelling:
smell small

Jackson

a o c j k n s

MAKE WORDS

on
Jon
con
can
scan
Jack
jock
sock
sack
snack
Jason
Jackson

SORT WORDS

Beginning Letters (Optional)

Rhymes:

can	on	Jack	jock
scan	con	sack	sock
	Jon	snack	

TRANSFER WORDS

Reading:
knock crack

Spelling:
block stack

Make Words: Tell children how many letters to use to make each word. (A slash indicates words that can be made with the same letters.)

Emphasize how changing just one letter or rearranging letters makes a different word.

> "Change a letter in **sock** to spell **sack**."

> "Add 1 letter to **sack** to spell **snack**."

When children are not just adding or changing one letter, cue them to start over.

> "Start over and use 4 new letters to spell the name **Jack**."

Give a meaning or sentence clue, when needed, to clarify the word children are making.

> "Change 1 letter in **can** to spell **con**. The men were arrested for trying to **con** people out of their money."

Always alert children when they are making a name and expect them to use a capital letter.

> "Use 5 new letters to spell the name **Jason**."

Give children one minute to figure out the secret word and then give clues, if needed.

> "Our secret word is a name that can be made by adding your letters to **Jack**."

Sort Beginning Letters (Optional)

Sort Rhymes

Reading Transfer: "Pretend you are reading and come to a new word." Have children put the transfer words under the appropriate rhymes and use the rhymes to decode them.

Spelling Transfer: "Pretend you are writing and need to spell these words." Have children tell you how the words begin. Then, have children find and use the appropriate rhymes to finish spelling the transfer words.

Step-by-step directions for a sample *Making Names* lesson are on pages 8-12.

Making Names • CD-2429 • © Carson-Dellosa

Jacqueline

a e e i u c j l n q

Make Words: Tell children how many letters to use to make each word. (A slash indicates words that can be made with the same letters.)

Emphasize how changing just one letter or rearranging letters makes a different word.

"Change a letter in **lice** to spell **lace**."

"Use the same letters in **Jean** to spell the name **Jane**."

When children are not just adding or changing one letter, cue them to start over.

"Start over and use 4 new letters to spell **cane**."

Give a meaning or sentence clue, when needed, to clarify the word children are making.

"Use 6 letters to spell **unlace**. **Unlace** your shoes so you can clean them."

Always alert children when they are making a name and expect them to use a capital letter.

"Use 5 letters to spell the name **Julia**."

Give children one minute to figure out the secret word and then give clues, if needed.

"Our secret word is a name that begins with **J** and ends with **e**."

Sort Related Words

Sort Rhymes

Reading Transfer: "Pretend you are reading and come to a new word." Have children put the transfer words under the appropriate rhymes and use the rhymes to decode them.

Spelling Transfer: "Pretend you are writing and need to spell these words." Have children tell you how the words begin. Then, have children find and use the appropriate rhymes to finish spelling the transfer words.

Step-by-step directions for a sample *Making Names* lesson are on pages 8-12.

MAKE WORDS

ice
ace
Jan
Jen
Jean/Jane
June
cane
lice
lace
clean
Julia
Julian
unlace
Jacqueline

SORT WORDS

Related Words:
lace, unlace

Rhymes:
ice	ace	Jane	Jean
lice	lace	cane	clean

TRANSFER WORDS

Reading:
mean Shane

Spelling:
space spice

Janet

a e j n t

an
ant/tan
Jan
Jen
ten/net
jet
eat
neat
Jean/Jane
Janet

SORT WORDS

Beginning Letters (Optional)

Rhymes:

an	Jen	net	eat
tan	ten	jet	neat
Jan			

TRANSFER WORDS

Reading:
vet seat

Spelling:
treat span

Make Words: Tell children how many letters to use to make each word. (A slash indicates words that can be made with the same letters.)

Emphasize how changing just one letter or rearranging letters makes a different word.

"Add a letter to **eat** to spell **neat**."

"Change 1 letter in **net** to spell **jet**."

When children are not just adding or changing one letter, cue them to start over.

"Start over and use 4 new letters to spell the name **Jean**."

Give a meaning or sentence clue, when needed, to clarify the word children are making.

"Change 1 letter in net to spell **jet**. My brother flies a **jet** fighter."

Always alert children when they are making a name and expect them to use a capital letter.

"Change 1 letter in **tan** to spell the name **Jan**."

Give children one minute to figure out the secret word and then give clues, if needed.

"Our secret word is a name that you can spell by adding your letters to **Jan**."

Sort Beginning Letters (Optional)

Sort Rhymes

Reading Transfer: "Pretend you are reading and come to a new word." Have children put the transfer words under the appropriate rhymes and use the rhymes to decode them.

Spelling Transfer: "Pretend you are writing and need to spell these words." Have children tell you how the words begin. Then, have children find and use the appropriate rhymes to finish spelling the transfer words.

Step-by-step directions for a sample *Making Names* lesson are on pages 8-12.

Jarrett

a e j r r t t

Make Words: Tell children how many letters to use to make each word. (A slash indicates words that can be made with the same letters.)

Emphasize how changing just one letter or rearranging letters makes a different word.

> "Change a letter in **eat** to spell **ear**."

> "Use the same letters in **ate** to spell **eat**."

When children are not just adding or changing one letter, cue them to start over.

> "Start over and use 5 new letters to spell **treat**."

Give a meaning or sentence clue, when needed, to clarify the word children are making.

> "Change a letter in **rate** to spell **rare**. He likes his steaks cooked **rare**."

Give children one minute to figure out the secret word and then give clues, if needed. Always alert children when they are making a name and expect them to use a capital letter.

> "Our secret word is a name that you can spell by adding your letters to **jar**."

Sort Beginning Letters (Optional)

Sort Rhymes

Reading Transfer: "Pretend you are reading and come to a new word." Have children put the transfer words under the appropriate rhymes and use the rhymes to decode them.

Spelling Transfer: "Pretend you are writing and need to spell these words." Have children tell you how the words begin. Then, have children find and use the appropriate rhymes to finish spelling the transfer words.

Step-by-step directions for a sample *Making Names* lesson are on pages 8-12.

MAKE WORDS

jar
jet
tea/ate/eat
ear
tear/rate
rare/rear
treat
Jarrett

SORT WORDS

Beginning Letters (Optional)

Rhymes:

ate	ear	eat
rate	tear	treat
	rear	

TRANSFER WORDS

Reading:
fear fate

Spelling:
gate cheat

Jasmine

a e i j m n s

MAKE WORDS

am
Sam
jam
Jim
sea
Jane/Jean
mean/name
same
sane
mine
Jamie
Jasmine

SORT WORDS

Beginning Letters (Optional)

Rhymes:

am	Jane	Jean	same
Sam	sane	mean	name
jam			

TRANSFER WORDS

Reading:
blame plane

Spelling:
shame slam

Make Words: Tell children how many letters to use to make each word. (A slash indicates words that can be made with the same letters.)

Emphasize how changing just one letter or rearranging letters makes a different word.

> "Change a letter in **name** to spell **same**."

> "Use the same letters in **mean** to spell **name**."

When children are not just adding or changing one letter, cue them to start over.

> "Start over and use 5 new letters to spell the name **Jamie**."

Give a meaning or sentence clue, when needed, to clarify the word children are making.

> "Change 1 letter in **same** to spell **sane**. The judge declared the man **sane** and able to stand trial."

Always alert children when they are making a name and expect them to use a capital letter.

> "Take 4 new letters and spell the name **Jane**."

Give children one minute to figure out the secret word and then give clues, if needed.

> "Our secret word is a name that you can make by adding your letters to **mine**."

Sort Beginning Letters (Optional)

Sort Rhymes

Reading Transfer: "Pretend you are reading and come to a new word." Have children put the transfer words under the appropriate rhymes and use the rhymes to decode them.

Spelling Transfer: "Pretend you are writing and need to spell these words." Have children tell you how the words begin. Then, have children find and use the appropriate rhymes to finish spelling the transfer words.

Step-by-step directions for a sample *Making Names* lesson are on pages 8-12.

Making Names • CD-2429 • © Carson-Dellosa

Jennifer

Make Words: Tell children how many letters to use to make each word. (A slash indicates words that can be made with the same letters.)

Emphasize how changing just one letter or rearranging letters makes a different word.

"Change a letter in **nine** to spell **fine**."

"Add a letter to **fee** to spell **free**."

When children are not just adding or changing one letter, cue them to start over.

"Start over and use 5 new letters to spell the name **Ernie**."

Give a meaning or sentence clue, when needed, to clarify the word children are making.

"Add a letter to **fine** to spell **finer**. Nothing could be **finer** than to live in North Carolina!"

Always alert children when they are making a name and expect them to use a capital letter.

"Take 4 new letters and spell the name **Erin**."

Give children one minute to figure out the secret word and then give clues, if needed.

"Our secret word is a name that you can make by adding your letters to **Jen**."

Sort Related Words

Sort Rhymes

Reading Transfer: "Pretend you are reading and come to a new word." Have children put the transfer words under the appropriate rhymes and use the rhymes to decode them.

Spelling Transfer: "Pretend you are writing and need to spell these words." Have children tell you how the words begin. Then, have children find and use the appropriate rhymes to finish spelling the transfer words.

Step-by-step directions for a sample *Making Names* lesson are on pages 8-12.

MAKE WORDS

if
in
fin
Jen
fee
free
Erin
fire
nine
fine
finer
Ernie
Jennie
Jennifer

SORT WORDS

Related Words:
fine, finer

Rhymes:
| in | fee | fine |
| fin | free | nine |

TRANSFER WORDS

Reading:
thin shine

Spelling:
three spine

Jermaine

MAKE WORDS

man
Jan
Jen
men
mean
Jean
Erin
mine
miner
Maine
Marie
marine
Jermaine

SORT WORDS

Beginning Letters (Optional)

Related Words:
mine, miner

Rhymes:

man	Jen	mean
Jan	men	Jean

TRANSFER WORDS

Reading:
than then

Spelling:
clean clan

Make Words: Tell children how many letters to use to make each word. (A slash indicates words that can be made with the same letters.)

Emphasize how changing just one letter or rearranging letters makes a different word.

> "Add a letter to **men** to spell **mean**."

> "Change a letter in **Jen** to spell **men**."

When children are not just adding or changing one letter, cue them to start over.

> "Start over and use 4 new letters to spell the name **Erin**."

Give a meaning or sentence clue, when needed, to clarify the word children are making.

> "Add 1 letter to **Marie** spell **marine**. My brother is a **marine** biologist."

Always alert children when they are making a name and expect them to use a capital letter.

> "Use 5 new letters to spell the state, **Maine**."

Give children one minute to figure out the secret word and then give clues, if needed.

> "Our secret word is a name that you can spell by adding your letters to **Maine**."

Sort Beginning Letters (Optional)

Sort Related Words

Sort Rhymes

Reading Transfer: "Pretend you are reading and come to a new word." Have children put the transfer words under the appropriate rhymes and use the rhymes to decode them.

Spelling Transfer: "Pretend you are writing and need to spell these words." Have children tell you how the words begin. Then, have children find and use the appropriate rhymes to finish spelling the transfer words.

Step-by-step directions for a sample *Making Names* lesson are on pages 8-12.

Jocelyn

e o c j l n y

Make Words: Tell children how many letters to use to make each word. (A slash indicates words that can be made with the same letters.)

Emphasize how changing just one letter or rearranging letters makes a different word.

"Add a letter to **Leo** to spell the name **Cleo**."

"Change a letter in **Joey** to spell the name **Joel**."

When children are not just adding or changing one letter, cue them to start over.

"Start over and use 5 new letters to spell **enjoy**."

Give a meaning or sentence clue, when needed, to clarify the word children are making.

"Add a letter to **cone** to spell **clone**. Do you think it is right to **clone** a human?"

Always alert children when they are making a name and expect them to use a capital letter.

"Use 4 new letters to spell the name **Joey**."

Give children one minute to figure out the secret word and then give clues, if needed.

"Our secret word is a name that begins with **J** and ends with **n**."

Sort Beginning Letters (Optional)

Sort Rhymes

Reading Transfer: "Pretend you are reading and come to a new word." Have children put the transfer words under the appropriate rhymes and use the rhymes to decode them.

Spelling Transfer: "Pretend you are writing and need to spell these words." Have children tell you how the words begin. Then, have children find and use the appropriate rhymes to finish spelling the transfer words.

Step-by-step directions for a sample *Making Names* lesson are on pages 8-12.

MAKE WORDS

Joy
Joe
Jon
Jen
Len
Leo
Cleo
Joey
Joel
cone
clone
enjoy
Joyce
Jocelyn

SORT WORDS

Beginning Letters (Optional)

Rhymes:

Jen	Leo	cone
Len	Cleo	clone

TRANSFER WORDS

Reading:
phone Theo

Spelling:
bone stone

Jonathan

a a o h j n n t

at
an
ant/tan
Jan
Nat
hat
hot
not
than
Noah
John
Jonah
Nathan
Jonathan

SORT WORDS

Beginning Letters (Optional)

Rhymes:

at	an	hot
hat	tan	not
Nat	Jan	
	than	

TRANSFER WORDS

Reading:
flat clot

Spelling:
spot chat

Make Words: Tell children how many letters to use to make each word. (A slash indicates words that can be made with the same letters.)

Emphasize how changing just one letter or rearranging letters makes a different word.

> "Add a letter to **an** to spell **ant**."

> "Change 1 letter in **hat** to spell **hot**."

When children are not just adding or changing one letter, cue them to start over.

> "Start over and use 4 new letters to spell the name **Noah**."

Give a meaning or sentence clue, when needed, to clarify the word children are making.

> "Take 4 new letters and spell **than**. My sister is older **than** me."

Always alert children when they are making a name and expect them to use a capital letter.

> "Use 3 letters to spell the name **Nat**."

Give children one minute to figure out the secret word and then give clues, if needed.

> "Our secret word is a name that you can spell by adding your letters to **Nathan**."

Sort Beginning Letters (Optional)

Sort Rhymes

Reading Transfer: "Pretend you are reading and come to a new word." Have children put the transfer words under the appropriate rhymes and use the rhymes to decode them.

Spelling Transfer: "Pretend you are writing and need to spell these words." Have children tell you how the words begin. Then, have children find and use the appropriate rhymes to finish spelling the transfer words.

Step-by-step directions for a sample *Making Names* lesson are on pages 8-12.

Joseph

e o h j p s

Make Words: Tell children how many letters to use to make each word. (A slash indicates words that can be made with the same letters.)

Emphasize how changing just one letter or rearranging letters makes a different word.

> "Add a letter to **he** to spell **she**."

> "Change 1 letter in **shoe** to spell **shop**."

When children are not just adding or changing one letter, cue them to start over.

> "Start over and use 4 new letters to spell **hope**."

Give a meaning or sentence clue, when needed, to clarify the word children are making.

> "Change 1 letter in **hose** to spell **pose**. It was hard to get my dog to **pose** for the picture."

Always alert children when they are making a name and expect them to use a capital letter.

> "Take 3 new letters and spell the name **Joe**."

Give children one minute to figure out the secret word and then give clues, if needed.

> "Our secret word is a name that begins with **J** and ends with **ph**."

Sort Rhymes

Reading Transfer: "Pretend you are reading and come to a new word." Have children put the transfer words under the appropriate rhymes and use the rhymes to decode them.

Spelling Transfer: "Pretend you are writing and need to spell these words." Have children tell you how the words begin. Then, have children find and use the appropriate rhymes to finish spelling the transfer words.

Step-by-step directions for a sample *Making Names* lesson are on pages 8-12.

MAKE WORDS

he
she
hop
Joe
Josh
hope
hose
pose
shoe
shop
Joseph

SORT WORDS

Rhymes:

| he | hop | pose |
| she | shop | hose |

TRANSFER WORDS

Reading:
close those

Spelling:
nose drop

J o s e p h i n e

e e i o h j n p s

▶ MAKE WORDS

Joe
Josh
John
join
jeep
phone
shone
shine
spine
sheep
Joseph
ponies
phonies
Josephine

▶ SORT WORDS

Ph Words (Optional):
phone, phonies, Joseph,
Josephine

Rhymes:
phone shine jeep   ponies
shone spine sheep   phonies

▶ TRANSFER WORDS

Reading:
zone steep

Spelling:
cone sweep

Make Words: Tell children how many letters to use to make each word. (A slash indicates words that can be made with the same letters.)

Emphasize how changing just one letter or rearranging letters makes a different word.

> "Change a letter in **phone** to spell **shone**."

When children are not just adding or changing one letter, cue them to start over.

> "Start over and use 5 new letters to spell **sheep**."

Give a meaning or sentence clue, when needed, to clarify the word children are making.

> "Add 1 letter to **ponies** to spell **phonies**. We realized that the tickets were not genuine. They were **phonies**."

Always alert children when they are making a name and expect them to use a capital letter.

> "Use 6 new letters to spell the name **Joseph**."

Give children one minute to figure out the secret word and then give clues, if needed.

> "Our secret word is a name that you can make by adding your letters to **Joseph**."

Sort Ph Words (Optional)

Sort Rhymes

Reading Transfer: "Pretend you are reading and come to a new word." Have children put the transfer words under the appropriate rhymes and use the rhymes to decode them.

Spelling Transfer: "Pretend you are writing and need to spell these words." Have children tell you how the words begin. Then, have children find and use the appropriate rhymes to finish spelling the transfer words.

Step-by-step directions for a sample *Making Names* lesson are on pages 8-12.

Making Names • CD-2429 • © Carson-Dellosa

Juanita

a a i u j n t

Make Words: Tell children how many letters to use to make each word. (A slash indicates words that can be made with the same letters.)

Emphasize how changing just one letter or rearranging letters makes a different word.

"Change a letter in **nut** to spell **jut**."

"Use the same letters in **tuna** to spell **aunt**."

Give a meaning or sentence clue, when needed, to clarify the word children are making.

"Change 1 letter in **Tina** to spell **tuna**. I like **tuna** sandwiches."

Always alert children when they are making a name and expect them to use a capital letter.

"Take 3 new letters and spell the name **Jan**."

Give children one minute to figure out the secret word and then give clues, if needed.

"Our secret word is a name that you can spell by adding your letters to **Anita**."

Sort Rhymes

Reading Transfer: "Pretend you are reading and come to a new word." Have children put the transfer words under the appropriate rhymes and use the rhymes to decode them.

Spelling Transfer: "Pretend you are writing and need to spell these words." Have children tell you how the words begin. Then, have children find and use the appropriate rhymes to finish spelling the transfer words.

Step-by-step directions for a sample *Making Names* lesson are on pages 8-12.

MAKE WORDS

an
at
Nat/ant/tan
nut
jut
Jan
Juan
Tina
tuna/aunt
Anita
Juanita

SORT WORDS

Rhymes:

an	nut	at
tan	jut	Nat
Jan		

TRANSFER WORDS

Reading:
strut splat

Spelling:
brat shut

Justine

e i u j n s t

MAKE WORDS

Sue/use
tie
sit
set
jet
jut
just
June
tune
untie/unite
Justin
Justine

SORT WORDS

Related Words:
tie, untie

Rhymes:

set	June
jet	tune

TRANSFER WORDS

Reading:
prune wet

Spelling:
dune Chet

Make Words: Tell children how many letters to use to make each word. (A slash indicates words that can be made with the same letters.)

Emphasize how changing just one letter or rearranging letters makes a different word.

"Add a letter to **jut** to spell **just**."

"Change a letter in **June** to spell **tune**."

When children are not just adding or changing one letter, cue them to start over.

"Start over and use 5 new letters to spell **untie**."

Give a meaning or sentence clue, when needed, to clarify the word children are making.

"Use the same letters in **untie** to spell **unite**. After their defeat, the leaders tried to **unite** their sides."

Always alert children when they are making a name and expect them to use a capital letter.

"Take 4 new letters and spell the name **June**."

Give children one minute to figure out the secret word and then give clues, if needed.

"Our secret word is a name that can be made by adding a letter to **Justin**."

Sort Related Words

Sort Rhymes

Reading Transfer: "Pretend you are reading and come to a new word." Have children put the transfer words under the appropriate rhymes and use the rhymes to decode them.

Spelling Transfer: "Pretend you are writing and need to spell these words." Have children tell you how the words begin. Then, have children find and use the appropriate rhymes to finish spelling the transfer words.

Step-by-step directions for a sample *Making Names* lesson are on pages 8-12.

Kaitlyn

a i k l n t y

Make Words: Tell children how many letters to use to make each word. (A slash indicates words that can be made with the same letters.)

Emphasize how changing just one letter or rearranging letters makes a different word.

> "Add a letter to **it** to spell **lit**."

> "Change a letter in **tank** to spell **yank**."

When children are not just adding or changing one letter, cue them to start over.

> "Start over and use 4 new letters to spell the name **Katy**."

Give a meaning or sentence clue, when needed, to clarify the word children are making.

> "Start over and use 5 new letters to spell **Latin**. **Latin** America includes many of the countries south of the United States."

Always alert children when they are making a name and expect them to use a capital letter.

> "Use 3 new letters to spell the name **Kay**."

Give children one minute to figure out the secret word and then give clues, if needed.

> "Our secret word is a name that begins with **K** and ends with **n**."

Sort Beginning Letters (Optional)

Sort Rhymes

Reading Transfer: "Pretend you are reading and come to a new word." Have children put the transfer words under the appropriate rhymes and use the rhymes to decode them.

Spelling Transfer: "Pretend you are writing and need to spell these words." Have children tell you how the words begin. Then, have children find and use the appropriate rhymes to finish spelling the transfer words.

Step-by-step directions for a sample *Making Names* lesson are on pages 8-12.

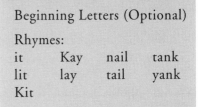

MAKE WORDS

it
lit
Kit
Ian
Kay
lay
nail
tail
talk
tank
yank
Katy
Latin
Kaitlyn

SORT WORDS

Beginning Letters (Optional)

Rhymes:

it	Kay	nail	tank
lit	lay	tail	yank
Kit			

TRANSFER WORDS

Reading:
trail plank

Spelling:
crank prank

Katherine

a e e i h k n r t

MAKE WORDS

eat/ate
hate/heat
rink
Erin
Keri
Kate
Katie
Karen
Irene
think
heater
thinker
Katherine

SORT WORDS

Related Words:
heat, heater; think, thinker

Rhymes:

eat	ate	rink
heat	hate	think
	Kate	

TRANSFER WORDS

Reading:
stink state

Spelling:
blink shrink

Make Words: Tell children how many letters to use to make each word. (A slash indicates words that can be made with the same letters.)

Emphasize how changing just one letter or rearranging letters makes a different word.

"Add a letter to **Kate** to spell the name **Katie**."

"Use the same letters in **hate** to spell **heat**."

When children are not just adding or changing one letter, cue them to start over.

"Start over and use 5 new letters to spell the name **Irene**."

Give a meaning or sentence clue, when needed, to clarify the word children are making.

"Start over and use 6 new letters to spell **heater**. It was cold in the car when the **heater** quit working."

Always alert children when they are making a name and expect them to use a capital letter.

"Use 4 new letters to spell the name **Erin**."

Give children one minute to figure out the secret word and then give clues, if needed.

"Our secret word is a name that begins with **K** and ends with **e**."

Sort Related Words

Sort Rhymes

Reading Transfer: "Pretend you are reading and come to a new word." Have children put the transfer words under the appropriate rhymes and use the rhymes to decode them.

Spelling Transfer: "Pretend you are writing and need to spell these words." Have children tell you how the words begin. Then, have children find and use the appropriate rhymes to finish spelling the transfer words.

Step-by-step directions for a sample *Making Names* lesson are on pages 8-12.

Kathleen

a e e h k l n t

Make Words: Tell children how many letters to use to make each word. (A slash indicates words that can be made with the same letters.)

Emphasize how changing just one letter or rearranging letters makes a different word.

> "Add a letter to **ten** to spell **then**."

> "Use the same letters in **ate** to spell **eat**."

When children are not just adding or changing one letter, cue them to start over.

> "Start over and use 4 new letters to spell the name **Hank**."

Give a meaning or sentence clue, when needed, to clarify the word children are making.

> "Use 5 new letters to spell **eaten**. Have you **eaten** dinner yet?"

Always alert children when they are making a name and expect them to use a capital letter.

> "Take 3 new letters and spell the name **Len**."

Give children one minute to figure out the secret word and then give clues, if needed.

> "Our secret word is a name that begins with **K** and ends with **n**."

Sort Related Words

Sort Rhymes

Reading Transfer: "Pretend you are reading and come to a new word." Have children put the transfer words under the appropriate rhymes and use the rhymes to decode them.

Spelling Transfer: "Pretend you are writing and need to spell these words." Have children tell you how the words begin. Then, have children find and use the appropriate rhymes to finish spelling the transfer words.

Step-by-step directions for a sample *Making Names* lesson are on pages 8-12.

MAKE WORDS

at
ate/eat
Len
Ken
ten
then
late
Kate
Hank
tank
thank
ankle
eaten
Kathleen

SORT WORDS

Related Words:
eat, eaten

Rhymes:

ate	Len	Hank
late	Ken	tank
Kate	ten	thank
	then	

TRANSFER WORDS

Reading:
plank plate

Spelling:
Frank skate

Kathryn

a h k n r t y

MAKE WORDS

ant
Art/rat
hat
hay
Kay
Ray
tray
Hank
rank
tank
thank
Kathy
Kathryn

SORT WORDS

Beginning Letters (Optional)

Rhymes:

rat	hay	Hank
hat	Kay	tank
	Ray	thank
	tray	rank

TRANSFER WORDS

Reading:
spray drank

Spelling:
blank stray

Make Words: Tell children how many letters to use to make each word. (A slash indicates words that can be made with the same letters.)

Emphasize how changing just one letter or rearranging letters makes a different word.

"Add a letter to **tank** to spell **thank**."

"Change 1 letter in **Hank** to spell **rank**."

When children are not just adding or changing one letter, cue them to start over.

"Start over and use 5 new letters to spell the name **Kathy**."

Give a meaning or sentence clue, when needed, to clarify the word children are making:

"Change 1 letter in **hat** to spell **hay**. The cows were eating **hay**."

Always alert children when they are making a name and expect them to use a capital letter.

"Take 4 new letters and spell the name **Hank**."

Give children one minute to figure out the secret word and then give clues, if needed.

"Our secret word is a name that begins with **K** and ends with **n**."

Sort Beginning Letters (Optional)

Sort Rhymes

Reading Transfer: "Pretend you are reading and come to a new word." Have children put the transfer words under the appropriate rhymes and use the rhymes to decode them.

Spelling Transfer: "Pretend you are writing and need to spell these words." Have children tell you how the words begin. Then, have children find and use the appropriate rhymes to finish spelling the transfer words.

Step-by-step directions for a sample *Making Names* lesson are on pages 8-12.

Kendall

a e d k l l n

Make Words: Tell children how many letters to use to make each word. (A slash indicates words that can be made with the same letters.)

Emphasize how changing just one letter or rearranging letters makes a different word.

> "Change a letter in **lean** to spell the name **Dean**."

> "Use the same letters in **Dale** to spell **deal**."

When children are not just adding or changing one letter, cue them to start over.

> "Start over and use 4 new letters to spell **lake**."

Give a meaning or sentence clue, when needed, to clarify the word children are making.

> "Start over and use 5 new letters to spell **ankle**. She wore a pretty **ankle** bracelet."

Always alert children when they are making a name and expect them to use a capital letter.

> "Use 2 letters to spell the name **Ed**."

Give children one minute to figure out the secret word and then give clues, if needed.

> "Our secret word is a name that you can spell by adding your letters to **Ken**."

Sort Beginning Letters (Optional)

Sort Rhymes

Reading Transfer: "Pretend you are reading and come to a new word." Have children put the transfer words under the appropriate rhymes and use the rhymes to decode them.

Spelling Transfer: "Pretend you are writing and need to spell these words." Have children tell you how the words begin. Then, have children find and use the appropriate rhymes to finish spelling the transfer words.

Step-by-step directions for a sample *Making Names* lesson are on pages 8-12.

MAKE WORDS

Ed
Ned/den
Ken
lake
Dale/deal/lead
lean
Dean
ankle
Kendall

SORT WORDS

Beginning Letters (Optional)

Rhymes:
Ed	den	lean
Ned	Ken	Dean

TRANSFER WORDS

Reading:
clean then

Spelling:
Fred sled

Kendra

a e d k n r

MAKE WORDS

ran
Dan/and
den
Ken
Dean
dear/dare
near
rank
Karen
ranked/Kendra

SORT WORDS

Beginning Letters (Optional)

Related Words:
rank, ranked

Rhymes:
ran   den   dear
Dan   Ken   near

TRANSFER WORDS

Reading:
fear when

Spelling:
then than

Make Words: Tell children how many letters to use to make each word. (A slash indicates words that can be made with the same letters.)

Emphasize how changing just one letter or rearranging letters makes a different word.

"Change a letter in **Dean** to spell **dear**."

"Use the same letters in **dear** to spell **dare**."

When children are not just adding or changing one letter, cue them to start over.

"Start over and use 4 new letters to spell **rank**."

Give a meaning or sentence clue, when needed, to clarify the word children are making.

"Start over and use 4 new letters to spell **rank**. How would you **rank** the team this year?"

Always alert children when they are making a name and expect them to use a capital letter.

"Take 4 new letters and spell the name **Dean**."

Today's lesson has two secret words. Give children one minute to figure out each secret word and then give clues, if needed.

"You can make one secret word by adding your letters to **rank**."

"The other secret word is a name that you can make by adding your letters to **Ken**."

Sort Beginning Letters (Optional)

Sort Related Words

Sort Rhymes

Reading Transfer: "Pretend you are reading and come to a new word." Have children put the transfer words under the appropriate rhymes and use the rhymes to decode them.

Spelling Transfer: "Pretend you are writing and need to spell these words." Have children tell you how the words begin. Then, have children find and use the appropriate rhymes to finish spelling the transfer words.

Step-by-step directions for a sample *Making Names* lesson are on pages 8-12.

Kendrick

e i c d k k n r

Make Words: Tell children how many letters to use to make each word. (A slash indicates words that can be made with the same letters.)

Emphasize how changing just one letter or rearranging letters makes a different word.

> "Change a letter in **dice** to spell **rice**."

> "Add a letter to **rink** to spell **drink**."

When children are not just adding or changing one letter, cue them to start over.

> "Start over and use 4 new letters to spell **nice**."

Give a meaning or sentence clue, when needed, to clarify the word children are making.

> "Start over and use 6 new letters to spell **kinder**. I am trying to be **kinder** to my little brother."

Always alert children when they are making a name and expect them to use a capital letter.

> "Change 1 letter in **rice** to spell the name **Rick**."

Give children one minute to figure out the secret word and then give clues, if needed.

> "Our secret word is a name that you can make by adding your letters to **Ken**."

Sort Beginning Letters (Optional)

Sort Related Words

Sort Rhymes

Reading Transfer: "Pretend you are reading and come to a new word." Have children put the transfer words under the appropriate rhymes and use the rhymes to decode them.

Spelling Transfer: "Pretend you are writing and need to spell these words." Have children tell you how the words begin. Then, have children find and use the appropriate rhymes to finish spelling the transfer words.

Step-by-step directions for a sample *Making Names* lesson are on pages 8-12.

MAKE WORDS

Ken
kin
kind
nice
Nick
neck
deck
Dick
dice
rice
Rick
rink
drink
kinder
Kendrick

SORT WORDS

Beginning Letters (Optional)

Related Words:
kind, kinder

Rhymes:

Rick	nice	rink	neck
Nick	dice	drink	deck
Dick	rice		

TRANSFER WORDS

Reading:
think twice

Spelling:
trick shrink

Kimball

MAKE WORDS

Kim
all
ball
mall
mill
kill
Bill
bail
mail
Lila
milk
Kimball

SORT WORDS

Beginning Letters (Optional)

Rhymes:

all	Bill	bail
mall	kill	mail
ball	mill	

TRANSFER WORDS

Reading:
still fail

Spelling:
thrill small

Make Words: Tell children how many letters to use to make each word. (A slash indicates words that can be made with the same letters.)

Emphasize how changing just one letter or rearranging letters makes a different word.

"Change a letter in **ball** to spell **mall**."

When children are not just adding or changing one letter, cue them to start over.

"Start over and use 4 new letters to spell **milk**."

Give a meaning or sentence clue, when needed, to clarify the word children are making.

"Change 1 letter in **Bill** to spell **bail**. The judge set the man's **bail** at $50,000."

Always alert children when they are making a name and expect them to use a capital letter.

"Change 1 letter in **kill** to spell the name **Bill**."

Give children one minute to figure out the secret word and then give clues, if needed.

"Our secret word is a name that you can make by adding your letters to **Kim**."

Sort Beginning Letters (Optional)

Sort Rhymes

Reading Transfer: "Pretend you are reading and come to a new word." Have children put the transfer words under the appropriate rhymes and use the rhymes to decode them.

Spelling Transfer: "Pretend you are writing and need to spell these words." Have children tell you how the words begin. Then, have children find and use the appropriate rhymes to finish spelling the transfer words.

Step-by-step directions for a sample *Making Names* lesson are on pages 8-12.

Kimberly

e i b k l m r y

Make Words: Tell children how many letters to use to make each word. (A slash indicates words that can be made with the same letters.)

Emphasize how changing just one letter or rearranging letters makes a different word.

"Add a letter to **rim** to spell **brim**."

When children are not just adding or changing one letter, cue them to start over.

"Start over and use 4 new letters to spell the name **Kyle**."

Give a meaning or sentence clue, when needed, to clarify the word children are making:

"Use 5 new letters to spell **biker**. Sometimes we call a person who rides a bike a **biker**."

Always alert children when they are making a name and expect them to use a capital letter.

"Take 3 letters and spell the name **Kim**."

Give children one minute to figure out the secret word and then give clues, if needed.

"Our secret word is a name that you can make by adding your letters to **Kim**."

Sort Beginning Letters (Optional)

Sort Related Words

Sort Rhymes

Reading Transfer: "Pretend you are reading and come to a new word." Have children put the transfer words under the appropriate rhymes and use the rhymes to decode them.

Spelling Transfer: "Pretend you are writing and need to spell these words." Have children tell you how the words begin. Then, have children find and use the appropriate rhymes to finish spelling the transfer words.

Step-by-step directions for a sample *Making Names* lesson are on pages 8-12.

MAKE WORDS

Kim
rim
brim
milk
bike
like
lime
Mike
Kyle
biker
Kimberly

SORT WORDS

Beginning Letters (Optional)

Related Words:
bike, biker

Rhymes:
Kim   bike
rim   like
brim

TRANSFER WORDS

Reading:
trim spike

Spelling:
strike slim

Kirsten/Kristen

MAKE WORDS

ink
ski
ten
Ken
kin
Kit
Kris
rink
sink/skin
skier
stink
strike
Kirsten/Kristen

SORT WORDS

Related Words:
ski, skier

Rhymes:
ink	ten	kin
rink	Ken	skin
sink		
stink		

TRANSFER WORDS

Reading:
brink blink

Spelling:
think clink

Make Words: Tell children how many letters to use to make each word. (A slash indicates words that can be made with the same letters.)

Emphasize how changing just one letter or rearranging letters makes a different word.

"Change 1 letter in **rink** to spell **sink**."

"Use the same letters in **sink** to spell **skin**."

When children are not just adding or changing one letter, cue them to start over.

"Start over and use 5 new letters to spell **skier**."

Give a meaning or sentence clue, when needed, to clarify the word children are making.

"Start over and use 6 new letters to spell **strike**. The first pitch was a **strike**."

Always alert children when they are making a name and expect them to use a capital letter.

"Change 1 letter in **ten** to spell the name **Ken**."

This lesson has two secret words, and they are both names. Give children one minute to figure out each secret word and then give clues, if needed.

"Both names begin with **K** and end with **n**."

Sort Related Words

Sort Rhymes

Reading Transfer: "Pretend you are reading and come to a new word." Have children put the transfer words under the appropriate rhymes and use the rhymes to decode them.

Spelling Transfer: "Pretend you are writing and need to spell these words." Have children tell you how the words begin. Then, have children find and use the appropriate rhymes to finish spelling the transfer words.

Step-by-step directions for a sample *Making Names* lesson are on pages 8-12.

Kristina

Make Words: Tell children how many letters to use to make each word. (A slash indicates words that can be made with the same letters.)

Emphasize how changing just one letter or rearranging letters makes a different word.

> "Add a letter to **tan** to spell the name **Stan**."

When children are not just adding or changing one letter, cue them to start over.

> "Start over and use 5 new letters to spell **train**."

Give a meaning or sentence clue, when needed, to clarify the word children are making.

> "Use 6 new letters to spell **raisin**. My grandma makes **raisin** pudding."

Always alert children when they are making a name and expect them to use a capital letter.

> "Take 4 new letters and spell the name **Tina**."

Give children one minute to figure out the secret word and then give clues, if needed.

> "Our secret word is a name that you can make by adding your letters to **Tina**."

Sort Rhymes

Reading Transfer: "Pretend you are reading and come to a new word." Have children put the transfer words under the appropriate rhymes and use the rhymes to decode them.

Spelling Transfer: "Pretend you are writing and need to spell these words." Have children tell you how the words begin. Then, have children find and use the appropriate rhymes to finish spelling the transfer words.

Step-by-step directions for a sample *Making Names* lesson are on pages 8-12.

MAKE WORDS

tan
Stan
Tina
Rita
skin/sink
rink
rank
sank
rain
stink
train
strain
raisin
Kristina

SORT WORDS

Rhymes:

Stan	sink	rank	train
tan	rink	sank	strain
	stink		rain

TRANSFER WORDS

Reading:
blank blink

Spelling:
brain brink

Lakesha

a a e h k l s

MAKE WORDS

he
she
has/ash
ask
seal
heal
lake/leak
leash
shake/Kesha
Lakesha

SORT WORDS

Sh Words (Optional):
she, shake, ash, leash, Kesha, Lakesha

Rhymes:
| he | seal | lake |
| she | heal | shake |

TRANSFER WORDS

Reading:
steal brake

Spelling:
quake squeal

Make Words: Tell children how many letters to use to make each word. (A slash indicates words that can be made with the same letters.)

Emphasize how changing just one letter or rearranging letters makes a different word.

> "Use the same letters in **has** to spell **ash**."

> "Change 1 letter in **seal** to spell **heal**."

When children are not just adding or changing one letter, cue them to start over.

> "Start over and use 4 new letters to spell **lake**."

Give a meaning or sentence clue, when needed, to clarify the word children are making.

> "Start over and use 4 new letters to spell **seal**. We saw a **seal** at the zoo."

Always alert children when they are making a name and expect them to use a capital letter.

> "Use the same letters in **shake** to spell the name **Kesha**."

Give children one minute to figure out the secret word and then give clues if needed.

> "Our secret word is a name that you can make by adding your letters to **Kesha**."

Sort Sh Words (Optional)

Sort Rhymes

Reading Transfer: "Pretend you are reading and come to a new word." Have children put the transfer words under the appropriate rhymes and use the rhymes to decode them.

Spelling Transfer: "Pretend you are writing and need to spell these words." Have children tell you how the words begin. Then, have children find and use the appropriate rhymes to finish spelling the transfer words.

Step-by-step directions for a sample *Making Names* lesson are on pages 8-12.

Langston

a o g l n n s t

Make Words: Tell children how many letters to use to make each word. (A slash indicates words that can be made with the same letters.)

Emphasize how changing just one letter or rearranging letters makes a different word.

"Add a letter to **tag** to spell **Tang**®."

"Use the same letters in **sang** to spell **snag**."

When children are not just adding or changing one letter, cue them to start over.

"Start over and use 4 new letters to spell **lost**."

Give a meaning or sentence clue, when needed, to clarify the word children are making.

"Start over and use 6 new letters to spell **slogan**. The D. A. R. E. **slogan** is 'Say NO to drugs!'"

Always alert children when they are making a name and expect them to use a capital letter.

"Use the same letters in **loan** to spell the name **Nola**."

Give children one minute to figure out the secret word and then give clues, if needed.

"Our secret word is a name that begins with **L** and ends with **n**."

Sort Beginning Letters (Optional)

Sort Rhymes

Reading Transfer: "Pretend you are reading and come to a new word." Have children put the transfer words under the appropriate rhymes and use the rhymes to decode them.

Spelling Transfer: "Pretend you are writing and need to spell these words." Have children tell you how the words begin. Then, have children find and use the appropriate rhymes to finish spelling the transfer words.

Step-by-step directions for a sample *Making Names* lesson are on pages 8-12.

MAKE WORDS

lot
not
Nat
nag
tag
Tang®
sang/snag
Stan
lost
loan/Nola
slogan
Langston

SORT WORDS

Beginning Letters (Optional)

Rhymes:

lot	nag	Tang®
not	tag	sang
	snag	

TRANSFER WORDS

Reading:
drag slang

Spelling:
flag clang

Lawrence

MAKE WORDS

new
war/raw
law
claw
crew
Lane/
lean
clean
renew
cereal
leaner
cleaner
renewal
Lawrence

SORT WORDS

Related Words:
new, renew, renewal;
lean, leaner; clean, cleaner

Rhymes:
raw   new   lean   leaner
law   crew   clean   cleaner
claw

TRANSFER WORDS

Reading:
blew straw

Spelling:
grew meaner

Make Words: Tell children how many letters to use to make each word. (A slash indicates words that can be made with the same letters.)

Emphasize how changing just one letter or rearranging letters makes a different word.

"Add a letter to **law** to spell **claw**."

"Use the same letters in **Lane** to spell **lean**."

When children are not just adding or changing one letter, cue them to start over.

"Start over and use 7 new letters to spell **renewal**."

Give a meaning or sentence clue, when needed, to clarify the word children are making.

"Start over and use 5 new letters to spell **renew**. I will **renew** my subscription to the magazine."

Always alert children when they are making a name and expect them to use a capital letter.

"Take 4 new letters and spell the name **Lane**."

Give children one minute to figure out the secret word and then give clues, if needed.

"Our secret word is a name that you can make by adding your letters to **law**."

Sort Related Words

Sort Rhymes

Reading Transfer: "Pretend you are reading and come to a new word." Have children put the transfer words under the appropriate rhymes and use the rhymes to decode them.

Spelling Transfer: "Pretend you are writing and need to spell these words." Have children tell you how the words begin. Then, have children find and use the appropriate rhymes to finish spelling the transfer words.

Step-by-step directions for a sample *Making Names* lesson are on pages 8-12.

Leonardo

a e o o d l n r

Make Words: Tell children how many letters to use to make each word. (A slash indicates words that can be made with the same letters.)

Emphasize how changing just one letter or rearranging letters makes a different word.

> "Add a letter to **Leo** to spell the name **Leon**."

> "Change 1 letter in **Dean** to spell **dear**."

When children are not just adding or changing one letter, cue them to start over.

> "Start over and use 5 new letters to spell **alone**."

Give a meaning or sentence clue, when needed, to clarify the word children are making.

> "Use 6 new letters to spell **noodle**. I like chicken **noodle** soup."

Always alert children when they are making a name and expect them to use a capital letter.

> "Take 3 letters and spell the name **Don**."

Give children one minute to figure out the secret word and then give clues, if needed.

> "Our secret word is a name that you can make by adding your letters to **Leonard**."

Sort Beginning Letters (Optional)

Sort Rhymes

Reading Transfer: "Pretend you are reading and come to a new word." Have children put the transfer words under the appropriate rhymes and use the rhymes to decode them.

Spelling Transfer: "Pretend you are writing and need to spell these words." Have children tell you how the words begin. Then, have children find and use the appropriate rhymes to finish spelling the transfer words.

Step-by-step directions for a sample *Making Names* lesson are on pages 8-12.

MAKE WORDS

Don
Ron
Leo
Leon
lean
Dean
dear
near
Dale
rodeo
alone
older
noodle
Leonard
Leonardo

SORT WORDS

Beginning Letters (Optional)

Rhymes:

Don	lean	dear
Ron	Dean	near

TRANSFER WORDS

Reading:
spear clean

Spelling:
gear Jean

Linda

a i d l n

MAKE WORDS

an
ad
and/Dan
Ida/aid
ail
lad
land
nail
Dina
Linda

SORT WORDS

Beginning Letters (Optional)

Rhymes:

an	and	ail	ad
Dan	land	nail	lad

TRANSFER WORDS

Reading:
brand glad

Spelling:
sad hail

Make Words: Tell children how many letters to use to make each word. (A slash indicates words that can be made with the same letters.)

Emphasize how changing just one letter or rearranging letters makes a different word.

"Change a letter in **aid** to spell **ail**."

"Use the same letters in **Ida** to spell **aid**."

When children are not just adding or changing one letter, cue them to start over.

"Start over and use 4 new letters to spell the name **Dina**."

Give a meaning or sentence clue, when needed, to clarify the word children are making.

"Use 3 new letters to spell **lad**. Sometimes a boy is called a **lad**."

Always alert children when they are making a name and expect them to use a capital letter.

"Take 3 new letters and spell the name **Ida**."

Give children one minute to figure out the secret word and then give clues, if needed.

"Our secret word is a name that begins with **L** and ends with **a**."

Sort Beginning Letters (Optional)

Sort Rhymes

Reading Transfer: "Pretend you are reading and come to a new word." Have children put the transfer words under the appropriate rhymes and use the rhymes to decode them.

Spelling Transfer: "Pretend you are writing and need to spell these words." Have children tell you how the words begin. Then, have children find and use the appropriate rhymes to finish spelling the transfer words.

Step-by-step directions for a sample *Making Names* lesson are on pages 8-12.

Making Names • CD-2429 • © Carson-Dellosa

Lindsey

Make Words: Tell children how many letters to use to make each word. (A slash indicates words that can be made with the same letters.)

Emphasize how changing just one letter or rearranging letters makes a different word.

> "Change a letter in **led** to spell **lid**."

> "Add a letter to **side** to spell **slide**."

When children are not just adding or changing one letter, cue them to start over.

> "Start over and use 4 new letters to spell **line**."

Give a meaning or sentence clue, when needed, to clarify the word children are making.

> "Use 5 new letters to spell **yield**. The accident happened because the truck driver did not **yield** the right of way."

Always alert children when they are making a name and expect them to use a capital letter.

> "Take 3 new letters and spell the name **Del**."

Give children one minute to figure out the secret word and then gives clues, if needed.

> "Our secret word is a name that begins with **L** and ends with **y**."

Sort Beginning Letters (Optional)

Sort Rhymes

Reading Transfer: "Pretend you are reading and come to a new word." Have children put the transfer words under the appropriate rhymes and use the rhymes to decode them.

Spelling Transfer: "Pretend you are writing and need to spell these words." Have children tell you how the words begin. Then, have children find and use the appropriate rhymes to finish spelling the transfer words.

Step-by-step directions for a sample *Making Names* lesson are on pages 8-12.

MAKE WORDS

yes
Del
den
Len
led
lid
slid
sled
line
dine
side
slide
yield
Lindsey

SORT WORDS

Beginning Letters (Optional)

Rhymes:

den	lid	led	line	side
Len	slid	sled	dine	slide

TRANSFER WORDS

Reading:
bride nine

Spelling:
glide Fred

Loraine

a e i o l n r

MAKE WORDS

Al
Len
Ira
ear
near
Erin
Nora
Lori
lion
rain
rail
nail
alone
alien
Loraine

SORT WORDS

Beginning Letters (Optional)

Rhymes:
rail   ear
nail   near

TRANSFER WORDS

Reading:
fear snail

Spelling:
trail year

Make Words: Tell children how many letters to use to make each word. (A slash indicates words that can be made with the same letters.)

Emphasize how changing just one letter or rearranging letters makes a different word.

"Change a letter in **rain** to spell **rail**."

"Add a letter to **ear** to spell **near**."

When children are not just adding or changing one letter, cue them to start over.

"Start over and use 4 new letters to spell the name **Erin**."

Give a meaning or sentence clue, when needed, to clarify the word children are making.

"Use 5 new letters to spell **alone**. The dog didn't like being left **alone**."

Always alert children when they are making a name and expect them to use a capital letter.

"Take 4 new letters and spell the name **Nora**."

Give children one minute to figure out the secret word and then give clues, if needed.

"Our secret word is a name that begins with **L** and ends with **e**."

Sort Beginning Letters (Optional)

Sort Rhymes

Reading Transfer: "Pretend you are reading and come to a new word." Have children put the transfer words under the appropriate rhymes and use the rhymes to decode them.

Spelling Transfer: "Pretend you are writing and need to spell these words." Have children tell you how the words begin. Then, have children find and use the appropriate rhymes to finish spelling the transfer words.

Step-by-step directions for a sample *Making Names* lesson are on pages 8-12.

Loretta

a e o l r t t

Make Words: Tell children how many letters to use to make each word. (A slash indicates words that can be made with the same letters.)

Emphasize how changing just one letter or rearranging letters makes a different word.

"Change a letter in **rate** to spell **late**."

"Add a letter to **late** to spell **later**."

When children are not just adding or changing one letter, cue them to start over.

"Start over and use 5 new letters to spell **treat**."

Give a meaning or sentence clue, when needed, to clarify the word children are making.

"Use 5 new letters to spell **otter**. The **otter** is a very good swimmer."

Always alert children when they are making a name and expect them to use a capital letter.

"Take 3 new letters and spell the name **Art**."

Give children one minute to figure out the secret word and then give clues, if needed.

"Our secret word is a name that begins with **L** and ends with **a**."

Sort Related Words

Sort Rhymes

Reading Transfer: "Pretend you are reading and come to a new word." Have children put the transfer words under the appropriate rhymes and use the rhymes to decode them.

Spelling Transfer: "Pretend you are writing and need to spell these words." Have children tell you how the words begin. Then, have children find and use the appropriate rhymes to finish spelling the transfer words.

Step-by-step directions for a sample *Making Names* lesson are on pages 8-12.

MAKE WORDS

eat/ate
Art/rat
rate
late
later/alert/alter
treat
total
otter
rotate
rattle
Loretta

SORT WORDS

Related Words:
late, later

Rhymes:

eat	ate
treat	rate
	late
	rotate

TRANSFER WORDS

Reading:
gate heat

Spelling:
cheat state

Mackenzie

MAKE WORDS

ice
Ian
man
men
Ken
mice
nice
Nick
Mick
Mack
Zack
cake
make
Mike
Mackenzie

SORT WORDS

Beginning Letters (Optional)

Rhymes:
ice Nick Mack cake men
nice Mick Zack make Ken
mice

TRANSFER WORDS

Reading:
quick quake

Spelling:
twice stack

Make Words: Tell children how many letters to use to make each word. (A slash indicates words that can be made with the same letters.)

Emphasize how changing just one letter or rearranging letters makes a different word.

"Change a letter in **Mick** to spell the name **Mack**."

When children are not just adding or changing one letter, cue them to start over.

"Start over and use 4 new letters to spell **cake**."

Give a meaning or sentence clue, when needed, to clarify the word children are making.

"Change 1 letter in **man** to spell **men**. The **men** raced to the finish line."

Always alert children when they are making a name and expect them to use a capital letter.

"Change 1 letter in **make** to spell the name **Mike**."

Give children one minute to figure out the secret word and then give clues, if needed.

"Our secret word is a name that starts with **M** and ends with **e**."

Sort Beginning Letters (Optional)

Sort Rhymes

Reading Transfer: "Pretend you are reading and come to a new word." Have children put the transfer words under the appropriate rhymes and use the rhymes to decode them.

Spelling Transfer: "Pretend you are writing and need to spell these words." Have children tell you how the words begin. Then, have children find and use the appropriate rhymes to finish spelling the transfer words.

Step-by-step directions for a sample *Making Names* lesson are on pages 8-12.

Madeline

a e e i d l m n

Make Words: Tell children how many letters to use to make each word. (A slash indicates words that can be made with the same letters.)

Emphasize how changing just one letter or rearranging letters makes a different word.

> "Change a letter in **name** to spell **lame**."

> "Use the same letters in **mane** to spell **name**."

When children are not just adding or changing one letter, cue them to start over.

> "Start over and use 5 new letters to spell **named**."

Give a meaning or sentence clue, when needed, to clarify the word children are making.

> "Use 5 new letters to spell **medal**. The fastest runner won the gold **medal**."

Always alert children when they are making a name and expect them to use a capital letter.

> "Take 4 new letters and spell the name **Neil**."

Give children one minute to figure out the secret word and then give clues, if needed.

> "Our secret word is a name that you can make by adding your letters to **line**."

Sort Related Words

Sort Rhymes

Reading Transfer: "Pretend you are reading and come to a new word." Have children put the transfer words under the appropriate rhymes and use the rhymes to decode them.

Spelling Transfer: "Pretend you are writing and need to spell these words." Have children tell you how the words begin. Then, have children find and use the appropriate rhymes to finish spelling the transfer words.

Step-by-step directions for a sample *Making Names* lesson are on pages 8-12.

MAKE WORDS

die
lie
lied
mine
line
Lane
mane/name
lame
Neil
named
medal
Delia
Elaine
Madeline

SORT WORDS

Related Words:
name, named; lie, lied

Rhymes:

die	mine	Lane	name
lie	line	mane	lame

TRANSFER WORDS

Reading:
blame pie

Spelling:
Jane pine

Madison

a i o d m n s

MAKE WORDS

an
Ian
man
Dan/and
mad
sad
Ida/aid
maid
moan/Mona
Madison

SORT WORDS

Rhymes:

an	sad	aid
Dan	mad	maid
man		

TRANSFER WORDS

Reading:
paid pad

Spelling:
raid braid

Make Words: Tell children how many letters to use to make each word. (A slash indicates words that can be made with the same letters.)

Emphasize how changing just one letter or rearranging letters makes a different word.

"Change a letter in **mad** to spell **sad**."

"Add a letter to **an** to spell the name **Ian**."

When children are not just adding or changing one letter, cue them to start over.

"Start over and use 4 new letters to spell **moan**."

Give a meaning or sentence clue, when needed, to clarify the word children are making

"Add 1 letter to **aid** to spell **maid**. When Mom got sick, we hired a **maid** to do the cleaning."

Always alert children when they are making a name and expect them to use a capital letter.

"Use the same letters in **moan** to spell the name **Mona**."

Give children one minute to figure out the secret word and then give clues if needed.

"Our secret word is a name that you can make by adding your letters to **mad**."

Sort Rhymes

Reading Transfer: "Pretend you are reading and come to a new word." Have children put the transfer words under the appropriate rhymes and use the rhymes to decode them.

Spelling Transfer: "Pretend you are writing and need to spell these words." Have children tell you how the words begin. Then, have children find and use the appropriate rhymes to finish spelling the transfer words.

Step-by-step directions for a sample *Making Names* lesson are on pages 8-12.

Madonna

Make Words: Tell children how many letters to use to make each word. (A slash indicates words that can be made with the same letters.)

Emphasize how changing just one letter or rearranging letters makes a different word.

> "Add a letter to **ad** to spell **mad**."

> "Use the same letters in **moan** to spell the name **Mona**."

When children are not just adding or changing one letter, cue them to start over.

> "Start over and use 5 new letters to spell the name **Donna**."

Give a meaning or sentence clue, when needed, to clarify the word children are making.

> "Use 2 letters to spell **ad**. We put an **ad** in the newspaper to sell the old truck."

Always alert children when they are making a name and expect them to use a capital letter.

> "Use the same letters in **and** to spell the name **Dan**."

Give children one minute to figure out the secret word and then give clues, if needed.

> "Our secret word is a name that you can make by adding your letters to **Donna**."

Sort Beginning Letters (Optional)

Sort Rhymes

Reading Transfer: "Pretend you are reading and come to a new word." Have children put the transfer words under the appropriate rhymes and use the rhymes to decode them.

Spelling Transfer: "Pretend you are writing and need to spell these words." Have children tell you how the words begin. Then, have children find and use the appropriate rhymes to finish spelling the transfer words.

Step-by-step directions for a sample *Making Names* lesson are on pages 8-12.

MAKE WORDS

ad
mad
man
Nan
and/Dan
Don
Anna
Adam
moan/Mona
Donna
Madonna

SORT WORDS

Beginning Letters (Optional)

Rhymes:
ad	man
mad	Nan
	Dan

TRANSFER WORDS

Reading:
glad plan

Spelling:
Chad Stan

Malcolm

a o c l l m m

▶ MAKE WORDS

am
Al
all
mom
mall
call
clam/calm
coma
comma
local
Malcolm

▶ SORT WORDS

Beginning Letters (Optional)

Rhymes:
all	am
call	clam
mall	

▶ TRANSFER WORDS

Reading:
small swam

Spelling:
stall slam

Make Words: Tell children how many letters to use to make each word. (A slash indicates words that can be made with the same letters.)

Emphasize how changing just one letter or rearranging letters makes a different word.

> "Add a letter to **coma** to spell **comma**."

> "Use the same letters in **clam** to spell **calm**."

When children are not just adding or changing one letter, cue them to start over.

> "Start over and use 5 new letters to spell **local**."

Give a meaning or sentence clue, when needed, to clarify the word children are making.

> "Use 4 letters to spell **coma**. After the accident, my uncle was in a **coma** for five days."

Always alert children when they are making a name and expect them to use a capital letter.

> "Change 1 letter in **am** to spell the name **Al**."

Give children one minute to figure out the secret word and then give clues, if needed.

> "Our secret word is a name that begins with **M** and ends with **m**."

Sort Beginning Letters (Optional)

Sort Rhymes

Reading Transfer: "Pretend you are reading and come to a new word." Have children put the transfer words under the appropriate rhymes and use the rhymes to decode them.

Spelling Transfer: "Pretend you are writing and need to spell these words." Have children tell you how the words begin. Then, have children find and use the appropriate rhymes to finish spelling the transfer words.

Step-by-step directions for a sample *Making Names* lesson are on pages 8-12.

Making Names • CD-2429 • © Carson-Dellosa

Manuel

a e u l m n

Make Words: Tell children how many letters to use to make each word. (A slash indicates words that can be made with the same letters.)

Emphasize how changing just one letter or rearranging letters makes a different word.

"Add a letter to **men** to spell **mean**."

"Use the same letters in **name** to spell **mane**."

When children are not just adding or changing one letter, cue them to start over.

"Start over and use 4 new letters to spell **menu**."

Give a meaning or sentence clue, when needed, to clarify the word children are making.

"Change 1 letter in **mean** to spell **lean**. Please don't **lean** on the table."

Always alert children when they are making a name and expect them to use a capital letter.

"Change 1 letter in **mane** to spell the name **Lane**."

Give children one minute to figure out the secret word and then give clues, if needed.

"Our secret word is a name that you can spell by adding your letters to **man**."

Sort Beginning Letters (Optional)

Sort Rhymes

Reading Transfer: "Pretend you are reading and come to a new word." Have children put the transfer words under the appropriate rhymes and use the rhymes to decode them.

Spelling Transfer: "Pretend you are writing and need to spell these words." Have children tell you how the words begin. Then, have children find and use the appropriate rhymes to finish spelling the transfer words.

Step-by-step directions for a sample *Making Names* lesson are on pages 8-12.

MAKE WORDS

Al
an
man
men
mean
lean
meal/lame
name/mane
Lane
menu
Manuel

SORT WORDS

Beginning Letters (Optional)
Rhymes:

| an | mean | lame | mane |
| man | lean | name | Lane |

TRANSFER WORDS

Reading:
plane plan

Spelling:
clean game

Margaret

MAKE WORDS

Meg
ate/eat
meat/team/tame/mate
gate
game
rate
Tara
tamer
Marge
Margaret

SORT WORDS

Beginning Letters (Optional)

Related Words:
tame, tamer

Rhymes:

ate	eat	tame
mate	meat	game
gate		
rate		

TRANSFER WORDS

Reading:
blame plate

Spelling:
skate frame

Make Words: Tell children how many letters to use to make each word. (A slash indicates words that can be made with the same letters.)

Emphasize how changing just one letter or rearranging letters makes a different word.

> "Add a letter to **eat** to spell **meat**."

> "Use the same letters in **meat** to spell **team**."

When children are not just adding or changing one letter, cue them to start over.

> "Start over and use 4 new letters to spell the name **Tara**."

Give a meaning or sentence clue, when needed, to clarify the word children are making.

> "Use 4 new letters to spell **rate**. We got a good interest **rate** on our loan."

Always alert children when they are making a name and expect them to use a capital letter.

> "Take 3 letters and spell the name **Meg**."

Give children one minute to figure out the secret word and then give clues, if needed.

> "Our secret word is a name that begins with **M** and ends with **t**."

Sort Beginning Letters (Optional)

Sort Related Words

Sort Rhymes

Reading Transfer: "Pretend you are reading and come to a new word." Have children put the transfer words under the appropriate rhymes and use the rhymes to decode them.

Spelling Transfer: "Pretend you are writing and need to spell these words." Have children tell you how the words begin. Then, have children find and use the appropriate rhymes to finish spelling the transfer words.

Step-by-step directions for a sample *Making Names* lesson are on pages 8-12.

Margie

a e i g m r

Make Words: Tell children how many letters to use to make each word. (A slash indicates words that can be made with the same letters.)

Emphasize how changing just one letter or rearranging letters makes a different word.

> "Add a letter to **gem** to spell **germ**."

> "Use the same letters in **Meg** to spell **gem**."

When children are not just adding or changing one letter, cue them to start over.

> "Start over and use 5 new letters to spell the name **Marie**."

Give a meaning or sentence clue, when needed, to clarify the word children are making.

> "Use 4 letters to spell **gear**. We packed up all of our camping **gear**."

Always alert children when they are making a name and expect them to use a capital letter.

> "Take 3 letters and spell the name **Meg**."

This lesson has two secret words. Give children one minute to figure out each secret word and then give clues, if needed.

> "One secret word begins with **m**, and it is when you think you see something like water in a desert, but the water isn't really there." (Omit **mirage** if the word is not known to children in your class.)

> "The other secret word is a name that begins with **M** and ends with **e**."

Sort G Words—both sounds (Optional)

Sort Rhymes

Reading Transfer: "Pretend you are reading and come to a new word." Have children put the transfer words under the appropriate rhymes and use the rhymes to decode them.

Spelling Transfer: "Pretend you are writing and need to spell these words." Have children tell you how the words begin. Then, have children find and use the appropriate rhymes to finish spelling the transfer words.

Step-by-step directions for a sample *Making Names* lesson are on pages 8-12.

MAKE WORDS

ear/are
age
Meg/gem
germ
gear/rage
game
Marie
Marge
mirage/Margie

SORT WORDS

G Words—both sounds (Optional):
game, gear, Meg;
gem, germ, age, rage, Marge, mirage, Margie

Rhymes:
ear   age
gear   rage

TRANSFER WORDS

Reading:
year page
Spelling:
stage smear

Marilyn

MAKE WORDS

any
Amy
Ian
Ray
May
Mary/army/Myra
rain
rail
mail
main
many
rainy
Marilyn

SORT WORDS

Related Words:
rain, rainy

Rhymes:
Ray   rain   rail
May   main   mail

TRANSFER WORDS

Reading:
stay stain

Spelling:
frail gray

Make Words: Tell children how many letters to use to make each word. (A slash indicates words that can be made with the same letters.)

Emphasize how changing just one letter or rearranging letters makes a different word.

"Change a letter in **rain** to spell **rail**."

"Use the same letters in **Mary** to spell **army**."

When children are not just adding or changing one letter, cue them to start over.

"Start over and use 4 new letters to spell **rain**."

Give a meaning or sentence clue, when needed, to clarify the word children are making.

"Start over and use 4 new letters to spell **many**. There are **many** wonderful places to visit in the United States."

Always alert children when they are making a name and expect them to use a capital letter.

"Change 1 letter in **any** to spell the name **Amy**."

Give children one minute to figure out the secret word and then give clues, if needed.

"Our secret word is a name that starts with **M** and ends with **n**."

Sort Related Words

Sort Rhymes

Reading Transfer: "Pretend you are reading and come to a new word." Have children put the words under the appropriate rhymes and use the rhymes to decode them.

Spelling Transfer: "Pretend you are writing and need to spell these words." Have children tell you how the words begin. Then, have children find and use the appropriate rhymes to finish spelling the new words.

Step-by-step directions for a sample *Making Names* lesson are on pages 8-12.

Marisol

Make Words: Tell children how many letters to use to make each word. (A slash indicates words that can be made with the same letters.)

Emphasize how changing just one letter or rearranging letters makes a different word.

> "Add a letter to **oil** to spell **soil**."

> "Use the same letters in **soil** to spell the name **Lois**."

When children are not just adding or changing one letter, cue them to start over.

> "Start over and use 4 new letters to spell the planet, **Mars**."

Give a meaning or sentence clue, when needed, to clarify the word children are making.

> "Use 5 new letters to spell **solar**. Some houses are heated by **solar** energy from the sun."

Always alert children when they are making a name and expect them to use a capital letter.

> "Take 3 letters and spell the name **Ira**."

Give children one minute to figure out the secret word and then give clues, if needed.

> "Our secret word is a name that begins with **M** and ends with **l**."

Sort Related Words

Sort Rhymes

Reading Transfer: "Pretend you are reading and come to a new word." Have children put the words under the appropriate rhymes and use the rhymes to decode them.

Spelling Transfer: "Pretend you are writing and need to spell these words." Have children tell you how the words begin. Then, have children find and use the appropriate rhymes to finish spelling the new words.

Step-by-step directions for a sample *Making Names* lesson are on pages 8-12.

MAKE WORDS

Ira
oil
soil/Lois
Lori
Mars
mail
sail/Lisa
solar
sailor
Marisol

SORT WORDS

Related Words:
sail, sailor

Rhymes:
oil   mail
soil   sail

TRANSFER WORDS

Reading:
trail spoil

Spelling:
jail boil

Marshall

MAKE WORDS

Al
am
Sam
ham
Hal
all
slam
hall
mall
small
alarm
llama
Marsha
Marshall

SORT WORDS

Beginning Letters (Optional)

Rhymes:

am	Al	hall
Sam	Hal	mall
ham		small
slam		all

TRANSFER WORDS

Reading:
squall Pam

Spelling:
stall pal

Make Words: Tell children how many letters to use to make each word. (A slash indicates words that can be made with the same letters.)

Emphasize how changing just one letter or rearranging letters makes a different word.

"Change a letter in **hall** to spell **mall**."

"Add a letter to **mall** to spell **small**."

When children are not just adding or changing one letter, cue them to start over.

"Start over and use 4 new letters to spell **hall**."

Give a meaning or sentence clue, when needed, to clarify the word children are making.

"Use 5 letters to spell **llama**. A **llama** is a strange-looking animal and has a strange spelling."

Always alert children when they are making a name and expect them to use a capital letter.

"Take 6 new letters and spell the name **Marsha**."

Give children one minute to figure out the secret word and then give clues, if needed.

"Our secret word is a name that you can make by adding your letters to **Marsha**."

Sort Beginning Letters (Optional)

Sort Rhymes

Reading Transfer: "Pretend you are reading and come to a new word." Have children put the transfer words under the appropriate rhymes and use the rhymes to decode them.

Spelling Transfer: "Pretend you are writing and need to spell these words." Have children tell you how the words begin. Then, have children find and use the appropriate rhymes to finish spelling the transfer words.

Step-by-step directions for a sample *Making Names* lesson are on pages 8-12.

Martin

a i m n r t

Make Words: Tell children how many letters to use to make each word. (A slash indicates words that can be made with the same letters.)

Emphasize how changing just one letter or rearranging letters makes a different word.

> "Add a letter to **mat** to spell **mart**."

> "Change a letter in **rat** to spell **ran**."

When children are not just adding or changing one letter, cue them to start over.

> "Start over and use 3 new letters to spell the name **Art**."

Give a meaning or sentence clue, when needed, to clarify the word children are making.

> "Change 1 letter in **Tim** to spell **rim**. They stood on the **rim** of the canyon and looked down."

Always alert children when they are making a name and expect them to use a capital letter.

> "Use 4 letters to spell the name **Rita**."

Give children one minute to figure out the secret word and then give clues, if needed.

> "Our secret word is a name that begins with **M** and ends with **n**."

Sort Beginning Letters (Optional)

Sort Rhymes

Reading Transfer: "Pretend you are reading and come to a new word." Have children put the transfer words under the appropriate rhymes and use the rhymes to decode them.

Spelling Transfer: "Pretend you are writing and need to spell these words." Have children tell you how the words begin. Then, have children find and use the appropriate rhymes to finish spelling the transfer words.

Step-by-step directions for a sample *Making Names* lesson are on pages 8-12.

MAKE WORDS

Tim
rim
Art/rat
ran
man
mat
mart
Rita
Tina
main
rain
train
Martin

SORT WORDS

Beginning Letters (Optional)

Rhymes:

Tim	ran	art	main	rat
rim	man	mart	rain	mat
			train	

TRANSFER WORDS

Reading:
chain chart

Spelling:
swim start

Martina

aaimnrt

MAKE WORDS

am
an
ran
ram
Ira
Tina
Rita
Tara
main
rain
train
Anita
Maria
Martin
Martina

SORT WORDS

Beginning Letters (Optional)

Rhymes:

an	main	am
ran	rain	ram
	train	

TRANSFER WORDS

Reading:
brain bran

Spelling:
clam drain

Make Words: Tell children how many letters to use to make each word. (A slash indicates words that can be made with the same letters.)

Emphasize how changing just one letter or rearranging letters makes a different word.

"Add a letter to **rain** to spell **train**."

"Change a letter in **main** to spell **rain**."

When children are not just adding or changing one letter, cue them to start over.

"Start over and use 5 new letters to spell the name **Anita**."

Give a meaning or sentence clue, when needed, to clarify the word children are making.

"Start over and use 4 new letters to spell **main**. Sometimes we read to understand the **main** idea."

Always alert children when they are making a name and expect them to use a capital letter.

"Use 3 letters to spell the name **Ira**."

Give children one minute to figure out the secret word and then give clues, if needed.

"Our secret word is a name that you can spell by adding a letter to **Martin**."

Sort Beginning Letters (Optional)

Sort Rhymes

Reading Transfer: "Pretend you are reading and come to a new word." Have children put the transfer words under the appropriate rhymes and use the rhymes to decode them.

Spelling Transfer: "Pretend you are writing and need to spell these words." Have children tell you how the words begin. Then, have children find and use the appropriate rhymes to finish spelling the transfer words.

Step-by-step directions for a sample *Making Names* lesson are on pages 8-12.

Marty

amrty

Make Words: Tell children how many letters to use to make each word. (A slash indicates words that can be made with the same letters.)

Emphasize how changing just one letter or rearranging letters makes a different word.

"Add a letter to **try** to spell **tray**."

"Change 1 letter in **mat** to spell **rat**."

When children are not just adding or changing one letter, cue them to start over.

"Start over and use 3 new letters to spell **mat**."

Give a meaning or sentence clue, when needed, to clarify the word children are making:

"Use 4 new letters to spell **army**. After high school, he joined the **army**."

Always alert children when they are making a name and expect them to use a capital letter.

"Use the same letters in **May** to spell the name **Amy**."

Give children one minute to figure out the secret word and then give clues, if needed.

"Our secret word is a name that you can make by adding a letter to **Mary**."

Sort Beginning Letters (Optional)

Sort Rhymes

Reading Transfer: "Pretend you are reading and come to a new word." Have children put the transfer words under the appropriate rhymes and use the rhymes to decode them.

Spelling Transfer: "Pretend you are writing and need to spell these words." Have children tell you how the words begin. Then, have children find and use the appropriate rhymes to finish spelling the transfer words.

Step-by-step directions for a sample *Making Names* lesson are on pages 8-12.

MAKE WORDS

my
mat
rat/Art
arm/ram
Ray
May/Amy
try
tray
army/Myra/Mary
Marty

SORT WORDS

Beginning Letters (Optional)

Rhymes:

mat	my	Ray
rat	try	May
		tray

TRANSFER WORDS

Reading:
fly flat

Spelling:
sky spray

Marvin

a i m n r v

MAKE WORDS

am
an
Ian
Ira
arm/ram
ran
van
man
main
rain
Marvin

SORT WORDS

Beginning Letters (Optional)

Rhymes:

an	rain	am
van	main	ram
ran		
man		

TRANSFER WORDS

Reading:
slam plan

Spelling:
tram train

Make Words: Tell children how many letters to use to make each word. (A slash indicates words that can be made with the same letters.)

Emphasize how changing just one letter or rearranging letters makes a different word.

> "Add a letter to **man** to spell **main**."

> "Change 1 letter in **main** to spell **rain**."

When children are not just adding or changing one letter, cue them to start over.

> "Start over and use 3 new letters to spell **arm**."

Give a meaning or sentence clue, when needed, to clarify the word children are making.

> "Use the same letters in **arm** to spell **ram**. I heard a noise and felt something **ram** into the back of our bus."

Always alert children when they are making a name and expect them to use a capital letter.

> "Take 3 letters and spell the name **Ian**."

Give children one minute to figure out the secret word and then give clues, if needed.

> "Our secret word is a name that begins with **M** and ends with **n**."

Sort Beginning Letters (Optional)

Sort Rhymes

Reading Transfer: "Pretend you are reading and come to a new word." Have children put the transfer words under the appropriate rhymes and use the rhymes to decode them.

Spelling Transfer: "Pretend you are writing and need to spell these words." Have children tell you how the words begin. Then, have children find and use the appropriate rhymes to finish spelling the transfer words.

Step-by-step directions for a sample *Making Names* lesson are on pages 8-12.

Matthew

Make Words: Tell children how many letters to use to make each word. (A slash indicates words that can be made with the same letters.)

Emphasize how changing just one letter or rearranging letters makes a different word.

> "Add a letter to **mat** to spell the name **Matt**."

> "Use the same letters in **mate** to spell **team**."

When children are not just adding or changing one letter, cue them to start over.

> "Start over and use 4 new letters to spell **meat**."

Give a meaning or sentence clue, when needed, to clarify the word children are making.

> "Start over and use 4 new letters to spell **what**. **What** would you like to eat?"

Always alert children when they are making a name and expect them to use a capital letter.

> "Add a letter to **mat** to spell the name **Matt**."

Give children one minute to figure out the secret word and then give clues, if needed.

> "Our secret word is a name that you can make by adding your letters to **Matt**."

Sort Beginning Letters (Optional)

Sort Rhymes

Reading Transfer: "Pretend you are reading and come to a new word." Have children put the transfer words under the appropriate rhymes and use the rhymes to decode them.

Spelling Transfer: "Pretend you are writing and need to spell these words." Have children tell you how the words begin. Then, have children find and use the appropriate rhymes to finish spelling the transfer words.

Step-by-step directions for a sample *Making Names* lesson are on pages 8-12.

MAKE WORDS

eat/ate
mat
Matt
math
meat
heat/hate
mate/team
them
what
wheat
Matthew

SORT WORDS

Beginning Letters (Optional)

Rhymes:
eat	ate
heat	hate
wheat	mate
meat	

TRANSFER WORDS

Reading:
cheat late

Spelling:
skate treat

Maxwell

a e l l m w x

am
ax
wax
Max
law
Lew
all
wall
mall
meal/lame/male
exam
axle
Maxwell

SORT WORDS

X Words (Optional):
ax, wax, Max, exam, axle,
Maxwell

Rhymes:
ax   all
wax   wall
Max   mall

TRANSFER WORDS

Reading:
tax tall

Spelling:
fax small

Make Words: Tell children how many letters to use to make each word. (A slash indicates words that can be made with the same letters.)

Emphasize how changing just one letter or rearranging letters makes a different word.

"Add a letter to **all** to spell **wall**."

"Use the same letters in **meal** to spell **lame**. Use the same letters again to spell **male**."

When children are not just adding or changing one letter, cue them to start over.

"Start over and use 3 new letters to spell **law**."

Give a meaning or sentence clue, when needed, to clarify the word children are making.

"Start over and use 4 new letters to spell **axle**. The **axle** broke and the wheel fell off the car."

Always alert children when they are making a name and expect them to use a capital letter.

"Change a letter in **wax** to spell the name **Max**."

Give children one minute to figure out the secret word and then give clues, if needed.

"Our secret word is a name that you can spell by adding your letters to **Max**."

Sort X Words (Optional)

Sort Rhymes

Reading Transfer: "Pretend you are reading and come to a new word." Have children put the transfer words under the appropriate rhymes and use the rhymes to decode them.

Spelling Transfer: "Pretend you are writing and need to spell these words." Have children tell you how the words begin. Then, have children find and use the appropriate rhymes to finish spelling the transfer words.

Step-by-step directions for a sample *Making Names* lesson are on pages 8-12.

Melanie

Make Words: Tell children how many letters to use to make each word. (A slash indicates words that can be made with the same letters.)

Emphasize how changing just one letter or rearranging letters makes a different word.

> "Add a letter to **an** to spell **man**."

> "Use the same letters in **mane** to spell **name**."

When children are not just adding or changing one letter, cue them to start over.

> "Start over and use 4 new letters to spell the name **Neil**."

Give a meaning or sentence clue, when needed, to clarify the word children are making.

> "Change 1 letter in **Lane** to spell **mane**. The horse had a thick **mane** of hair on its neck."

Always alert children when they are making a name and expect them to use a capital letter.

> "Start over and use 4 new letters to spell the name **Neil**."

Give children one minute to figure out the secret word and then give clues, if needed.

> "Our secret word is a name that starts with **M** and ends with **e**."

Sort Beginning Letters (Optional)

Sort Rhymes

Reading Transfer: "Pretend you are reading and come to a new word." Have children put the transfer words under the appropriate rhymes and use the rhymes to decode them.

Spelling Transfer: "Pretend you are writing and need to spell these words." Have children tell you how the words begin. Then, have children find and use the appropriate rhymes to finish spelling the transfer words.

Step-by-step directions for a sample *Making Names* lesson are on pages 8-12.

MAKE WORDS

an
man
men
Neil
Lane
mane/name
lame
mine
line
alien
Elaine
Melanie

SORT WORDS

Beginning Letters (Optional)

Rhymes:

an	Lane	name	mine
man	mane	lame	line

TRANSFER WORDS

Reading:
shame Shane

Spelling:
shine blame

Melissa

a e i l m s s

Al
Sal
Sam
slam
Lisa
meal
seal
miss
mess
less
lime/mile
smile/slime
Melissa

SORT WORDS

Beginning Letters (Optional)

Rhymes:
Al   Sam   meal   mess   lime
Sal   slam   seal   less   slim

mile
smile

TRANSFER WORDS

Reading:
chess chime

Spelling:
while crime

Make Words: Tell children how many letters to use to make each word. (A slash indicates words that can be made with the same letters.)

Emphasize how changing just one letter or rearranging letters makes a different word.

> "Add a letter to **mile** to spell **smile**."

> "Use the same letters in **lime** to spell **mile**."

When children are not just adding or changing one letter, cue them to start over.

> "Start over and use 4 new letters to spell **miss**."

Give a meaning or sentence clue, when needed, to clarify the word children are making.

> "Use the same letters in **smile** to spell **slime**. There was a green **slime** all over the fish tank."

Always alert children when they are making a name and expect them to use a capital letter.

> "Take 4 letters and spell the name **Lisa**."

Give children one minute to figure out the secret word and then give clues, if needed.

> "Our secret word is a name that begins with **M** and ends with **a**."

Sort Beginning Letters (Optional)

Sort Rhymes

Reading Transfer: "Pretend you are reading and come to a new word." Have children put the transfer words under the appropriate rhymes and use the rhymes to decode them.

Spelling Transfer: "Pretend you are writing and need to spell these words." Have children tell you how the words begin. Then, have children find and use the appropriate rhymes to finish spelling the transfer words.

Step-by-step directions for a sample *Making Names* lesson are on pages 8-12.

Meredith

Make Words: Tell children how many letters to use to make each word. (A slash indicates words that can be made with the same letters.)

Emphasize how changing just one letter or rearranging letters makes a different word.

> "Add a letter to **Tim** to spell **time**."

> "Change a letter in **hire** to spell **tire**."

When children are not just adding or changing one letter, cue them to start over.

> "Start over and use 3 new letters to spell **him**."

Give a meaning or sentence clue, when needed, to clarify the word children are making.

> "Start over and use 5 new letters to spell **timer**. We set the **timer** for 20 minutes."

Always alert children when they are making a name and expect them to use a capital letter.

> "Use 5 letters to spell the name **Edith**."

Give children one minute to figure out the secret word and then give clues, if needed.

> "Our secret word is a name that you can make by adding your letters to **Edith**."

Sort Related Words

Sort Rhymes

Reading Transfer: "Pretend you are reading and come to a new word." Have children put the transfer words under the appropriate rhymes and use the rhymes to decode them.

Spelling Transfer: "Pretend you are writing and need to spell these words." Have children tell you how the words begin. Then, have children find and use the appropriate rhymes to finish spelling the transfer words.

Step-by-step directions for a sample *Making Names* lesson are on pages 8-12.

MAKE WORDS

Ed
Ted
him
Tim
time
dime
ride
hide
hire
tire
tired
hired
timer
Edith
Meredith

SORT WORDS

Related Words:
hire, hired; tire, tired;
time, timer

Rhymes:

Ed	him	time	ride
Ted	Tim	dime	hide

hire	tired
tire	hired

TRANSFER WORDS

Reading:
slide slime

Spelling:
prime pride

Michael

a e i c h l m

MAKE WORDS

Al
Hal
heal
meal/male/lame
came
clam/calm
lime/mile
mice
camel
Celia
Michael

SORT WORDS

Beginning Letters (Optional)

Rhymes:

Al	heal	lame
Hal	meal	came

TRANSFER WORDS

Reading:
flame frame

Spelling:
blame shame

Make Words: Tell children how many letters to use to make each word. (A slash indicates words that can be made with the same letters.)

Emphasize how changing just one letter or rearranging letters makes a different word.

"Add a letter to **Hal** to spell **heal**."

"Use the same letters in **clam** to spell **calm**."

When children are not just adding or changing one letter, cue them to start over.

"Start over and use 4 new letters to spell **lime**."

Give a meaning or sentence clue, when needed, to clarify the word children are making.

"Use 5 new letters to spell **camel**. We rode a **camel** across the desert."

Always alert children when they are making a name and expect them to use a capital letter.

"Take 5 letters and spell the name **Celia**."

Give children one minute to figure out the secret word and then give clues, if needed.

"Our secret word is a name that begins with **M** and ends with **l**."

Sort Beginning Letters (Optional)

Sort Rhymes

Reading Transfer: "Pretend you are reading and come to a new word." Have children put the transfer words under the appropriate rhymes and use the rhymes to decode them.

Spelling Transfer: "Pretend you are writing and need to spell these words." Have children tell you how the words begin. Then, have children find and use the appropriate rhymes to finish spelling the transfer words.

Step-by-step directions for a sample *Making Names* lesson are on pages 8-12.

Michelle

e e i c h l l m

Make Words: Tell children how many letters to use to make each word. (A slash indicates words that can be made with the same letters.)

Emphasize how changing just one letter or rearranging letters makes a different word.

"Change a letter in **lice** to spell **lime**."

"Use the same letters in **lime** to spell **mile**."

When children are not just adding or changing one letter, cue them to start over.

"Start over and use 3 new letters to spell **ice**."

Give a meaning or sentence clue, when needed, to clarify the word children are making.

"Start over and use 5 new letters to spell **chime**. I love to hear the bells **chime**."

Always alert children when they are making a name and expect them to use a capital letter.

"Use the same letters in **eel** to spell the name **Lee**."

Give children one minute to figure out the secret word and then give clues, if needed.

"Our secret word is a name that begins with **M** and ends with **e**."

Sort Beginning Letters (Optional)

Sort Rhymes

Reading Transfer: "Pretend you are reading and come to a new word." Have children put the transfer words under the appropriate rhymes and use the rhymes to decode them.

Spelling Transfer: "Pretend you are writing and need to spell these words." Have children tell you how the words begin. Then, have children find and use the appropriate rhymes to finish spelling the transfer words.

Step-by-step directions for a sample *Making Names* lesson are on pages 8-12.

MAKE WORDS

eel/Lee
lie
ill
ice
lice
lime/mile
mill
hill
chill
chime
Michelle

SORT WORDS

Beginning Letters (Optional)

Rhymes:

ice	lime	ill
lice	chime	hill
		mill
		chill

TRANSFER WORDS

Reading:
thrill price

Spelling:
shrill grime

Miranda

a a i d m n r

MAKE WORDS

Ira
Ian
Dan
man
ran
ram
rim
dim
rain
drain
Maria
marina
Miranda

SORT WORDS

Beginning Letters (Optional)

Rhymes:

Dan	rim	rain
man	dim	drain
ran		

TRANSFER WORDS

Reading:
brain brim

Spelling:
trim grain

Make Words: Tell children how many letters to use to make each word. (A slash indicates words that can be made with the same letters.)

Emphasize how changing just one letter or rearranging letters makes a different word.

"Change a letter in **rim** to spell **dim**."

When children are not just adding or changing one letter, cue them to start over.

"Start over and use 5 new letters to spell the name **Maria**."

Give a meaning or sentence clue, when needed, to clarify the word children are making.

"Add 1 letter to **Maria** to spell **marina**. We walked along the **marina** and looked at all of the sailboats."

Always alert children when they are making a name and expect them to use a capital letter.

"Take 3 letters and spell the name **Ira**."

Give children one minute to figure out the secret word and then give clues, if needed.

"Our secret word is a name that begins with **M** and ends with **a**."

Sort Beginning Letters (Optional)

Sort Rhymes

Reading Transfer: "Pretend you are reading and come to a new word." Have children put the transfer words under the appropriate rhymes and use the rhymes to decode them.

Spelling Transfer: "Pretend you are writing and need to spell these words." Have children tell you how the words begin. Then, have children find and use the appropriate rhymes to finish spelling the transfer words.

Step-by-step directions for a sample *Making Names* lesson are on pages 8-12.

Making Names • CD-2429 • © Carson-Dellosa

Mitchell

Make Words: Tell children how many letters to use to make each word. (A slash indicates words that can be made with the same letters.)

Emphasize how changing just one letter or rearranging letters makes a different word.

"Add a letter to **hill** to spell **chill**."

"Change 1 letter in **mill** to spell **hill**."

When children are not just adding or changing one letter, cue them to start over.

"Start over and use 4 new letters to spell **hill**."

Give meaning or sentence clues when needed to clarify the word they are making:

"Change 1 letter in **tell** to spell **cell**. They locked the criminal in a jail **cell**."

Always alert children when they are making a name and expect them to use a capital letter.

"Use 5 letters to spell the name **Mitch**."

Give them one minute to figure out the secret words and then gives clues if needed.

"Our secret word is a name that you can make by adding your letters to **Mitch**."

Sort Ch Words (Optional)

Sort Rhymes

Reading Transfer: "Pretend you are reading and come to a new word." Have children put the transfer words under the appropriate rhymes and use the rhymes to decode them.

Spelling Transfer: "Pretend you are writing and need to spell these words." Have children tell you how the words begin. Then, have children find and use the appropriate rhymes to finish spelling the transfer words.

Step-by-step directions for a sample *Making Names* lesson are on pages 8-12.

MAKE WORDS

Tim
him
let
met
Chet
itch
tell
cell
time
hill
mill
chill
chime
Mitch
Mitchell

SORT WORDS

Ch Words (Optional):
Chet, chill, chime, itch, Mitch, Mitchell

Rhymes:
Tim   let   tell   hill   itch
him   met   cell   mill   Mitch
    Chet   chill

time
chime

TRANSFER WORDS

Reading:
switch grill

Spelling:
pitch hitch

Mohammed

a e o d h m m m

MAKE WORDS

Mo
Ed
am
ad
had
mad
ham
mom
home
dome
head
memo
modem
Mohammed

SORT WORDS

Beginning Letters (Optional)

Rhymes:
ad	am	home
had	ham	dome
mad		

TRANSFER WORDS

Reading:
chrome spam

Spelling:
Chad scram

Make Words: Tell children how many letters to use to make each word. (A slash indicates words that can be made with the same letters.)

Emphasize how changing just one letter or rearranging letters makes a different word.

"Change a letter in **home** to spell **dome**."

"Add a letter to **ad** to spell **had**."

When children are not just adding or changing one letter, cue them to start over.

"Start over and use 4 new letters to spell **head**."

Give a meaning or sentence clue, when needed, to clarify the word children are making.

"Start over and use 5 new letters to spell **modem**. You can use a **modem** to connect to the Internet."

Always alert children when they are making a name and expect them to use a capital letter.

"Take 2 letters and spell the name **Mo**."

Give children one minute to figure out the secret word and then give clues, if needed.

"Our secret word is a name that you can make by adding your letters to **Mo**."

Sort Beginning Letters (Optional)

Sort Rhymes

Reading Transfer: "Pretend you are reading and come to a new word." Have children put the transfer words under the appropriate rhymes and use the rhymes to decode them.

Spelling Transfer: "Pretend you are writing and need to spell these words." Have children tell you how the words begin. Then, have children find and use the appropriate rhymes to finish spelling the transfer words.

Step-by-step directions for a sample *Making Names* lesson are on pages 8-12.

Morgan

a o g m n r

Make Words: Tell children how many letters to use to make each word. (A slash indicates words that can be made with the same letters.)

Emphasize how changing just one letter or rearranging letters makes a different word.

"Add a letter to **an** to spell **man**."

"Change a letter in **rag** to spell **nag**."

When children are not just adding or changing one letter, cue them to start over.

"Start over and use 4 new letters to spell **moan**."

Give a meaning or sentence clue, when needed, to clarify the word children are making.

"Start over and use 5 new letters to spell **among**. She divided the candy **among** the five children."

Always alert children when they are making a name and expect them to use a capital letter.

"Change a letter in **ran** to spell the name **Ron**."

Give children one minute to figure out the secret word and then give clues, if needed.

"Our secret word is a name that begins with **M** and ends with **n**."

Sort Beginning Letters (Optional)

Sort Rhymes

Reading Transfer: "Pretend you are reading and come to a new word." Have children put the transfer words under the appropriate rhymes and use the rhymes to decode them.

Spelling Transfer: "Pretend you are writing and need to spell these words." Have children tell you how the words begin. Then, have children find and use the appropriate rhymes to finish spelling the transfer words.

Step-by-step directions for a sample *Making Names* lesson are on pages 8-12.

MAKE WORDS

on
an
man
ran
Ron
rag
nag
Nora
moan
groan/organ
among
Morgan

SORT WORDS

Beginning Letters (Optional)

Rhymes:

an	on	rag	moan
man	Ron	nag	groan
ran			

TRANSFER WORDS

Reading:
loan flag

Spelling:
brag drag

Natalie

a a e i l n t

▶ **MAKE WORDS**

at
Nat
eat/ate
Ali/ail
tail
nail
Nate/neat
Tina
Anita
Elaina
Natalie

▶ SORT WORDS

Beginning Letters (Optional)

Rhymes:

eat	ate	ail	at
neat	Nate	tail	Nat
		nail	

▶ TRANSFER WORDS

Reading:
bleat skate

Spelling:
cheat state

Make Words: Tell children how many letters to use to make each word. (A slash indicates words that can be made with the same letters.)

Emphasize how changing just one letter or rearranging letters makes a different word.

"Change a letter in **tail** to spell **nail**."

"Use the same letters in **Ali** to spell **ail**."

When children are not just adding or changing one letter, cue them to start over.

"Start over and use 5 new letters to spell the name **Anita**."

Give a meaning or sentence clue, when needed, to clarify the word children are making.

"Add 1 letter to **ail** and spell **tail**. The dog was wagging her **tail**."

Always alert children when they are making a name and expect them to use a capital letter.

"Take 3 new letters and spell the name **Ali**."

Give children one minute to figure out the secret word and then give clues, if needed.

"Our secret word is a name that you can spell by adding your letters to **Nat**."

Sort Beginning Letters (Optional)

Sort Rhymes

Reading Transfer: "Pretend you are reading and come to a new word." Have children put the transfer words under the appropriate rhymes and use the rhymes to decode them.

Spelling Transfer: "Pretend you are writing and need to spell these words." Have children tell you how the words begin. Then, have children find and use the appropriate rhymes to finish spelling the transfer words.

Step-by-step directions for a sample *Making Names* lesson are on pages 8-12.

Making Names • CD-2429 • © Carson-Dellosa

Nathaniel

a a e i h l n n t

Make Words: Tell children how many letters to use to make each word. (A slash indicates words that can be made with the same letters.)

Emphasize how changing just one letter or rearranging letters makes a different word.

"Change a letter in **late** to spell the name **Lane**."

"Use the same letters in **line** to spell the name **Neil**."

When children are not just adding or changing one letter, cue them to start over.

"Start over and use 4 new letters to spell the name **Alan**."

Give a meaning or sentence clue, when needed, to clarify the word children are making.

"Start over and use 5 new letters to spell **alien**. The story was about an **alien** from the planet Mars."

Always alert children when they are making a name and expect them to use a capital letter.

"Use the same letters in **line** to spell the name **Neil**."

Give children one minute to figure out the secret word and then give clues, if needed.

"Our secret word is a name that you can make by adding your letters to **Nathan**."

Sort Beginning Letters (Optional)

Sort Related Words

Sort Rhymes

Reading Transfer: "Pretend you are reading and come to a new word." Have children put the transfer words under the appropriate rhymes and use the rhymes to decode them.

Spelling Transfer: "Pretend you are writing and need to spell these words." Have children tell you how the words begin. Then, have children find and use the appropriate rhymes to finish spelling the transfer words.

Step-by-step directions for a sample *Making Names* lesson are on pages 8-12.

MAKE WORDS

ten
Len
hat
Nat
Nate
late
Lane
line/Neil
Alan
nine
ninth
alien
Nathan
Nathaniel

SORT WORDS

Beginning Letters (Optional)

Related Words:
nine, ninth

Rhymes:
| ten | hat | Nate | line |
| Len | Nat | late | nine |

TRANSFER WORDS

Reading:
Ken Kate

Spelling:
plate fine

Nicholas

a i o c h l n s

MAKE WORDS

Al
Hal
Sal
oil
Lois/soil
coil
Lisa
also
hail
nail
sail
snail
lions
Nicholas

SORT WORDS

Beginning Letters (Optional)

Rhymes:

Al	oil	hail
Hal	soil	nail
Sal	coil	snail
		sail

TRANSFER WORDS

Reading:
tail toil

Spelling:
spoil fail

Make Words: Tell children how many letters to use to make each word. (A slash indicates words that can be made with the same letters.)

Emphasize how changing just one letter or rearranging letters makes a different word.

> "Add a letter to **sail** to spell **snail**."

> "Use the same letters in **Lois** to spell **soil**."

When children are not just adding or changing one letter, cue them to start over.

> "Start over and use 5 new letters to spell **lions**."

Give a meaning or sentence clue, when needed, to clarify the word children are making.

> "Start over and use 4 new letters to spell **also**. I like to ice-skate, and I **also** like to roller-skate."

Always alert children when they are making a name and expect them to use a capital letter.

> "Use 4 letters to spell the name **Lois**."

Give children one minute to figure out the secret word and then give clues, if needed.

> "Our secret word is a name that begins with **N** and ends with **s**."

Sort Beginning Letters (Optional)

Sort Rhymes

Reading Transfer: "Pretend you are reading and come to a new word." Have children put the transfer words under the appropriate rhymes and use the rhymes to decode them.

Spelling Transfer: "Pretend you are writing and need to spell these words." Have children tell you how the words begin. Then, have children find and use the appropriate rhymes to finish spelling the transfer words.

Step-by-step directions for a sample *Making Names* lesson are on pages 8-12.

Nicole

e i o c l n

Make Words: Tell children how many letters to use to make each word. (A slash indicates words that can be made with the same letters.)

Emphasize how changing just one letter or rearranging letters makes a different word.

"Add a letter to **Len** to spell the name **Leon**."

"Use the same letters in **Neil** to spell **line**."

When children are not just adding or changing one letter, cue them to start over.

"Start over and use 4 new letters to spell the name **Cole**."

Give a meaning or sentence clue, when needed, to clarify the word children are making.

"Add a letter to **cone** to spell **clone**. Scientists have learned how to **clone** sheep."

Always alert children when they are making a name and expect them to use a capital letter.

"Use 3 letters to spell the name **Len**."

Give children one minute to figure out the secret word and then give clues, if needed.

"Our secret word is a name that you can spell by adding your letters to **Cole**."

Sort Beginning Letters (Optional)

Sort Rhymes

Reading Transfer: "Pretend you are reading and come to a new word." Have children put the transfer words under the appropriate rhymes and use the rhymes to decode them.

Spelling Transfer: "Pretend you are writing and need to spell these words." Have children tell you how the words begin. Then, have children find and use the appropriate rhymes to finish spelling the transfer words.

Step-by-step directions for a sample *Making Names* lesson are on pages 8-12.

MAKE WORDS

line
ice
Len
Leon
lion
Neil/line
lice
nice
Cole
cone
clone
Nicole

SORT WORDS

Beginning Letters (Optional)

Rhymes:

ice	cone
lice	clone
nice	

TRANSFER WORDS

Reading:
spice phone

Spelling:
stone twice

Othello

MAKE WORDS

to
toe
Leo
let
lot
hot
hoot
loot/tool
toll
tell
Theo
hotel
hello
Othello

SORT WORDS

Beginning Letters (Optional)

Rhymes:
lot   hoot
hot   loot

TRANSFER WORDS

Reading:
boot plot

Spelling:
shoot scoot

Make Words: Tell children how many letters to use to make each word. (A slash indicates words that can be made with the same letters.)

Emphasize how changing just one letter or rearranging letters makes a different word.

"Add a letter to **hot** to spell **hoot**."

"Use the same letters in **loot** to spell **tool**."

When children are not just adding or changing one letter, cue them to start over.

"Start over and use 4 new letters to spell the name **Theo**."

Give a meaning or sentence clue, when needed, to clarify the word children are making.

"Start over and use 5 new letters to spell **hotel**. When we went to Disneyland®, we stayed at a big **hotel**."

Always alert children when they are making a name and expect them to use a capital letter.

"Use 3 letters to spell the name **Leo**."

Give children one minute to figure out the secret word and then give clues, if needed.

"Our secret word is a name that begins and ends with the letter **O**."

Sort Beginning Letters (Optional)

Sort Rhymes

Reading Transfer: "Pretend you are reading and come to a new word." Have children put the transfer words under the appropriate rhymes and use the rhymes to decode them.

Spelling Transfer: "Pretend you are writing and need to spell these words." Have children tell you how the words begin. Then, have children find and use the appropriate rhymes to finish spelling the transfer words.

Step-by-step directions for a sample *Making Names* lesson are on pages 8-12.

Pamela

a a e l m p

Make Words: Tell children how many letters to use to make each word. (A slash indicates words that can be made with the same letters.)

Emphasize how changing just one letter or rearranging letters makes a different word.

> "Add a letter to **lap** to spell **lamp**."

> "Use the same letters in **meal** to spell **lame**."

When children are not just adding or changing one letter, cue them to start over.

> "Start over and use 4 new letters to spell **leap**."

Give a meaning or sentence clue, when needed, to clarify the word children are making.

> "Add 1 letter to **male** to spell **maple**. We have a big **maple** tree in our yard."

Always alert children when they are making a name and expect them to use a capital letter.

> "Change one letter in **pal** to spell the name **Pam**."

Give children one minute to figure out the secret word and then give clues, if needed.

> "The secret word is a name that you can make by adding your letters to **Pam**."

Sort Beginning Letters (Optional)

Sort Rhymes

Reading Transfer: "Pretend you are reading and come to a new word." Have children put the transfer words under the appropriate rhymes and use the rhymes to decode them.

Spelling Transfer: "Pretend you are writing and need to spell these words." Have children tell you how the words begin. Then, have children find and use the appropriate rhymes to finish spelling the transfer words.

Step-by-step directions for a sample *Making Names* lesson are on pages 8-12.

MAKE WORDS

am
Al
pal
Pam/map
lap
lamp
leap/peal
meal/lame/male
maple
Pamela

SORT WORDS

Beginning Letters (Optional)

Rhymes:

am	Al	map	peal
Pam	pal	lap	meal

TRANSFER WORDS

Reading:
slam deal

Spelling:
trap strap

Patricia

a a i i c p r t

MAKE WORDS

car
cat
Art/tar
tap/Pat
air
pair
Rita
Tara
trip
trap/part
apart
Patricia

SORT WORDS

Related Words:
part, apart

Rhymes:

cat	air	Art	car	tap
Pat	pair	part	tar	trap
		apart		

TRANSFER WORDS

Reading:
smart wrap

Spelling:
snap Blair

Make Words: Tell children how many letters to use to make each word. (A slash indicates words that can be made with the same letters.)

Emphasize how changing just one letter or rearranging letters makes a different word.

"Add a letter to **air** to spell **pair**."

"Use the same letters in **trap** to spell **part**."

When children are not just adding or changing one letter, cue them to start over.

"Start over and use 4 new letters to spell the name **Rita**."

Give a meaning or sentence clue, when needed, to clarify the word children are making.

"Add 1 letter to **part** to spell **apart**. We had to take the desk **apart** to move it out of the room."

Always alert children when they are making a name and expect them to use a capital letter.

"Use the same letters in **tap** to spell the name **Pat**."

Give children one minute to figure out the secret word and then give clues, if needed.

"Our secret word is a name that you can make by adding your letters to **Pat**."

Sort Related Words

Sort Rhymes

Reading Transfer: "Pretend you are reading and come to a new word." Have children put the transfer words under the appropriate rhymes and use the rhymes to decode them.

Spelling Transfer: "Pretend you are writing and need to spell these words." Have children tell you how the words begin. Then, have children find and use the appropriate rhymes to finish spelling the transfer words.

Step-by-step directions for a sample *Making Names* lesson are on pages 8-12.

Patrick

a i c k p r t

Make Words: Tell children how many letters to use to make each word. (A slash indicates words that can be made with the same letters.)

Emphasize how changing just one letter or rearranging letters makes a different word.

> "Add a letter to **Rick** to spell **trick**."

> "Change 1 letter in **trick** to spell **track**."

When children are not just adding or changing one letter, cue them to start over.

> "Start over and use 3 new letters to spell **cat**."

Give a meaning or sentence clue, when needed, to clarify the word children are making.

> "Change 1 letter in **trick** to spell **track**. We heard the train coming down the **track**."

Always alert children when they are making a name and expect them to use a capital letter.

> "Change 1 letter in **pick** to spell the name **Rick**."

Give children one minute to figure out the secret word and then give clues, if needed.

> "Our secret word is a name that you can make by adding your letters to **Pat**."

Sort Tr Words (Optional)

Sort Rhymes

Reading Transfer: "Pretend you are reading and come to a new word." Have children put the transfer words under the appropriate rhymes and use the rhymes to decode them.

Spelling Transfer: "Pretend you are writing and need to spell these words." Have children tell you how the words begin. Then, have children find and use the appropriate rhymes to finish spelling the transfer words.

Step-by-step directions for a sample *Making Names* lesson are on pages 8-12.

MAKE WORDS

Ira
cat
Pat/tap
tip
trip
trap/part
park
pack
pick
Rick
trick
track
Patrick

SORT WORDS

Tr Words (Optional):
trip, trap, trick, track, Patrick

Rhymes:

cat	tap	pack	pick	tip
Pat	trap	track	trick	trip
				Rick

TRANSFER WORDS

Reading:
brick crack

Spelling:
strip thick

Patsy

a p s t y

MAKE WORDS

Ty
at
sat
Pat
pay
say
spy
sap
tap
yap
past
stay
Patsy

SORT WORDS

Beginning Letters (Optional)

Rhymes:

Ty	at	sap	pay
spy	sat	tap	say
	Pat	yap	stay

TRANSFER WORDS

Reading:
why pray

Spelling:
tray trap

Make Words: Tell children how many letters to use to make each word. (A slash indicates words that can be made with the same letters.)

Emphasize how changing just one letter or rearranging letters makes a different word.

"Add a letter to **at** to spell **sat**."

"Change a letter in **tap** to spell **yap**."

When children are not just adding or changing one letter, cue them to start over.

"Start over and use 4 new letters to spell **stay**."

Give a meaning or sentence clue, when needed, to clarify the word children are making.

"Start over and use new 4 letters to spell **past**. We drove **past** the new mall."

Always alert children when they are making a name and expect them to use a capital letter.

"Change a letter in **sat** to spell the name **Pat**."

Give children one minute to figure out the secret word and then give clues, if needed.

"Our secret word is a name that you can make by adding your letters to **Pat**."

Sort Beginning Letters (Optional)

Sort Rhymes

Reading Transfer: "Pretend you are reading and come to a new word." Have children put the transfer words under the appropriate rhymes and use the rhymes to decode them.

Spelling Transfer: "Pretend you are writing and need to spell these words." Have children tell you how the words begin. Then, have children find and use the appropriate rhymes to finish spelling the transfer words.

Step-by-step directions for a sample *Making Names* lesson are on pages 8-12.

Pauline

a e i u l n p

Make Words: Tell children how many letters to use to make each word. (A slash indicates words that can be made with the same letters.)

Emphasize how changing just one letter or rearranging letters makes a different word.

"Add a letter to **Lane** to spell **plane**."

"Use the same letters in **nap** to spell **pan**."

When children are not just adding or changing one letter, cue them to start over.

"Start over and use 3 new letters to spell **pie**."

Give a meaning or sentence clue, when needed, to clarify the word children are making.

"Start over and use 4 new letters to spell **pine**. The lightning struck the big **pine** tree."

Always alert children when they are making a name and expect them to use a capital letter.

"Take 4 letters and spell the name **Paul**."

Give children one minute to figure out the secret word and then give clues, if needed.

"Our secret word is a name that you can make by adding your letters to **Paul**."

Sort Beginning Letters (Optional)

Sort Rhymes

Reading Transfer: "Pretend you are reading and come to a new word." Have children put the transfer words under the appropriate rhymes and use the rhymes to decode them.

Spelling Transfer: "Pretend you are writing and need to spell these words." Have children tell you how the words begin. Then, have children find and use the appropriate rhymes to finish spelling the transfer words.

Step-by-step directions for a sample *Making Names* lesson are on pages 8-12.

MAKE WORDS

Ian
pie
lie
lip
lap
nap/pan
plan
Paul
pine
line
Lane
plane
Pauline

SORT WORDS

Beginning Letters (Optional)

Rhymes:

pie	lap	pan	pine	Lane
lie	nap	plan	line	plane

TRANSFER WORDS

Reading:
shine clap

Spelling:
die Shane

Phyllis

MAKE WORDS

is
his
shy
sly
lip
slip
ship
pill
hill
hilly
silly
spill
Phyllis

SORT WORDS

Related Words:
hill, hilly

Rhymes:

is	shy	lip	pill	hilly
his	sly	slip	hill	silly
		ship	spill	

TRANSFER WORDS

Reading:
grill grip

Spelling:
chill chilly

Make Words: Tell children how many letters to use to make each word. (A slash indicates words that can be made with the same letters.)

Emphasize how changing just one letter or rearranging letters makes a different word.

"Add a letter to **lip** to spell **slip**."

"Change a letter in **hilly** to spell **silly**."

When children are not just adding or changing one letter, cue them to start over.

"Start over and use 4 new letters to spell **pill**."

Give a meaning or sentence clue, when needed, to clarify the word children are making.

"Add a letter to **hill** to spell **hilly**. When a place has a lot of hills, we say it is **hilly**."

Give children one minute to figure out the secret word and then give clues, if needed. Always alert children when they are making a name and expect them to use a capital letter.

"Our secret word is a name that starts with **Ph** and ends with **s**."

Sort Related Words

Sort Rhymes

Reading Transfer: "Pretend you are reading and come to a new word." Have children put the transfer words under the appropriate rhymes and use the rhymes to decode them.

Spelling Transfer: "Pretend you are writing and need to spell these words." Have children tell you how the words begin. Then, have children find and use the appropriate rhymes to finish spelling the transfer words.

Step-by-step directions for a sample *Making Names* lesson are on pages 8-12.

Prescott

e o c p r s t t

Make Words: Tell children how many letters to use to make each word. (A slash indicates words that can be made with the same letters.)

Emphasize how changing just one letter or rearranging letters makes a different word.

> "Change a letter in **pest** to spell **post**."

> "Use the same letters in **poster** to spell **presto**."

When children are not just adding or changing one letter, cue them to start over.

> "Start over and use 6 new letters to spell **poster**."

Give a meaning or sentence clue, when needed, to clarify the word children are making.

> "Start over and use 7 new letters to spell **protect**. A mother lion will **protect** her cubs."

Always alert children when they are making a name and expect them to use a capital letter.

> "Take 5 new letters and spell the name **Scott**."

This lesson has two secret words. Give children one minute to figure out each secret word and then give clues, if needed.

> "You can make one secret word by adding a letter to **protect**."

> "The other secret word is a name that you can make by adding your letters to **Scott**."

Sort Pr Words (Optional)

Sort Related Words

Sort Rhymes

Reading Transfer: "Pretend you are reading and come to a new word." Have children put the transfer words under the appropriate rhymes and use the rhymes to decode them.

Spelling Transfer: "Pretend you are writing and need to spell these words." Have children tell you how the words begin. Then, have children find and use the appropriate rhymes to finish spelling the transfer words.

Step-by-step directions for a sample *Making Names* lesson are on pages 8-12.

MAKE WORDS

test
pest
post
port
sore
tore
core
score
store
Scott
poster/presto
protect
protects/Prescott

SORT WORDS

Pr Words (Optional):
presto, protect, protects, Prescott

Related Words:
post, poster; protect, protects

Rhymes:

test	sore
pest	tore
	core
	store
	score

TRANSFER WORDS

Reading:
vest more

Spelling:
chest shore

Preston

MAKE WORDS

Ron
rot
pot
pet
pest
nest/sent
rent
note/tone
stone
store
snore
person
Preston

SORT WORDS

Beginning Letters (Optional)

Rhymes:

rot	pest	sent	tone	store
pot	nest	rent	stone	snore

TRANSFER WORDS

Reading:
chore spot

Spelling:
shore clot

Make Words: Tell children how many letters to use to make each word. (A slash indicates words that can be made with the same letters.)

Emphasize how changing just one letter or rearranging letters makes a different word.

"Add a letter to **pet** to spell **pest**."

"Use the same letters in **nest** to spell **sent**."

When children are not just adding or changing one letter, cue them to start over.

"Start over and use 6 new letters to spell **person**."

Give a meaning or sentence clue, when needed, to clarify the word children are making.

"Use the same letters in **note** to spell **tone**. I could tell my mom was mad by the **tone** of her voice."

Always alert children when they are making a name and expect them to use a capital letter.

"Take 3 letters and spell the name **Ron**."

Give children one minute to figure out the secret word and then give clues, if needed.

"Our secret word is a name that starts with **Pr** and ends with **n**."

Sort Beginning Letters (Optional)

Sort Rhymes

Reading Transfer: "Pretend you are reading and come to a new word." Have children put the transfer words under the appropriate rhymes and use the rhymes to decode them.

Spelling Transfer: "Pretend you are writing and need to spell these words." Have children tell you how the words begin. Then, have children find and use the appropriate rhymes to finish spelling the transfer words.

Step-by-step directions for a sample *Making Names* lesson are on pages 8-12.

Priscilla

a i i c l l p r s

Make Words: Tell children how many letters to use to make each word. (A slash indicates words that can be made with the same letters.)

Emphasize how changing just one letter or rearranging letters makes a different word.

> "Add a letter to **pill** to spell **spill**."

> "Change 1 letter in **clap** to spell **clip**."

When children are not just adding or changing one letter, cue them to start over.

> "Start over and use 4 new letters to spell **pill**."

Give a meaning or sentence clue, when needed, to clarify the word children are making.

> "Start over and use 6 new letters to spell **spiral**. The old house had a long, **spiral** staircase."

Always alert children when they are making a name and expect them to use a capital letter.

> "Take 5 new letters and spell the name **April**."

Give children one minute to figure out the secret word and then give clues, if needed.

> "Our secret word is a name that starts with **Pr** and ends with **a**."

Sort Cl Words (Optional)

Sort Sl Words (Optional)

Sort Sp Words (Optional)

Sort Rhymes

Reading Transfer: "Pretend you are reading and come to a new word." Have children put the transfer words under the appropriate rhymes and use the rhymes to decode them.

Spelling Transfer: "Pretend you are writing and need to spell these words." Have children tell you how the words begin. Then, have children find and use the appropriate rhymes to finish spelling the transfer words.

Step-by-step directions for a sample *Making Names* lesson are on pages 8-12.

MAKE WORDS

Al
pal/lap
lip
all
call
clap
clip
slip
slap
Lisa
pill
spill
April
spiral
Priscilla

SORT WORDS

Cl Words (Optional):
clap, clip

Sl Words (Optional):
slip, slap

Sp Words (Optional):
spill, spiral

Rhymes:
Al   lap   lip   pill   all
pal   clap   slip   spill   call
        slap   clip

TRANSFER WORDS

Reading:
strap thrill

Spelling:
scrap skill

Quentin

eiunnqt

MAKE WORDS

it
in
tin
ten
net
nut
tie
tune
quit
quite/quiet
untie/unite
Quentin

SORT WORDS

Qu Words:
quit, quite, quiet, Quentin

Related Words:
tie, untie

Rhymes:
it   in
quit   tin

TRANSFER WORDS

Reading:
spit   spin

Spelling:
chin   split

Make Words: Tell children how many letters to use to make each word. (A slash indicates words that can be made with the same letters.)

Emphasize how changing just one letter or rearranging letters makes a different word.

> "Add a letter to **quit** to spell **quite**."

> "Use the same letters in **quite** to spell **quiet**."

When children are not just adding or changing one letter, cue them to start over.

> "Start over and use new 5 letters to spell **untie**."

Give a meaning or sentence clue, when needed, to clarify the word children are making.

> "Use the same letters in **untie** to spell **unite**. After the disaster, the mayor worked with everyone to **unite** the community."

Give children one minute to figure out the secret word and then give clues, if needed. Always alert children when they are making a name and expect them to use a capital letter.

> "Our secret word is a name that you can make by adding your letters to **tin**."

Sort Qu Words

Sort Related Words

Sort Rhymes

Reading Transfer: "Pretend you are reading and come to a new word." Have children put the transfer words under the appropriate rhymes and use the rhymes to decode them.

Spelling Transfer: "Pretend you are writing and need to spell these words." Have children tell you how the words begin. Then, have children find and use the appropriate rhymes to finish spelling the transfer words.

Step-by-step directions for a sample *Making Names* lesson are on pages 8-12.

Rachel

Make Words: Tell children how many letters to use to make each word. (A slash indicates words that can be made with the same letters.)

Emphasize how changing just one letter or rearranging letters makes a different word.

"Add a letter to **each** to spell **reach**."

"Use the same letters in **heal** to spell the name **Leah**."

When children are not just adding or changing one letter, cue them to start over.

"Start over and use 4 new letters to spell **race**."

Give a meaning or sentence clue, when needed, to clarify the word children are making.

"Change 1 letter in **race** to spell **lace**. My grandma has a **lace** tablecloth."

Always alert children when they are making a name and expect them to use a capital letter.

"Add 1 letter to **ear** to spell the name **Earl**."

Give children one minute to figure out the secret word and then give clues, if needed.

"Our secret word is a name that begins with **R** and ends with **l**."

Sort Beginning Letters (Optional)

Sort Rhymes

Reading Transfer: "Pretend you are reading and come to a new word." Have children put the transfer words under the appropriate rhymes and use the rhymes to decode them.

Spelling Transfer: "Pretend you are writing and need to spell these words." Have children tell you how the words begin. Then, have children find and use the appropriate rhymes to finish spelling the transfer words.

Step-by-step directions for a sample *Making Names* lesson are on pages 8-12.

MAKE WORDS

ace
are/ear
Earl/real
heal/Leah
hear
race
lace
each
reach
Rachel

SORT WORDS

Beginning Letters (Optional)

Rhymes:

ace	each	real	ear
lace	reach	heal	hear
race			

TRANSFER WORDS

Reading:
brace steal

Spelling:
beach bleach

Randolph

MAKE WORDS

Don
Ron
ran
Dan
pan
plan
road
load
loan
apron
Ralph
polar
Poland
orphan
Randolph

SORT WORDS

Ph Words—f sound:
Ralph, orphan, Randolph

Rhymes:

Don	ran	road
Ron	Dan	load
	pan	
	plan	

TRANSFER WORDS

Reading:
bran toad

Spelling:
con than

Make Words: Tell children how many letters to use to make each word. (A slash indicates words that can be made with the same letters.)

Emphasize how changing just one letter or rearranging letters makes a different word.

> "Change a letter in **road** to spell **load**."

> "Add one letter to **pan** to spell **plan**."

When children are not just adding or changing one letter, cue them to start over.

> "Start over and use 5 new letters to spell **apron**."

Give a meaning or sentence clue, when needed, to clarify the word children are making.

> "Change a letter in **load** to spell **loan**. We got a **loan** from the bank to buy the truck."

Always alert children when they are making a name and expect them to use a capital letter.

> "Take 5 new letters and spell the name **Ralph**."

Give children one minute to figure out the secret word and then give clues, if needed.

> "Our secret word is a name that you can make by adding your letters to **ran**."

Sort Ph Words—f sound

Sort Rhymes

Reading Transfer: "Pretend you are reading and come to a new word." Have children put the transfer words under the appropriate rhymes and use the rhymes to decode them.

Spelling Transfer: "Pretend you are writing and need to spell these words." Have children tell you how the words begin. Then, have children find and use the appropriate rhymes to finish spelling the transfer words.

Step-by-step directions for a sample *Making Names* lesson are on pages 8-12.

Raphael

a a e h l p r

Make Words: Tell children how many letters to use to make each word. (A slash indicates words that can be made with the same letters.)

Emphasize how changing just one letter or rearranging letters makes a different word.

"Change a letter in **heap** to spell **leap**."

"Use the same letters in **heal** to spell the name **Leah**."

When children are not just adding or changing one letter, cue them to start over.

"Start over and use 5 new letters to spell the name **Ralph**."

Give a meaning or sentence clue, when needed, to clarify the word children are making.

"Start over and use 4 new letters to spell the word **heap**. The clothes were all in a **heap** on the floor."

Always alert children when they are making a name and expect them to use a capital letter.

"Add 1 letter to **Al** to spell the name **Hal**."

Give children one minute to figure out the secret word and then give clues, if needed.

"Our secret word is a name that starts with **R** and ends with **l**."

Sort Beginning Letters (Optional)

Sort Rhymes

Reading Transfer: "Pretend you are reading and come to a new word." Have children put the transfer words under the appropriate rhymes and use the rhymes to decode them.

Spelling Transfer: "Pretend you are writing and need to spell these words." Have children tell you how the words begin. Then, have children find and use the appropriate rhymes to finish spelling the transfer words.

Step-by-step directions for a sample *Making Names* lesson are on pages 8-12.

MAKE WORDS

Al
Hal
pal/lap
rap
heap
leap/peal
real
heal/Leah
Ralph
Raphael

SORT WORDS

Beginning Letters (Optional)

Rhymes:

Al	lap	heap	peal
Hal	rap	leap	real
pal			heal

TRANSFER WORDS

Reading:
cheap squeal

Spelling:
steal strap

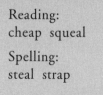

Raymond

MAKE WORDS

day
Ray
May/Amy
Don
Ron
Nora
Dora
army/Mary
Mandy
Randy
mayor
Monday
Raymond

SORT WORDS

Beginning Letters (Optional)

Rhymes:

day	Don	Nora	Mandy
Ray	Ron	Dora	Randy
May			

TRANSFER WORDS

Reading:
candy gray

Spelling:
sandy stray

Make Words: Tell children how many letters to use to make each word. (A slash indicates words that can be made with the same letters.)

Emphasize how changing just one letter or rearranging letters makes a different word.

> "Use the same letters in **May** to spell the name **Amy**."

> "Change one letter in **Nora** and spell the name **Dora**."

When children are not just adding or changing one letter, cue them to start over.

> "Start over and use 4 new letters to spell the name **Nora**."

Give a meaning or sentence clue, when needed, to clarify the word children are making.

> "Start over and use 6 new letters to spell **Monday**. **Monday** is the first day of the school week."

Always alert children when they are making a name and expect them to use a capital letter.

> "Take 5 new letters and spell the name **Mandy**."

Give children one minute to figure out the secret word and then give clues, if needed.

> "Our secret word is a name that you can make by adding your letters to **Ray**."

Sort Beginning Letters (Optional)

Sort Rhymes

Reading Transfer: "Pretend you are reading and come to a new word." Have children put the transfer words under the appropriate rhymes and use the rhymes to decode them.

Spelling Transfer: "Pretend you are writing and need to spell these words." Have children tell you how the words begin. Then, have children find and use the appropriate rhymes to finish spelling the transfer words.

Step-by-step directions for a sample *Making Names* lesson are on pages 8-12.

Rebecca

a e e b c c r

Make Words: Tell children how many letters to use to make each word. (A slash indicates words that can be made with the same letters.)

Emphasize how changing just one letter or rearranging letters makes a different word.

> "Change a letter in **bar** to spell **car**."

> "Use the same letters in **care** to spell **race**."

When children are not just adding or changing one letter, cue them to start over.

> "Start over and use 4 new letters to spell **care**."

Give a meaning or sentence clue, when needed, to clarify the word children are making.

> "Add a letter to **race** to spell **brace**. After the operation, the boy wore a **brace** on his leg."

Always alert children when they are making a name and expect them to use a capital letter.

> "Add a letter to **be** to spell the name **Bea**."

Give children one minute to figure out the secret word and then give clues, if needed.

> "Our secret word is a name that begins with **R** and ends with **a**."

Sort Rhymes

Reading Transfer: "Pretend you are reading and come to a new word." Have children put the transfer words under the appropriate rhymes and use the rhymes to decode them.

Spelling Transfer: "Pretend you are writing and need to spell these words." Have children tell you how the words begin. Then, have children find and use the appropriate rhymes to finish spelling the transfer words.

Step-by-step directions for a sample *Making Names* lesson are on pages 8-12.

MAKE WORDS

be
Bea/Abe
ace
bar
car
cab
crab
care/race
brace
Rebecca

SORT WORDS

Rhymes:

ace	bar	cab
race	car	crab
brace		

TRANSFER WORDS

Reading:
Grace jar

Spelling:
scar trace

Reginald

a e i d g l n r

MAKE WORDS

Dan
rain
read
lead
Gina
Gail
drain
Diane
rained
Daniel
Regina
reading
leading
Ireland
Reginald

SORT WORDS

Related Words:
read, reading; lead, leading;
rain, rained

Rhymes:
rain   lead   reading
drain   read   leading

TRANSFER WORDS

Reading:
strain bead

Spelling:
pleading brain

Make Words: Tell children how many letters to use to make each word. (A slash indicates words that can be made with the same letters.)

Emphasize how changing just one letter or rearranging letters makes a different word.

> "Change a letter in **reading** to spell **leading**."

When children are not just adding or changing one letter, cue them to start over.

> "Start over and use 6 new letters to spell the name **Daniel**."

Give a meaning or sentence clue, when needed, to clarify the word children are making.

> "Use 7 new letters to spell **Ireland**. **Ireland** is the country St. Patrick came from."

Always alert children when they are making a name and expect them to use a capital letter.

> "Take 4 new letters and spell the name **Gina**."

Give children one minute to figure out the secret word and then give clues, if needed.

> "Our secret word is a name that you can make by adding your letters to **Regina**."

Sort Related Words

Sort Rhymes

Reading Transfer: "Pretend you are reading and come to a new word." Have children put the transfer words under the appropriate rhymes and use the rhymes to decode them.

Spelling Transfer: "Pretend you are writing and need to spell these words." Have children tell you how the words begin. Then, have children find and use the appropriate rhymes to finish spelling the transfer words.

Step-by-step directions for a sample *Making Names* lesson are on pages 8-12.

R i c h a r d

a i c d h r r

Make Words: Tell children how many letters to use to make each word. (A slash indicates words that can be made with the same letters.)

Emphasize how changing just one letter or rearranging letters makes a different word.

> "Add a letter to **hair** to spell **chair**."

> "Change a letter in **card** to spell **hard**."

When children are not just adding or changing one letter, cue them to start over.

> "Start over and use 4 new letters to spell **hair**."

Give a meaning or sentence clue, when needed, to clarify the word children are making.

> "Start over and use 3 new letters to spell **air**. We opened the windows to let in some cool **air**."

Always alert children when they are making a name and expect them to use a capital letter.

> "Use 4 new letters to spell the name **Chad**."

Give children one minute to figure out the secret word and then give clues, if needed.

> "Our secret word is a name that that you can spell by adding your letters to **Rich**."

Sort Beginning Letters (Optional)

Sort Rhymes

Reading Transfer: "Pretend you are reading and come to a new word." Have children put the transfer words under the appropriate rhymes and use the rhymes to decode them.

Spelling Transfer: "Pretend you are writing and need to spell these words." Have children tell you how the words begin. Then, have children find and use the appropriate rhymes to finish spelling the transfer words.

Step-by-step directions for a sample *Making Names* lesson are on pages 8-12.

MAKE WORDS

ad
had
hid
rid
air
car
card
hard
Rich
Chad
hair
chair
Richard

SORT WORDS

Beginning Letters (Optional)

Rhymes:

ad	hid	card	hair
had	rid	hard	chair
Chad			air

TRANSFER WORDS

Reading:
glad yard

Spelling:
slid pair

Roberta

aeobrrt

MAKE WORDS

Bo
boa
bat
rat
eat/ate
Rob
Art
Bart/brat
boat
beat
rate
Robert
Roberta

SORT WORDS

Beginning Letters (Optional)

Rhymes:

bat	eat	ate	Art
rat	beat	rate	Bart
brat			

TRANSFER WORDS

Reading:
start wheat

Spelling:
cheat chart

Make Words: Tell children how many letters to use to make each word. (A slash indicates words that can be made with the same letters.)

Emphasize how changing just one letter or rearranging letters makes a different word.

> "Add a letter to **Art** to spell the name **Bart**."

> "Change a letter in **boat** to spell **beat**."

When children are not just adding or changing one letter, cue them to start over.

> "Start over and use 3 new letters to spell the name **Rob**."

Give a meaning or sentence clue, when needed, to clarify the word children are making.

> "Add 1 letter to **Bo** to spell **boa**. We saw a **boa** constrictor at the zoo."

Always alert children when they are making a name and expect them to use a capital letter.

> "Use 6 new letters to spell the name **Robert**."

Give children one minute to figure out the secret word and then give clues, if needed.

> "Our secret word is a name that you can make by adding a letter to **Robert**."

Sort Beginning Letters (Optional)

Sort Rhymes

Reading Transfer: "Pretend you are reading and come to a new word." Have children put the transfer words under the appropriate rhymes and use the rhymes to decode them.

Spelling Transfer: "Pretend you are writing and need to spell these words." Have children tell you how the words begin. Then, have children find and use the appropriate rhymes to finish spelling the transfer words.

Step-by-step directions for a sample *Making Names* lesson are on pages 8-12.

Roland/Ronald

Make Words: Tell children how many letters to use to make each word. (A slash indicates words that can be made with the same letters.)

Emphasize how changing just one letter or rearranging letters makes a different word.

> "Add a letter to **and** to spell **land**."

> "Change 1 letter in **load** to spell **road**."

When children are not just adding or changing one letter, cue them to start over.

> "Start over and use 4 new letters to spell **load**."

Give a meaning or sentence clue, when needed, to clarify the word children are making.

> "Take 4 letters to spell **load**. I helped my dad **load** and unload the truck."

Always alert children when they are making a name and expect them to use a capital letter.

> "Take 4 letters and spell the name **Nora**."

This lesson has two secret words. Give children one minute to figure out each secret word and then give clues, if needed.

> "Today we have two secret words, and they are both names. You can make one secret word by adding your letters to **land** and the other by adding your letters to **Ron**."

Sort Beginning Letters (Optional)

Sort Rhymes

Reading Transfer: "Pretend you are reading and come to a new word." Have children put the transfer words under the appropriate rhymes and use the rhymes to decode them.

Spelling Transfer: "Pretend you are writing and need to spell these words." Have children tell you how the words begin. Then, have children find and use the appropriate rhymes to finish spelling the transfer words.

Step-by-step directions for a sample *Making Names* lesson are on pages 8-12.

MAKE WORDS

Al
an
Dan
Don
Ron
ran
and
land
load
road
Nora
Nola
Roland/Ronald

SORT WORDS

Beginning Letters (Optional)

Rhymes:

an	Don	and	load
Dan	Ron	land	road
ran			

TRANSFER WORDS

Reading:
plan grand

Spelling:
toad strand

Roosevelt

MAKE WORDS

Lee/eel
Eve
ever
Rose
rove
tool
vote/veto
steel
stool
stove
Steve
voters
Roosevelt

SORT WORDS

St Words (Optional):
steel, stool, stove, Steve

Related Words:
vote, voters

Rhymes:
Eve   rove   tool   eel
Steve   stove   stool   steel

TRANSFER WORDS

Reading:
kneel drool

Spelling:
wheel drove

Make Words: Tell children how many letters to use to make each word. (A slash indicates words that can be made with the same letters.)

Emphasize how changing just one letter or rearranging letters makes a different word.

> "Add a letter to **Eve** to spell **ever**."

> "Change 1 letter in **Rose** to spell **rove**."

When children are not just adding or changing one letter, cue them to start over.

> "Start over and use 5 new letters to spell **stove**."

Give a meaning or sentence clue, when needed, to clarify the word children are making.

> "Use the same letters in **vote** to spell **veto**. The president threatened to **veto** the bill if it was not changed."

Always alert children when they are making a name and expect them to use a capital letter.

> "Take 3 letters and spell the name **Eve**."

Give children one minute to figure out the secret word and then give clues, if needed.

> "Our secret word is a name that begins with **R** and ends with **t**."

Sort St Words (Optional)

Sort Related Words

Sort Rhymes

Reading Transfer: "Pretend you are reading and come to a new word." Have children put the transfer words under the appropriate rhymes and use the rhymes to decode them.

Spelling Transfer: "Pretend you are writing and need to spell these words." Have children tell you how the words begin. Then, have children find and use the appropriate rhymes to finish spelling the transfer words.

Step-by-step directions for a sample *Making Names* lesson are on pages 8-12.

Rosalind

a i o d l n r s

Make Words: Tell children how many letters to use to make each word. (A slash indicates words that can be made with the same letters.)

Emphasize how changing just one letter or rearranging letters makes a different word.

"Add a letter to **nail** to spell **snail**."

"Use the same letters in **soil** to spell the name **Lois**."

When children are not just adding or changing one letter, cue them to start over.

"Start over and use 4 new letters to spell **nail**."

Give a meaning or sentence clue, when needed, to clarify the word children are making.

"Use 4 letters to spell **soil**. We planted the seeds in good, rich **soil**."

Always alert children when they are making a name and expect them to use a capital letter.

"Use 4 letters to spell the name **Lisa**."

Give children one minute to figure out the secret word and then give clues, if needed.

"Our secret word is a name that you can make by adding your letters to **Rosa**."

Sort Beginning Letters (Optional)

Sort Rhymes

Reading Transfer: "Pretend you are reading and come to a new word." Have children put the transfer words under the appropriate rhymes and use the rhymes to decode them.

Spelling Transfer: "Pretend you are writing and need to spell these words." Have children tell you how the words begin. Then, have children find and use the appropriate rhymes to finish spelling the transfer words.

Step-by-step directions for a sample *Making Names* lesson are on pages 8-12.

MAKE WORDS

Dan
Don
Ron
oil
old
sold
soil/Lois
Lisa
Rosa
nail
snail
Linda
island
Rosalind

SORT WORDS

Beginning Letters (Optional)

Rhymes:

Don	oil	old	nail
Ron	soil	sold	snail

TRANSFER WORDS

Reading:
broil bold

Spelling:
spoil trail

Rosemary

MAKE WORDS

am
Sam
say
Ray
Roy
Amy/May
Mary/army/Myra
Rose
Rosa
ears
years
Rosemary

SORT WORDS

Beginning Letters (Optional)

Rhymes:

am	say	ears
Sam	Ray	years
	May	

TRANSFER WORDS

Reading:
spray spears

Spelling:
clay clam

Make Words: Tell children how many letters to use to make each word. (A slash indicates words that can be made with the same letters.)

Emphasize how changing just one letter or rearranging letters makes a different word.

"Change a letter in **Rose** to spell the name **Rosa**."

"Use the same letters in **Mary** to spell **army**."

Give a meaning or sentence clue, when needed, to clarify the word children are making.

"Add 1 letter to **ears** to spell **years**. How many **years** have you lived here?"

Always alert children when they are making a name and expect them to use a capital letter.

"Change a letter in **say** to spell the name **Ray**."

Give children one minute to figure out the secret word and then give, clues, if needed.

"Our secret word is a name that you can make by adding your letters to **Rose**."

Sort Beginning Letters (Optional)

Sort Rhymes

Reading Transfer: "Pretend you are reading and come to a new word." Have children put the transfer words under the appropriate rhymes and use the rhymes to decode them.

Spelling Transfer: "Pretend you are writing and need to spell these words." Have children tell you how the words begin. Then, have children find and use the appropriate rhymes to finish spelling the transfer words.

Step-by-step directions for a sample *Making Names* lesson are on pages 8-12.

Rudolph

oudhlpr

Make Words: Tell children how many letters to use to make each word. (A slash indicates words that can be made with the same letters.)

Emphasize how changing just one letter or rearranging letters makes a different word.

"Add a letter to **old** to spell **hold**."

"Use the same letters in **drop** to spell **prod**."

When children are not just adding or changing one letter, cue them to start over.

"Start over and use 4 new letters to spell **drop**."

Give a meaning or sentence clue, when needed, to clarify the word children are making.

"Use the same letters in **holdup** to spell **uphold**. The deputies were sworn to **uphold** the law."

Always alert children when they are making a name and expect them to use a capital letter.

"Change 1 letter in **pod** to spell the name **Rod**."

Give children one minute to figure out the secret word and then give clues, if needed.

"Our secret word is a name that begins with **R** and ends with **ph**."

Sort Related Words

Sort Rhymes

Reading Transfer: "Pretend you are reading and come to a new word." Have children put the transfer words under the appropriate rhymes and use the rhymes to decode them.

Spelling Transfer: "Pretend you are writing and need to spell these words." Have children tell you how the words begin. Then, have children find and use the appropriate rhymes to finish spelling the transfer words.

Step-by-step directions for a sample *Making Names* lesson are on pages 8-12.

MAKE WORDS

hop
pod
Rod
old
hold
drop/prod
loud
proud
holdup/uphold
Rudolph

SORT WORDS

Related Words:
hold, uphold, holdup

Rhymes:

pod	old	loud	hop
Rod	hold	proud	drop
prod	uphold		

TRANSFER WORDS

Reading:
cloud crop

Spelling:
scold chop

Salvador

a a o d l r s v

MAKE WORDS

Al
Sal
Val
Rod
old
sold
soda
also
load
road/Dora
solar
Salvador

SORT WORDS

Beginning Letters (Optional)

Rhymes:

Al	old	load
Sal	sold	road
Val		

TRANSFER WORDS

Reading:
gold gal

Spelling:
toad told

Make Words: Tell children how many letters to use to make each word. (A slash indicates words that can be made with the same letters.)

Emphasize how changing just one letter or rearranging letters makes a different word.

"Add a letter to **old** to spell **sold**."

"Change a letter in **load** to spell **road**."

When children are not just adding or changing one letter, cue them to start over.

"Start over and use 4 new letters to spell **also**."

Give a meaning or sentence clue, when needed, to clarify the word children are making.

"Start over and use 5 new letters to spell **solar**. We get **solar** energy from the sun."

Always alert children when they are making a name and expect them to use a capital letter.

"Use 2 letters to spell the name **Al**."

Give children one minute to figure out the secret word and then give clues, if needed.

"Our secret word is a name that you can make by adding your letters to **Sal**."

Sort Beginning Letters (Optional)

Sort Rhymes

Reading Transfer: "Pretend you are reading and come to a new word." Have children put the transfer words under the appropriate rhymes and use the rhymes to decode them.

Spelling Transfer: "Pretend you are writing and need to spell these words." Have children tell you how the words begin. Then, have children find and use the appropriate rhymes to finish spelling the transfer words.

Step-by-step directions for a sample *Making Names* lesson are on pages 8-12.

Samantha

a a a h m n s t

Make Words: Tell children how many letters to use to make each word. (A slash indicates words that can be made with the same letters.)

Emphasize how changing just one letter or rearranging letters makes a different word.

> "Change a letter in **math** to spell **mash**."

> "Use the same letters in **ant** to spell **tan**."

When children are not just adding or changing one letter, cue them to start over.

> "Start over and use 4 new letters to spell **math**."

Give a meaning or sentence clue, when needed, to clarify the word children are making.

> "Add a letter to **tan** to spell **than**. I am older **than** my brother."

Always alert children when they are making a name and expect them to use a capital letter.

> "Add a letter to **am** to spell the name **Sam**."

Give children one minute to figure out the secret word and then give clues, if needed.

> "Our secret word is a name that you can make by adding your letters to **Sam**."

Sort Beginning Letters (Optional)

Sort Rhymes

Reading Transfer: "Pretend you are reading and come to a new word." Have children put the transfer words under the appropriate rhymes and use the rhymes to decode them.

Spelling Transfer: "Pretend you are writing and need to spell these words." Have children tell you how the words begin. Then, have children find and use the appropriate rhymes to finish spelling the transfer words.

Step-by-step directions for a sample *Making Names* lesson are on pages 8-12.

MAKE WORDS

am
Sam
ham
hat
sat
mat
ash
ant/tan
than
math
mash
Samantha

SORT WORDS

Beginning Letters (Optional)

Rhymes:

am	hat	ash	tan
Sam	sat	mash	than
ham	mat		

TRANSFER WORDS

Reading:
splash slam

Spelling:
plan crash

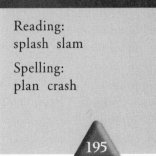

Samuel

a e u l m s

Al
Sal
Sam
use/Sue
slam
same
lame/meal
seal/sale
male
mules
Samuel

Beginning Letters (Optional)

Rhymes:

Al	Sam	same	seal	sale
Sal	slam	lame	meal	male

Reading:
cram blame

Spelling:
scale flame

Make Words: Tell children how many letters to use to make each word. (A slash indicates words that can be made with the same letters.)

Emphasize how changing just one letter or rearranging letters makes a different word.

"Change a letter in **Sal** to spell **Sam**."

"Use the same letters in **lame** to spell **meal**."

When children are not just adding or changing one letter, cue them to start over.

"Start over and use 4 new letters to spell **slam**."

Give a meaning or sentence clue, when needed, to clarify the word children are making.

"Change a letter in **sale** to spell **male**. My dog had three puppies; two are female and one is **male**."

Always alert children when they are making a name and expect them to use a capital letter.

"Take 2 letters and spell the name **Al**."

Give children one minute to figure out the secret word and then give clues, if needed.

"Our secret word is a name that you can make by adding your letters to **Sam**."

Sort Beginning Letters (Optional)

Sort Rhymes

Reading Transfer: "Pretend you are reading and come to a new word." Have children put the transfer words under the appropriate rhymes and use the rhymes to decode them.

Spelling Transfer: "Pretend you are writing and need to spell these words." Have children tell you how the words begin. Then, have children find and use the appropriate rhymes to finish spelling the transfer words.

Step-by-step directions for a sample *Making Names* lesson are on pages 8-12.

Sanford

a o d f n r s

Make Words: Tell children how many letters to use to make each word. (A slash indicates words that can be made with the same letters.)

Emphasize how changing just one letter or rearranging letters makes a different word.

"Add a letter to **an** to spell **and**."

"Use the same letters in **and** to spell the name **Dan**."

When children are not just adding or changing one letter, cue them to start over.

"Start over and use 4 new letters to spell **soda**."

Give a meaning or sentence clue, when needed, to clarify the word children are making.

"Use 5 new letters to spell **sonar**. They used **sonar** to find the submarines."

Always alert children when they are making a name and expect them to use a capital letter.

"Take 4 new letters and spell the name **Nora**."

Give children one minute to figure out the secret word and then give clues, if needed.

"Our secret word is a name that you can spell by adding your letters to **Ford**®."

Sort Beginning Letters (Optional)

Sort Rhymes

Reading Transfer: "Pretend you are reading and come to a new word." Have children put the transfer words under the appropriate rhymes and use the rhymes to decode them.

Spelling Transfer: "Pretend you are writing and need to spell these words." Have children tell you how the words begin. Then, have children find and use the appropriate rhymes to finish spelling the transfer words.

Step-by-step directions for a sample *Making Names* lesson are on pages 8-12.

MAKE WORDS

an
and/Dan
Don
Ron
ran
fan
sand
soda
sofa
Ford®
Nora
Dora
sonar
Sanford

SORT WORDS

Beginning Letters (Optional)

Rhymes:
an	Don	and
Dan	Ron	sand
fan		
ran		

TRANSFER WORDS

Reading:
plan stand

Spelling:
brand con

Scarlet

a e c l r s t

MAKE WORDS

act
eat
east/seat
seal
real
Carl
care
scare
stare
steal/least
react
castle
Scarlet

SORT WORDS

Related Words:
act, react

Rhymes:

eat	seal	care	east
seat	real	scare	least
	steal	stare	

TRANSFER WORDS

Reading:
beast square

Spelling:
feast squeal

Make Words: Tell children how many letters to use to make each word. (A slash indicates words that can be made with the same letters.)

Emphasize how changing just one letter or rearranging letters makes a different word.

"Add a letter to **eat** to spell **east**."

"Use the same letters in **steal** to spell **least**."

When children are not just adding or changing one letter, cue them to start over.

"Start over and use 6 new letters to spell **castle**."

Give a meaning or sentence clue, when needed, to clarify the word children are making.

"Use 5 new letters to spell **react**. When the tornado alarm sounded, we all had to **react** quickly."

Always alert children when they are making a name and expect them to use a capital letter.

"Use 4 letters to make the name **Carl**."

Give children one minute to figure out the secret word and then give clues, if needed.

"Our secret word is a name that begins with **Sc** and ends with **t**."

Sort Related Words

Sort Rhymes

Reading Transfer: "Pretend you are reading and come to a new word." Have children put the transfer words under the appropriate rhymes and use the rhymes to decode them.

Spelling Transfer: "Pretend you are writing and need to spell these words." Have children tell you how the words begin. Then, have children find and use the appropriate rhymes to finish spelling the transfer words.

Step-by-step directions for a sample *Making Names* lesson are on pages 8-12.

Shandra

a a d h n r s

Make Words: Tell children how many letters to use to make each word. (A slash indicates words that can be made with the same letters.)

Emphasize how changing just one letter or rearranging letters makes a different word.

> "Add a letter to **sad** to spell **sand**."

> "Use the same letters in **and** to spell the name **Dan**."

When children are not just adding or changing one letter, cue them to start over.

> "Start over and use 3 new letters to spell **had**."

Give a meaning or sentence clue, when needed, to clarify the word children are making.

> "Start over and use 4 letters to spell **rash**. The baby had diaper **rash**."

Always alert children when they are making a name and expect them to use a capital letter.

> "Use 4 letters to spell the name **Sara**."

Give children one minute to figure out the secret word and then give clues, if needed.

> "Our secret word is a name that begins with **Sh** and ends with **a**."

Sort Beginning Letters (Optional)

Sort Rhymes

Reading Transfer: "Pretend you are reading and come to a new word." Have children put the transfer words under the appropriate rhymes and use the rhymes to decode them.

Spelling Transfer: "Pretend you are writing and need to spell these words." Have children tell you how the words begin. Then, have children find and use the appropriate rhymes to finish spelling the transfer words.

Step-by-step directions for a sample *Making Names* lesson are on pages 8-12.

MAKE WORDS

an
ash
and/Dan
ran
had
sad
sand
hand
hard
rash
Sara
Sarah
Sandra
Shandra

SORT WORDS

Beginning Letters (Optional)

Rhymes:

an	had	ash	and
Dan	sad	rash	hand
ran			sand

TRANSFER WORDS

Reading:
smash grand

Spelling:
glad stash

Shaquille

a e i u h l l q s

MAKE WORDS

Al
Sal
Hal
all
ill
hill
hall
heal/Leah
Ella
Lisa
seal
sell
shell
Shaquille

SORT WORDS

Beginning Letters (Optional)

Rhymes:

Al	seal	all	ill	sell
Hal	heal	hall	hill	shell
Sal				

TRANSFER WORDS

Reading:
spill swell

Spelling:
stall still

Make Words: Tell children how many letters to use to make each word. (A slash indicates words that can be made with the same letters.)

Emphasize how changing just one letter or rearranging letters makes a different word.

"Add a letter to **sell** to spell **shell**."

"Use the same letters in **heal** to spell the name **Leah**."

When children are not just adding or changing one letter, cue them to start over.

"Start over and use 4 new letters to spell the name **Ella**."

Give a meaning or sentence clue, when needed, to clarify the word children are making.

"Start over and use 4 new letters to spell **seal**. The **seal** dove into the icy water and caught a fish."

Always alert children when they are making a name and expect them to use a capital letter.

"Take 4 new letters and spell the name **Lisa**."

Give children one minute to figure out the secret word and then give clues, if needed.

"Our secret word is a name and begins with **Sh** and ends with **e**."

Sort Beginning Letters (Optional)

Sort Rhymes

Reading Transfer: "Pretend you are reading and come to a new word." Have children put the transfer words under the appropriate rhymes and use the rhymes to decode them.

Spelling Transfer: "Pretend you are writing and need to spell these words." Have children tell you how the words begin. Then, have children find and use the appropriate rhymes to finish spelling the transfer words.

Step-by-step directions for a sample *Making Names* lesson are on pages 8-12.

Sheila

a e i h l s

Make Words: Tell children how many letters to use to make each word. (A slash indicates words that can be made with the same letters.)

Emphasize how changing just one letter or rearranging letters makes a different word.

"Change a letter in **seal** to spell **heal**."

"Use the same letters in **Lisa** to spell **sail**."

When children are not just adding or changing one letter, cue them to start over.

"Start over and use 5 new letters to spell **leash**."

Give a meaning or sentence clue, when needed, to clarify the word children are making.

"Start over and use 5 new letters to spell **leash**. We put the **leash** on our dog and took her for a walk."

Always alert children when they are making a name and expect them to use a capital letter.

"Use 4 new letters to spell the name **Lisa**."

Give children one minute to figure out the secret word and then give clues, if needed.

"Our secret word is a name that begins with **Sh** and ends with **a**."

Sort Beginning Letters (Optional)

Sort Rhymes

Reading Transfer: "Pretend you are reading and come to a new word." Have children put the transfer words under the appropriate rhymes and use the rhymes to decode them.

Spelling Transfer: "Pretend you are writing and need to spell these words." Have children tell you how the words begin. Then, have children find and use the appropriate rhymes to finish spelling the transfer words.

Step-by-step directions for a sample *Making Names* lesson are on pages 8-12.

MAKE WORDS

Al
as
has
Hal
Sal
seal
heal
Lisa/sail
hail
leash
Sheila

SORT WORDS

Beginning Letters (Optional)

Rhymes:

Al	seal	as
Hal	heal	has
Sal		

TRANSFER WORDS

Reading:
steal gal

Spelling:
squeal deal

Shelley

e e h l l s y

see
Lee/eel
yes
shy
sly
yell
sell
shell
Shelley

Beginning Letters (Optional)

Rhymes:

Lee	shy	yell
see	sly	sell
		shell

Reading:
free fry

Spelling:
flee swell

Make Words: Tell children how many letters to use to make each word. (A slash indicates words that can be made with the same letters.)

Emphasize how changing just one letter or rearranging letters makes a different word.

"Change a letter in **yell** to spell **sell**."

"Use the same letters in **Lee** to spell **eel**."

When children are not just adding or changing one letter, cue them to start over.

"Start over and use 3 new letters to spell **shy**."

Give a meaning or sentence clue, when needed, to clarify the word children are making.

"Change 1 letter in **shy** to spell **sly**. The magician was very clever and **sly**."

Always alert children when they are making a name and expect them to use a capital letter.

"Change 1 letter in **see** to spell the name **Lee**."

Give children one minute to figure out the secret word and then give clues, if needed.

"Our secret word is a name that you can make by adding your letters to **shell**."

Sort Beginning Letters (Optional)

Sort Rhymes

Reading Transfer: "Pretend you are reading and come to a new word." Have children put the transfer words under the appropriate rhymes and use the rhymes to decode them.

Spelling Transfer: "Pretend you are writing and need to spell these words." Have children tell you how the words begin. Then, have children find and use the appropriate rhymes to finish spelling the transfer words.

Step-by-step directions for a sample *Making Names* lesson are on pages 8-12.

Stacey

Make Words: Tell children how many letters to use to make each word. (A slash indicates words that can be made with the same letters.)

Emphasize how changing just one letter or rearranging letters makes a different word.

> "Add a letter to **eat** to spell **seat**."

> "Use the same letters in **seat** to spell **east**."

When children are not just adding or changing one letter, cue them to start over.

> "Start over and use 4 new letters to spell **cats**."

Give a meaning or sentence clue, when needed, to clarify the word children are making.

> "Use the same letters in **cats** to spell **scat**. I told the cat to **scat**."

Always alert children when they are making a name and expect them to use a capital letter.

> "Use 5 new letters to spell the name **Casey**."

Give children one minute to figure out the secret word and then give clues, if needed.

> "Our secret word is a name that starts with **St** and ends with **y**."

Sort Beginning Letters (Optional)

Sort Rhymes

Reading Transfer: "Pretend you are reading and come to a new word." Have children put the transfer words under the appropriate rhymes and use the rhymes to decode them.

Spelling Transfer: "Pretend you are writing and need to spell these words." Have children tell you how the words begin. Then, have children find and use the appropriate rhymes to finish spelling the transfer words.

Step-by-step directions for a sample *Making Names* lesson are on pages 8-12.

MAKE WORDS

at
cat
sat
set
yet
yes
eat
seat/east
easy
cats/scat
Casey
Stacey

SORT WORDS

Beginning Letters (Optional)

Rhymes:

at	set	eat
cat	yet	seat
sat		
scat		

TRANSFER WORDS

Reading:
wheat treat

Spelling:
cheat flat

Stephanie

a e e i h n p s t

MAKE WORDS

ape
hip
Nat
Nate
ship
this
these
shine
Shane
shape
sheep
sheet
Stephen
Stephanie

SORT WORDS

Sh Words (Optional):
ship, shine, Shane, shape,
sheet, sheep

Rhymes:
ape   hip
shape   ship

TRANSFER WORDS

Reading:
grape clip

Spelling:
scrape strip

Make Words: Tell children how many letters to use to make each word. (A slash indicates words that can be made with the same letters.)

Emphasize how changing just one letter or rearranging letters makes a different word.

"Add a letter to **Nat** to spell the name **Nate**."

"Change 1 letter in **sheep** to spell **sheet**."

When children are not just adding or changing one letter, cue them to start over.

"Start over and use 7 new letters to spell the name **Stephen**."

Give a meaning or sentence clue, when needed, to clarify the word children are making.

"Change 1 letter in **Shane** to spell **shape**. A triangle is a **shape**."

Always alert children when they are making a name and expect them to use a capital letter.

"Use 7 new letters to spell the name **Stephen**."

Give children one minute to figure out the secret word and then give clues, if needed.

"Our secret word is a name that begins with **St** and ends with **ie**."

Sort Sh Words (Optional)

Sort Rhymes

Reading Transfer: "Pretend you are reading and come to a new word." Have children put the transfer words under the appropriate rhymes and use the rhymes to decode them.

Spelling Transfer: "Pretend you are writing and need to spell these words." Have children tell you how the words begin. Then, have children find and use the appropriate rhymes to finish spelling the transfer words.

Step-by-step directions for a sample *Making Names* lesson are on pages 8-12.

Making Names • CD-2429 • © Carson-Dellosa

Stephen

eehnpst

Make Words: Tell children how many letters to use to make each word. (A slash indicates words that can be made with the same letters.)

Emphasize how changing just one letter or rearranging letters makes a different word.

> "Change a letter in **nest** to spell **pest**."

> "Use the same letters in **ten** to spell **net**."

When children are not just adding or changing one letter, cue them to start over.

> "Start over and use 4 new letters to spell **nest**."

Give a meaning or sentence clue, when needed, to clarify the word children are making.

> "Add a letter to **step** to spell **steep**. It was hard work to climb the **steep** hill."

Always alert children when they are making a name and expect them to use a capital letter.

> "Add a letter to **set** to spell the name **Seth**."

Give children one minute to figure out the secret word and then give clues, if needed.

> "Our secret word is a name that begins with **St** and ends with **n**."

Sort Beginning Letters (Optional)

Sort Rhymes

Reading Transfer: "Pretend you are reading and come to a new word." Have children put the transfer words under the appropriate rhymes and use the rhymes to decode them.

Spelling Transfer: "Pretend you are writing and need to spell these words." Have children tell you how the words begin. Then, have children find and use the appropriate rhymes to finish spelling the transfer words.

Step-by-step directions for a sample *Making Names* lesson are on pages 8-12.

MAKE WORDS

pet
pen
hen
ten/net
set
Seth
nest
pest/step
steep
sheep
sheet
Stephen

SORT WORDS

Beginning Letters (Optional)

Rhymes:

pet	pen	nest	steep
set	hen	pest	sheep
net	ten		

TRANSFER WORDS

Reading:
quest sleep

Spelling:
then sweep

Sterling

e i g l n r s t

MAKE WORDS

girl
Erin
ring
sing
sting
string
singer
single
tingle
linger
silent/listen
glisten
stinger
Sterling

SORT WORDS

Related Words:
sing, singer; sting, stinger

Rhymes:
ring   singer single listen
sing   linger tingle glisten
sting   stinger
string

TRANSFER WORDS

Reading:
jingle zinger

Spelling:
finger shingle

Make Words: Tell children how many letters to use to make each word. (A slash indicates words that can be made with the same letters.)

Emphasize how changing just one letter or rearranging letters makes a different word.

"Add a letter to **sting** to spell **string**."

"Use the same letters in **silent** to spell **listen**."

When children are not just adding or changing one letter, cue them to start over.

"Start over and use 6 new letters to spell **linger**."

Give a meaning or sentence clue when needed, to clarify the word children are making.

"Add 1 letter to **listen** to spell **glisten**. I love to see the snow **glisten** in the sun."

Always alert children when they are making a name and expect them to use a capital letter.

"Use 4 new letters to spell the name **Erin**."

Give children one minute to figure out the secret word and then give clues, if needed.

"Our secret word is a name that begins with **St** and ends with **ing**."

Sort Related Words

Sort Rhymes

Reading Transfer: "Pretend you are reading and come to a new word." Have children put the transfer words under the appropriate rhymes and use the rhymes to decode them.

Spelling Transfer: "Pretend you are writing and need to spell these words." Have children tell you how the words begin. Then, have children find and use the appropriate rhymes to finish spelling the transfer words.

Step-by-step directions for a sample *Making Names* lesson are on pages 8-12.

Steven

e e n s t v

Make Words: Tell children how many letters to use to make each word. (A slash indicates words that can be made with the same letters.)

Emphasize how changing just one letter or rearranging letters makes a different word.

> "Change a letter in **net** to spell **set**."

> "Use the same letters in **nest** to spell **sent**."

When children are not just adding or changing one letter, cue them to start over.

> "Start over and use 4 new letters to spell **teen**."

Give a meaning or sentence clue, when needed, to clarify the word children are making.

> "Start over and use 5 new letters to spell **event**. A big **event** in our town was when the President of the United States came to give a speech."

Always alert children when they are making a name and expect them to use a capital letter.

> "Take 3 letters and spell the name **Eve**."

This lesson has two secret words. Give children one minute to figure out each secret word and then give clues, if needed.

> "One secret word is the plural of **event**."

> "The other secret word is a name that you can make by adding a letter to **Steve**."

Sort Related Words

Sort Rhymes

Reading Transfer: "Pretend you are reading and come to a new word." Have children put the transfer words under the appropriate rhymes and use the rhymes to decode them.

Spelling Transfer: "Pretend you are writing and need to spell these words." Have children tell you how the words begin. Then, have children find and use the appropriate rhymes to finish spelling the transfer words.

Step-by-step directions for a sample *Making Names* lesson are on pages 8-12.

MAKE WORDS

Eve
net
set
vet
vest
nest/sent
vent
teen
seen
seven
Steve
event
events/Steven

SORT WORDS

Related Words:
event, events

Rhymes:
Eve	net	sent	vest	teen
Steve	set	vent	nest	seen
		vet		

TRANSFER WORDS

Reading:
quest queen

Spelling:
west spent

Tameka

a a e k m t

MAKE WORDS

at
mat
eat/ate
mate/meat/team/tame
take
make
Kate
Tameka

SORT WORDS

Beginning Letters (Optional)

Rhymes:

at	eat	ate	take
mat	meat	mate	make
		Kate	

TRANSFER WORDS

Reading:
treat skate

Spelling:
plate brake

Make Words: Tell children how many letters to use to make each word. (A slash indicates words that can be made with the same letters.)

Emphasize how changing just one letter or rearranging letters makes a different word.

"Change a letter in **take** to spell **make**."

"Use the same letters in **mate** to spell **meat**."

When children are not just adding or changing one letter, cue them to start over.

"Start over and use 4 new letters to spell the name **Kate**."

Give a meaning or sentence clue, when needed, to clarify the word children are making.

"Add a letter to **ate** to spell **mate**. Most penguins **mate** for life."

Always alert children when they are making a name and expect them to use a capital letter.

"Take 4 letters and spell the name **Kate**."

Give children one minute to figure out the secret word and then give clues, if needed.

"Our secret word is a name that you can make by adding your letters to **tame**."

Sort Beginning Letters (Optional)

Sort Rhymes

Reading Transfer: "Pretend you are reading and come to a new word." Have children put the transfer words under the appropriate rhymes and use the rhymes to decode them.

Spelling Transfer: "Pretend you are writing and need to spell these words." Have children tell you how the words begin. Then, have children find and use the appropriate rhymes to finish spelling the transfer words.

Step-by-step directions for a sample *Making Names* lesson are on pages 8-12.

Taylor

a o l r t y

Make Words: Tell children how many letters to use to make each word. (A slash indicates words that can be made with the same letters.)

Emphasize how changing just one letter or rearranging letters makes a different word.

> "Add a letter to **toy** to spell the name **Troy**."

> "Use the same letters in **Art** to spell **rat**."

When children are not just adding or changing one letter, cue them to start over.

> "Start over and use 5 new letters to spell **royal**."

Give a meaning or sentence clue, when needed, to clarify the word children are making:

> "Start over and use 5 new letters to spell **royal**. The prince wanted to marry a woman of **royal** blood."

Always alert children when they are making a name and expect them to use a capital letter.

> "Use 4 new letters to spell the name **Arlo**."

Give children one minute to figure out the secret word and then give clues, if needed.

> "Our secret word is a name that begins with **T** and ends with **r**."

Sort Beginning Letters (Optional)

Sort Rhymes

Reading Transfer: "Pretend you are reading and come to a new word." Have children put the transfer words under the appropriate rhymes and use the rhymes to decode them.

Spelling Transfer: "Pretend you are writing and need to spell these words." Have children tell you how the words begin. Then, have children find and use the appropriate rhymes to finish spelling the transfer words.

Step-by-step directions for a sample *Making Names* lesson are on pages 8-12.

MAKE WORDS

at
Art/rat
rot
lot
Ray
Roy
toy
Troy
tray
Arlo
royal
Taylor

SORT WORDS

Beginning Letters (Optional)

Rhymes:

at	rot	Roy	Ray
rat	lot	toy	tray
		Troy	

TRANSFER WORDS

Reading:
trot clay

Spelling:
joy spray

Theodore

MAKE WORDS

Ed
Ted
her
here
herd
hero
Theo
hoot
root
tree
three/there
other
rodeo
Theodore

SORT WORDS

Th words (Optional):
Theo, three, there,
Theodore, other

Rhymes:

Ed	hoot	tree
Ted	root	three

TRANSFER WORDS

Reading:
knee free

Spelling:
shed shred

Make Words: Tell children how many letters to use to make each word. (A slash indicates words that can be made with the same letters.)

Emphasize how changing just one letter or rearranging letters makes a different word.

"Add a letter to **tree** to spell **three**."

"Change a letter in **here** to spell **herd**."

When children are not just adding or changing one letter, cue them to start over.

"Start over and use 5 new letters to spell **other**."

Give a meaning or sentence clue, when needed, to clarify the word children are making.

"Use the same letters in **three** to spell **there**. **There** are 12 months in a year."

Always alert children when they are making a name and expect them to use a capital letter.

"Use 4 letters to spell the name **Theo**."

Give children one minute to figure out the secret word and then give clues, if needed.

"Our secret word is a name that you can make by adding your letters to **Theo**."

Sort Th Words (Optional)

Sort Rhymes

Reading Transfer: "Pretend you are reading and come to a new word." Have children put the transfer words under the appropriate rhymes and use the rhymes to decode them.

Spelling Transfer: "Pretend you are writing and need to spell these words." Have children tell you how the words begin. Then, have children find and use the appropriate rhymes to finish spelling the transfer words.

Step-by-step directions for a sample *Making Names* lesson are on pages 8-12.

Thomas

a o h m s t

Make Words: Tell children how many letters to use to make each word. (A slash indicates words that can be made with the same letters.)

Emphasize how changing just one letter or rearranging letters makes a different word.

> "Add a letter to **ash** to spell **mash**."

> "Change 1 letter in **math** to spell **moth**."

When children are not just adding or changing one letter, cue them to start over.

> "Start over and use 3 new letters to spell **ash**."

Give a meaning or sentence clue, when needed, to clarify the word children are making.

> "Use 4 letters to spell **shot**. Every year I get a flu **shot**."

Always alert children when they are making a name and expect them to use a capital letter.

> "Take 3 letters and spell the name **Tom**."

Give children one minute to figure out the secret word and then give clues, if needed.

> "Our secret word is a name that begins with **T** and ends with **s**."

Sort Rhymes

Reading Transfer: "Pretend you are reading and come to a new word." Have children put the transfer words under the appropriate rhymes and use the rhymes to decode them.

Spelling Transfer: "Pretend you are writing and need to spell these words." Have children tell you how the words begin. Then, have children find and use the appropriate rhymes to finish spelling the transfer words.

Step-by-step directions for a sample *Making Names* lesson are on pages 8-12.

MAKE WORDS

at
am
ham
hat
sat
mat
hot
Tom
ash
mash
math
moth
most
shot
Thomas

SORT WORDS

Rhymes:

at	am	ash	hot
hat	ham	mash	shot
sat			
mat			

TRANSFER WORDS

Reading:
crash clam

Spelling:
scram clot

Tiffany

a i f f n t y

MAKE WORDS

it
at
fat
fit
fin
fan
tan/Nat
Fay
tiny
faint
fifty
nifty
Taffy
Tiffany

SORT WORDS

Beginning Letters (Optional)

Rhymes:

it	at	fan	nifty
fit	fat	tan	fifty
		Nat	

TRANSFER WORDS

Reading:
shifty Fran

Spelling:
split splat

Make Words: Tell children how many letters to use to make each word. (A slash indicates words that can be made with the same letters.)

Emphasize how changing just one letter or rearranging letters makes a different word.

> "Add a letter to **at** to spell **fat**."

> "Change 1 letter in **fat** to spell **fit**."

When children are not just adding or changing one letter, cue them to start over.

> "Start over and use 5 new letters to spell **fifty**."

Give a meaning or sentence clue, when needed, to clarify the word children are making.

> "Use 5 new letters to spell **faint**. The heat was so bad that people started to **faint**."

Always alert children when they are making a name and expect them to use a capital letter.

> "Use 5 new letters to spell the name **Taffy**."

Give children one minute to figure out the secret word and then give clues, if needed.

> "Our secret word is a name that begins with **T** and ends with **y**."

Sort Beginning Letters (Optional)

Sort Rhymes

Reading Transfer: "Pretend you are reading and come to a new word." Have children put the transfer words under the appropriate rhymes and use the rhymes to decode them.

Spelling Transfer: "Pretend you are writing and need to spell these words." Have children tell you how the words begin. Then, have children find and use the appropriate rhymes to finish spelling the transfer words.

Step-by-step directions for a sample *Making Names* lesson are on pages 8-12.

212

Tracy

Make Words: Tell children how many letters to use to make each word. (A slash indicates words that can be made with the same letters.)

Emphasize how changing just one letter or rearranging letters makes a different word.

> "Change a letter in **car** to spell **cat**."

> "Use the same letters in **cat** to spell **act**."

When children are not just adding or changing one letter, cue them to start over.

> "Start over and use 4 new letters to spell **cart**."

Give a meaning or sentence clue, when needed, to clarify the word children are making.

> "Add l letter to **try** to spell **tray**. I put my lunch on a **tray**."

Always alert children when they are making a name and expect them to use a capital letter.

> "Change a letter in **act** to spell the name **Art**."

Give children one minute to figure out the secret word and then give clues, if needed.

> "Our secret word is a name that begins with **Tr** and ends with **y**."

Sort Tr Words (Optional)

Sort Rhymes

Reading Transfer: "Pretend you are reading and come to a new word." Have children put the transfer words under the appropriate rhymes and use the rhymes to decode them.

Spelling Transfer: "Pretend you are writing and need to spell these words." Have children tell you how the words begin. Then, have children find and use the appropriate rhymes to finish spelling the transfer words.

Step-by-step directions for a sample *Making Names* lesson are on pages 8-12.

MAKE WORDS

.car
cat/act
Art/rat
Ray
cry
try
tray
cart
Cary
Tracy

SORT WORDS

Tr Words (Optional):
try, tray, Tracy

Rhymes:

cat	Art	Ray	cry
rat	cart	tray	try

TRANSFER WORDS

Reading:
sky gray

Spelling:
shy chart

Trisha

a i h r s t

MAKE WORDS

Art/rat/tar
hat
sat
Ira
ash
rash
rats/star
Rita
trash
shirt
Trisha

SORT WORDS

Beginning Letters (Optional)

Rhymes:

rat	ash	tar
hat	rash	star
sat	trash	

TRANSFER WORDS

Reading:
crash thrash

Spelling:
splash chat

Make Words: Tell children how many letters to use to make each word. (A slash indicates words that can be made with the same letters.)

Emphasize how changing just one letter or rearranging letters makes a different word.

> "Change a letter in **hat** to spell **sat**."

> "Use the same letters in **rats** to spell **star**."

When children are not just adding or changing one letter, cue them to start over.

> "Start over and use 4 new letters to spell **trash**."

Give a meaning or sentence clue, when needed, to clarify the word children are making.

> "Add 1 letter to **ash** to spell **rash**. The **rash** was very itchy, but I didn't scratch it."

Always alert children when they are making a name and expect them to use a capital letter.

> "Use 4 letters to spell the name **Rita**."

Give children one minute to figure out the secret word and then give clues, if needed.

> "Our secret word is a name that begins with **Tr** and ends with **a**."

Sort Beginning Letters (Optional)

Sort Rhymes

Reading Transfer: "Pretend you are reading and come to a new word." Have children put the transfer words under the appropriate rhymes and use the rhymes to decode them.

Spelling Transfer: "Pretend you are writing and need to spell these words." Have children tell you how the words begin. Then, have children find and use the appropriate rhymes to finish spelling the transfer words.

Step-by-step directions for a sample *Making Names* lesson are on pages 8-12.

Making Names • CD-2429 • © Carson-Dellosa

Tucker

Make Words: Tell children how many letters to use to make each word. (A slash indicates words that can be made with the same letters.)

Emphasize how changing just one letter or rearranging letters makes a different word.

> "Change a letter in **cut** to spell **cue**."

> "Add a letter to **tuck** to spell **truck**."

When children are not just adding or changing one letter, cue them to start over.

> "Start over and use 4 new letters to spell **true**."

Give a meaning or sentence clue, when needed, to clarify the word children are making.

> "Add 1 letter to **cue** to spell **cure**. Scientists were trying to find a **cure** for the disease."

Always alert children when they are making a name and expect them to use a capital letter.

> "Take 4 letters and spell the name **Kurt**."

Give children one minute to figure out the secret word and then give clues, if needed.

> "Our secret word is a name that you can make by adding your letters to **tuck**."

Sort Related Words

Sort Rhymes

Reading Transfer: "Pretend you are reading and come to a new word." Have children put the transfer words under the appropriate rhymes and use the rhymes to decode them.

Spelling Transfer: "Pretend you are writing and need to spell these words." Have children tell you how the words begin. Then, have children find and use the appropriate rhymes to finish spelling the transfer words.

Step-by-step directions for a sample *Making Names* lesson are on pages 8-12.

MAKE WORDS

rut
cut
cue
cure
cute
true
Kurt
tuck
truck
truce
cuter
Tucker

SORT WORDS

Related Words:
cute   cuter

Rhymes:
| rut | cue | tuck |
| cut | true | truck |

TRANSFER WORDS

Reading:
struck   clue

Spelling:
strut   glue

Tyrone

Ty
on
Ron
rot
not
net
yet
try
toy
Troy/Tory
Tony
note/tone
tore
entry
Tyrone

SORT WORDS

Beginning Letters (Optional)

Rhymes:

on	rot	net	toy
Ron	not	yet	Troy

TRANSFER WORDS

Reading:
knot joy

Spelling:
trot bet

Make Words: Tell children how many letters to use to make each word. (A slash indicates words that can be made with the same letters.)

Emphasize how changing just one letter or rearranging letters makes a different word.

"Add a letter to **toy** to spell the name **Troy**."

"Use the same letters in **Troy** to spell the name **Tory**."

When children are not just adding or changing one letter, cue them to start over.

"Start over and use 4 new letters to spell **note**."

Give a meaning or sentence clue, when needed, to clarify the word children are making.

"Start over and use 5 new letters to spell **entry**. A tree fell and blocked the **entry** to the driveway."

Always alert children when they are making a name and expect them to use a capital letter.

"Use 2 letters to spell the name **Ty**."

Give children one minute to figure out the secret word and then give clues, if needed.

"Our secret word is a name that you can make by adding your letters to **Ty**."

Sort Beginning Letters (Optional)

Sort Rhymes

Reading Transfer: "Pretend you are reading and come to a new word." Have children put the transfer words under the appropriate rhymes and use the rhymes to decode them.

Spelling Transfer: "Pretend you are writing and need to spell these words." Have children tell you how the words begin. Then, have children find and use the appropriate rhymes to finish spelling the transfer words.

Step-by-step directions for a sample *Making Names* lesson are on pages 8-12.

Making Names • CD-2429 • © Carson-Dellosa

Veronica

a e i o c n r v

Make Words: Tell children how many letters to use to make each word. (A slash indicates words that can be made with the same letters.)

Emphasize how changing just one letter or rearranging letters makes a different word.

"Add a letter to **nice** to spell **nicer**."

"Use the same letters in **rave** to spell the name **Vera**."

When children are not just adding or changing one letter, cue them to start over.

"Start over and use 4 new letters to spell the name **Eric**."

Give a meaning or sentence clue, when needed, to clarify the word children are making.

"Start over and use 5 new letters to spell **crane**. They needed a **crane** to lift the heavy truck out of the ditch."

Always alert children when they are making a name and expect them to use a capital letter.

"Use 5 new letters to spell the name **Erica**."

Give children one minute to figure out the secret word and then give clues, if needed.

"Our secret word is a name that begins with **V** and ends with **a**."

Sort Related Words

Sort Rhymes

Reading Transfer: "Pretend you are reading and come to a new word." Have children put the transfer words under the appropriate rhymes and use the rhymes to decode them.

Spelling Transfer: "Pretend you are writing and need to spell these words." Have children tell you how the words begin. Then, have children find and use the appropriate rhymes to finish spelling the transfer words.

Step-by-step directions for a sample *Making Names* lesson are on pages 8-12.

MAKE WORDS

Ron
ran
van
can
cane
cave
rave/Vera
Eric/rice
nice
nicer
crane
Erica
Veronica

SORT WORDS

Related Words:
nice, nicer

Rhymes:

ran	cave	rice	cane
van	rave	nice	crane
can			

TRANSFER WORDS

Reading:
shave plane

Spelling:
brave slave

Victoria

a i i o c r t v

MAKE WORDS

Ira
car
tar/rat
cat/act
Art
cart
coat/taco
Cora
actor
Victor
Victoria

SORT WORDS

Related Words:
act, actor

Rhymes:
car   rat   Art
tar   cat   cart

TRANSFER WORDS

Reading:
star start

Spelling:
smart scar

Make Words: Tell children how many letters to use to make each word. (A slash indicates words that can be made with the same letters.)

Emphasize how changing just one letter or rearranging letters makes a different word.

> "Add a letter to **Art** to spell **cart**."

> "Use the same letters in **cat** to spell **act**."

When children are not just adding or changing one letter, cue them to start over.

> "Start over and use 4 new letters to spell **coat**."

Give a meaning or sentence clue, when needed, to clarify the word children are making.

> "Use 5 letters to spell **actor**. Who is your favorite movie **actor**?"

Always alert children when they are making a name and expect them to use a capital letter.

> "Take 6 letters and spell the name **Victor**."

Give children one minute to figure out the secret word and then give clues, if needed.

> "Our secret word is a name that you can spell by adding your letters to **Victor**."

Sort Related Words

Sort Rhymes

Reading Transfer: "Pretend you are reading and come to a new word." Have children put the words under the appropriate rhymes and use the rhymes to decode them.

Spelling Transfer: "Pretend you are writing and need to spell these words." Have children tell you how the words begin. Then, have children find and use the appropriate rhymes to finish spelling the new words.

Step-by-step directions for a sample *Making Names* lesson are on pages 8-12.

Vincent

e i c n n t v

Make Words: Tell children how many letters to use to make each word. (A slash indicates words that can be made with the same letters.)

Emphasize how changing just one letter or rearranging letters makes a different word.

"Add a letter to **ice** to spell **nice**."

"Use the same letters in **ten** to spell **net**."

When children are not just adding or changing one letter, cue them to start over.

"Start over and use 3 new letters to spell **ice**."

Give a meaning or sentence clue, when needed, to clarify the word children are making.

"Add 2 letters to **vent** to spell **invent**. It is fun to try to **invent** something new."

Give children one minute to figure out the secret word and then give clues, if needed. Always alert children when they are making a name and expect them to use a capital letter.

"Our secret word is a name that you can spell by adding your letters to **cent**."

Sort Beginning Letters (Optional)

Sort Rhymes

Reading Transfer: "Pretend you are reading and come to a new word." Have children put the transfer words under the appropriate rhymes and use the rhymes to decode them.

Spelling Transfer: "Pretend you are writing and need to spell these words." Have children tell you how the words begin. Then, have children find and use the appropriate rhymes to finish spelling the transfer words.

Step-by-step directions for a sample *Making Names* lesson are on pages 8-12.

MAKE WORDS

in
tin
ten/net
vet
ice
nice
nine
vine
cent
vent
invent
Vincent

SORT WORDS

Beginning Letters (Optional)

Rhymes:

in	net	ice	nine	cent
tin	vet	nice	vine	vent
				invent

TRANSFER WORDS

Reading:
twice   shine

Spelling:
twine   shrine

Whitney

e i h n t w y

wet
yet
net/ten
tin
win
twin
tiny
they
thin
with
went
when
white
Whitney

Beginning Letters (Optional)

Rhymes:

wet	tin	ten
yet	win	when
net	thin	
	twin	

Reading:
chin fret

Spelling:
spin skin

Make Words: Tell children how many letters to use to make each word. (A slash indicates words that can be made with the same letters.)

Emphasize how changing just one letter or rearranging letters makes a different word.

"Change a letter in **yet** to spell **net**."

"Use the same letters in **net** to spell **ten**."

When children are not just adding or changing one letter, cue them to start over.

"Start over and use 4 new letters to spell **they**."

Give a meaning or sentence clue, when needed, to clarify the word children are making.

"Start over and use 4 new letters to spell **tiny**. The newborn kittens were very **tiny**."

Give children one minute to figure out the secret word and then give clues, if needed. Always alert children when they are making a name and expect them to use a capital letter.

"Our secret word is a name that begins with **Wh** and ends with **y**."

Sort Beginning Letters (Optional)

Sort Rhymes

Reading Transfer: "Pretend you are reading and come to a new word." Have children put the transfer words under the appropriate rhymes and use the rhymes to decode them.

Spelling Transfer: "Pretend you are writing and need to spell these words." Have children tell you how the words begin. Then, have children find and use the appropriate rhymes to finish spelling the transfer words.

Step-by-step directions for a sample *Making Names* lesson are on pages 8-12.

Willard

a i d l l r w

Make Words: Tell children how many letters to use to make each word. (A slash indicates words that can be made with the same letters.)

Emphasize how changing just one letter or rearranging letters makes a different word.

"Change a letter in **dill** to spell **dial**."

"Use the same letters in **Ward** to spell **draw**."

When children are not just adding or changing one letter, cue them to start over.

"Start over and use 3 new letters to spell **all**."

Give a meaning or sentence clue, when needed, to clarify the word children are making.

"Start over and use 5 new letters to spell **drill**. The dentist had to **drill** my tooth to fill the cavity."

Always alert children when they are making a name and expect them to use a capital letter.

"Take 4 new letters and spell the name **Will**."

Give children one minute to figure out the secret word and then give clues, if needed.

"Our secret word is a name that you can make by adding your letters to **Will**."

Sort Beginning Letters (Optional)

Sort Rhymes

Reading Transfer: "Pretend you are reading and come to a new word." Have children put the transfer words under the appropriate rhymes and use the rhymes to decode them.

Spelling Transfer: "Pretend you are writing and need to spell these words." Have children tell you how the words begin. Then, have children find and use the appropriate rhymes to finish spelling the transfer words.

Step-by-step directions for a sample *Making Names* lesson are on pages 8-12.

MAKE WORDS

war/raw
all
ill
dill
dial
Will
wall
Ward/draw
wild
Lila
drill
Willard

SORT WORDS

Beginning Letters (Optional)

Rhymes:
raw	ill	all
draw	dill	wall
	drill	
	Will	

TRANSFER WORDS

Reading:
still thaw

Spelling:
straw small

William

a i i l l m w

MAKE WORDS

all
ill
law
mall
mill
Will
wall
wail
mail
Lila
Wilma
William

SORT WORDS

Beginning Letters (Optional)

Rhymes:

all	Will	wail
mall	ill	mail
wall	mill	

TRANSFER WORDS

Reading:
spill fail

Spelling:
thrill stall

Make Words: Tell children how many letters to use to make each word. (A slash indicates words that can be made with the same letters.)

Emphasize how changing just one letter or rearranging letters makes a different word.

"Change a letter in **mall** to spell **mill**."

When children are not just adding or changing one letter, cue them to start over.

"Start over and use 3 new letters to spell **law**."

Give a meaning or sentence clue, when needed, to clarify the word children are making.

"Change 1 letter in **wall** to spell **wail**. The wind blew very hard and began to **wail**."

Always alert children when they are making a name and expect them to use a capital letter.

"Change 1 letter in **mill** to spell the name **Will**."

Give children one minute to figure out the secret word and then give clues, if needed.

"Our secret word is a name that you can make by adding your letters to **Will**."

Sort Beginning Letters (Optional)

Sort Rhymes

Reading Transfer: "Pretend you are reading and come to a new word." Have children put the words under the appropriate rhymes and use the rhymes to decode them.

Spelling Transfer: "Pretend you are writing and need to spell these words." Have children tell you how the words begin. Then, have children find and use the appropriate rhymes to finish spelling the new words.

Step-by-step directions for a sample *Making Names* lesson are on pages 8-12.

Wolfgang

a o f g g l n w

Make Words: Tell children how many letters to use to make each word. (A slash indicates words that can be made with the same letters.)

Emphasize how changing just one letter or rearranging letters makes a different word.

> "Add a letter to **lag** to spell **flag**."

> "Use the same letters in **flow** to spell **wolf**."

When children are not just adding or changing one letter, cue them to start over.

> "Start over and use 4 new letters to spell **gang**."

Give a meaning or sentence clue, when needed, to clarify the word children are making.

> "Change a letter in **gang** to spell **fang**. A **fang** is a very large tooth."

Give children one minute to figure out the secret word and then give clues, if needed. Always alert children when they are making a name and expect them to use a capital letter.

> "Our secret word is a name that you can make by adding your letters to **wolf**."

Sort Beginning Letters (Optional)

Sort Rhymes

Reading Transfer: "Pretend you are reading and come to a new word." Have children put the transfer words under the appropriate rhymes and use the rhymes to decode them.

Spelling Transfer: "Pretend you are writing and need to spell these words." Have children tell you how the words begin. Then, have children find and use the appropriate rhymes to finish spelling the transfer words.

Step-by-step directions for a sample *Making Names* lesson are on pages 8-12.

MAKE WORDS

owl/low
law
lag
flag
lawn
gang
fang
glow
flow/wolf
wagon
Wolfgang

SORT WORDS

Beginning Letters (Optional)

Rhymes:
low	lag	gang
flow	flag	fang
glow		

TRANSFER WORDS

Reading:
brag know

Spelling:
clang grow

Yolanda

a a o d l n y

MAKE WORDS

no/on
Don
Dan/and
any
day
lay
lady
Lana
land
Andy
only
Dylan
Yolanda

SORT WORDS

Beginning Letters (Optional)

Rhymes:

on	and	day
Don	land	lay

TRANSFER WORDS

Reading:
strand stray

Spelling:
clan clay

Make Words: Tell children how many letters to use to make each word. (A slash indicates words that can be made with the same letters.)

Emphasize how changing just one letter or rearranging letters makes a different word.

> "Add a letter to **lay** to spell **lady**."

> "Use the same letters in **Dan** to spell **and**."

When children are not just adding or changing one letter, cue them to start over.

> "Start over and use 4 new letters to spell the name **Lana**."

Give a meaning or sentence clue, when needed, to clarify the word children are making.

> "Start over and use 4 new letters to spell **only**. There was **only** one cookie left."

Always alert children when they are making a name and expect them to use a capital letter.

> "Add a letter to **on** to spell the name **Don**."

Give children one minute to figure out the secret word and then give clues, if needed.

> "Our secret word is a name that begins with **Y** and ends with **a**."

Sort Beginning Letters (Optional)

Sort Rhymes

Reading Transfer: "Pretend you are reading and come to a new word." Have children put the transfer words under the appropriate rhymes and use the rhymes to decode them.

Spelling Transfer: "Pretend you are writing and need to spell these words." Have children tell you how the words begin. Then, have children find and use the appropriate rhymes to finish spelling the transfer words.

Step-by-step directions for a sample *Making Names* lesson are on pages 8-12.

Name	Lesson(s) Containing That Name
Abe	Belinda* Bernard* Bertha* Bethany* Bradley* Gabriel* Gabriella* Isabella* Rebecca*
Abigail*	
Adam	Madonna*
Al	Abigail* Albert* Alfred* Alisha* Alison* Angelina* Ashley* Carlos* Gabriella* Isabella* Loraine* Malcolm* Manuel* Marshall* Melissa* Michael* Nicholas* Pamela* Priscilla* Rafael* Roland/Ronald* Salvador* Samuel* Shaquille* Sheila*
Alan	Alexander* Alexandra* Nathaniel*
Albert*	
Alex	Alexander* Alexandra*
Alexander*	
Alexandra*	
Alfred*	
Ali	Alison* Natalie*
Alisha*	
Alison*	
Amy	Marilyn* Marty* Raymond* Rosemary*
Andrea	Alexander* Alexandra*
Andrew*	
Andy	Brandy* Yolanda*
Angel	Angelina*
Angela	Angelina*
Angelina*	
Angie	Angelina*
Anita	Juanita* Martina* Natalie*
Ann	Angelina* Anthony* Fernando*
Anna	Angelina* Brianna* Madonna*
Anne	Fernando*
Anthony*	
April	Priscilla*
Arlo	Carlos* Carlotta* Taylor*
Art	Bertha* Brittany* Bryant* Carlotta* Carlton* Carter* Crystal* Grant* Kathryn* Loretta* Martin* Marty* Patricia* Roberta* Taylor* Tracy* Trisha* Victoria*
Ashley*	
Ashton*	
Austin*	
Barney*	
Barry	Hildaberry*

(An asterisk indicates names that are secret words. A slash indicates names that can be made with the same letters.)

Name	Lesson(s) Containing That Name
Bart	Bertha* Brittany* Bryant* Roberta*
Bea	Belinda* Bernard* Bertha* Bethany* Blanche* Bradley* Gabriella* Isabella* Rebecca*
Belinda*	
Bella	Gabriella* Isabella*
Ben	Belinda* Benjamin* Blanche* Brenda* Brent*
Benjamin*	
Benji	Benjamin*
Bernard*	
Bert	Albert* Bertha* Brent*
Bertha*	
Beth	Bertha* Bethany* Elizabeth*
Bethany*	
Bill	Gabriella* Isabella* Kimball*
Blanche*	
Bo	Deborah* Roberta*
Brad	Bernard* Bradley* Brandon* Brandy* Brenda* Deborah* Hildaberry*
Bradley*	
Brandon*	
Brandy*	
Brenda*	Bernard*
Brent*	
Brian	Brianna* Brittany*
Brianna*	
Bridget*	
Brittany*	
Bryant*	
Cameron*	
Carl	Carlos* Carlotta* Carlton* Charles* Clarence* Scarlet*
Carlos*	
Carlotta*	
Carlton*	
Carol	Carlos* Carlotta* Carlton* Carolyn* Charlotte*
Carolyn*	
Carter*	
Cary	Carolyn* Crystal* Tracy*
Casey	Stacey*
Casper*	
Cassandra*	
Catherine*	
Cathy	Cynthia*
Celia	Michael*
Chad	Richard*

(An asterisk indicates names that are secret words. A slash indicates names that can be made with the same letters.)

Making Names • CD-2429 • © Carson-Dellosa

Name	Lesson(s) Containing That Name
Charisse*	
Charlene*	
Charles*	
Charlotte*	
Chester*	
Chet	Charlotte* Chester* Gretchen* Mitchell*
Chris	Charisse* Christian/Christina* Christopher* Christy*
Christian/Christina*	
Christopher*	
Christy*	
Clarence*	
Cleo	Jocelyn*
Cliff	Clifford*
Clifford*	
Clint	Clinton*
Clinton*	
Cole	Nicole*
Cora	Carlos* Carlotta* Carolyn* Charlotte* Victoria*
Courtney*	
Crystal*	
Cynthia*	
Dale	Alexandra* Alfred* Darlene* Darrell* Kendall* Leonardo*
Dameon*	
Dan	Brandy* Brenda* Cassandra* Dameon* Daniel* Danielle* Daphne* Darlene* Deshawn* Hernando* Kendra* Linda* Madison* Madonna* Miranda* Randolph* Reginald* Roland/Ronald* Rosalind* Sanford* Shandra* Yolanda*
Daniel*	Danielle* Geraldine* Reginald*
Danielle*	
Daphne*	
Darlene*	
Darrell*	
Dawn	Deshawn*
Dean	Alexandra* Andrew* Brenda* Dameon* Danielle* Daphne* Deshawn* Fernando* Hernando* Kendall* Kendra* Leonardo*
Deb	Deborah*
Deborah*	
Del	Darrell* Lindsey*
Delia	Danielle* Madeline*
Delores*	
Derrick*	Frederick*
Deshawn*	
Destiny*	

(An asterisk indicates names that are secret words. A slash indicates names that can be made with the same letters.)

Name	Lesson(s) Containing That Name
Diane	Belinda* Danielle* Geraldine* Reginald*
Dick	Derrick* Frederick* Kendrick*
Dina	Linda*
Dominique*	
Don	Brandon* Dameon* Dominique* Fernando* Gordon* Hernando* Leonardo* Madonna* Randolph* Raymond* Roland/Ronald* Rosalind* Sanford* Yolanda*
Donna	Brandon* Fernando* Hernando* Madonna*
Dora	Raymond* Salvador* Sanford*
Dorothy*	
Doug	Douglas*
Douglas*	
Drew	Andrew*
Dylan	Yolanda*
Earl	Charlene* Charlotte* Darrell* Garfield* Rachel*
Ed	Alexandra* Alfred* Bernard* Bridget* Dameon* Delores* Destiny* Dominique* Fernando* Kendall* Meredith* Mohammed* Theodore*
Edith	Meredith*
Edna	Belinda* Danielle* Daphne* Geraldine* Hernando*
Elaina	Natalie*
Elaine	Madeline* Melanie*
Eleanor*	
Eliza	Elizabeth*
Elizabeth*	
Ella	Darrell* Gabriella* Shaquille*
Eric	Charisse* Derrick* Frederick* Veronica*
Erica	Charisse* Veronica*
Erin	Geraldine* Hermione* Jennifer* Jermaine* Katherine* Loraine* Sterling*
Ernest*	
Ernie	Geraldine* Henrietta* Hermione* Jennifer*
Ethan*	
Eve	Roosevelt* Steven*
Fay	Tiffany*
Fernando*	
Fran	Frances* Francisco* Franklin*
Frances*	
Francis	Francisco*
Francisco*	
Frank	Franklin*
Franklin*	
Fred	Alfred* Fernando* Frederick*
Frederick*	
Gabe	Gabriel* Gabriella*

(An asterisk indicates names that are secret words. A slash indicates names that can be made with the same letters.)

Making Names • CD-2429 • © Carson-Dellosa

Name	Lesson(s) Containing That Name
Gabriel*	Gabriella*
Gabriella*	
Gail	Abigail* Gabriel* Garfield* Geraldine* Reginald*
Garfield*	
Georgia*	
Gerald	Geraldine*
Geraldine*	
Gina	Angelina* Reginald*
Gordon*	
Grace*	
Grant*	
Greg	Georgia*
Gretchen*	
Hal	Alisha* Ashley* Hildaberry* Marshall* Michael* Nicholas* Raphael* Shaquille* Sheila*
Hank	Kathleen* Kathryn*
Harold*	
Harriet*	
Harry	Hildaberry*
Hazel	Elizabeth*
Heather*	
Henrietta*	
Hermione*	
Hernando*	
Hilary	Hildaberry*
Hilda	Hildaberry*
Hildaberry*	
Homer	Hermione*
Hunter*	
Ian	Benjamin* Brianna* Francisco* Kaitlyn* Mackenzie* Madison* Marilyn* Marvin* Miranda* Pauline*
Ida	Linda* Madison*
Ira	Francisco* Georgia* Loraine* Marisol* Martina* Marvin* Miranda* Patrick* Trisha* Victoria*
Irene	Katherine*
Isabella*	
Jack	Jackson*
Jackson*	
Jacqueline*	
Jamie	Jasmine*
Jan	Benjamin* Jacqueline* Janet* Jermaine* Jonathan* Juanita*
Jane	Benjamin* Jacqueline* Janet* Jasmine*

(An asterisk indicates names that are secret words. A slash indicates names that can be made with the same letters.)

Name	Lesson(s) Containing That Name
Janet*	
Jarrett*	
Jasmine*	
Jason	Jackson*
Jean	Benjamin* Jacqueline* Janet* Jasmine* Jermaine*
Jen	Benjamin* Jacqueline* Janet* Jennifer* Jermaine* Jocelyn*
Jennie	Jennifer*
Jennifer*	
Jermaine*	
Jim	Jasmine*
Jocelyn*	
Joe	Jocelyn* Joseph* Josephine*
Joel	Jocelyn*
Joey	Jocelyn*
John	Jonathan* Josephine*
Jon	Jackson* Jocelyn*
Jonah	Jonathan*
Jonathan*	
Joseph*	Josephine*
Josephine*	
Josh	Joseph* Josephine*
Joy	Jocelyn*
Joyce	Jocelyn*
Juan	Juanita*
Juanita*	
Julia	Jacqueline*
Julian	Jacqueline*
June	Jacqueline* Justine*
Justin	Justine*
Justine*	
Kaitlyn*	
Karen	Katherine* Kendra*
Kate	Katherine* Kathleen* Tameka*
Katherine*	
Kathleen*	
Kathryn*	
Kathy	Kathryn*
Katie	Katherine*
Katy	Kaitlyn*
Kay	Kaitlyn* Kathryn*
Ken	Kathleen* Kendall* Kendra* Kendrick* Kirsten/Kristen* Mackenzie*
Kendall*	

(An asterisk indicates names that are secret words. A slash indicates names that can be made with the same letters.)

230

Name	Lesson(s) Containing That Name
Kendra*	
Kendrick*	
Keri	Derrick* Katherine*
Kesha	Lakesha*
Kim	Kimball* Kimberly*
Kimball*	
Kimberly*	
Kirsten/Kristen*	
Kit	Kaitlyn* Kirsten/Kristen*
Kris	Kirsten/Kristen*
Kristina*	
Kurt	Tucker*
Kyle	Kimberly*
Lakesha*	
Lana	Yolanda*
Lane	Blanche* Charlene* Daniel* Lawrence* Madeline* Manuel* Melanie* Nathaniel* Pauline*
Langston*	
Larry	Hildaberry*
Lawrence*	
Leah	Ashley* Rachel* Raphael* Shaquille*
Lee	Michelle* Roosevelt* Shelley
Len	Belinda* Jocelyn* Kathleen* Lindsey* Loraine* Nathaniel* Nicole*
Lena	Eleanor*
Leo	Jocelyn* Leonardo* Othello*
Leon	Leonardo* Nicole*
Leonard	Leonardo*
Leonardo*	
Lew	Maxwell*
Lila	Kimball* Willard* William*
Linda*	Belinda* Daniel* Danielle* Rosalind*
Lindsey*	
Lisa	Alisha* Alison* Isabella* Marisol* Melissa* Nicholas* Priscilla* Rosalind* Shaquille* Sheila*
Liz	Elizabeth*
Lois	Marisol* Nicholas* Rosalind*
Loraine*	
Loretta*	
Lori	Clifford* Loraine* Marisol*
Mack	Mackenzie*
Mackenzie*	
Madeline*	

(An asterisk indicates names that are secret words. A slash indicates names that can be made with the same letters.)

231

Name	Lesson(s) Containing That Name
Madison*	
Madonna*	
Malcolm*	
Mandy	Raymond*
Manuel*	
Margaret*	
Marge	Margaret* Margie*
Margie*	
Maria	Martina* Miranda*
Marie	Jermaine* Margie*
Marilyn*	
Marisol*	
Marsha	Marshall*
Marshall*	
Martin*	Martina*
Martina*	
Marty*	
Marvin*	
Mary	Marilyn* Marty* Raymond* Rosemary*
Matt	Matthew*
Matthew*	
Max	Maxwell*
Maxwell*	
May	Marilyn* Marty* Raymond* Rosemary*
Meg	Margaret* Margie*
Melanie*	
Melissa*	
Meredith*	
Michael*	
Michelle*	
Mick	Mackenzie*
Mike	Kimberly* Mackenzie*
Miranda*	
Mitch	Mitchell*
Mitchell*	
Mo	Mohammed*
Mohammed*	
Mona	Madison* Madonna*
Monique	Dominique*
Morgan*	
Myra	Marilyn* Marty* Rosemary*
Nan	Brianna* Hernando* Madonna*

(An asterisk indicates names that are secret words. A slash indicates names that can be made with the same letters.)

Making Names • CD-2429 • © Carson-Dellosa

Name	Lesson(s) Containing That Name
Nat	Anthony* Cynthia* Ethan* Grant* Jonathan* Juanita* Langston* Natalie* Nathaniel* Stephanie* Tiffany*
Natalie*	
Nate	Ethan* Natalie* Nathaniel* Stephanie*
Nathan	Jonathan* Nathaniel*
Nathaniel*	
Ned	Alexander* Alexandra* Bernard* Brenda* Destiny* Fernando* Kendall*
Neil	Belinda* Danielle* Madeline* Melanie* Nathaniel* Nicole*
Nellie	Danielle*
Nicholas*	
Nick	Kendrick* Mackenzie*
Nicole*	
Nina	Angelina* Franklin*
Noah	Anthony* Ashton* Jonathan*
Nola	Langston* Roland/Ronald*
Nora	Cameron* Eleanor* Loraine* Morgan* Raymond* Roland/Ronald* Sanford*
Ola	Douglas* Harold*
Oscar	Carlos*
Othello*	
Pam	Pamela*
Pamela*	
Pat	Patricia* Patrick* Patsy*
Patricia*	
Patrick*	
Patsy*	
Paul	Pauline*
Pauline*	
Phyllis*	
Prescott*	
Preston*	
Priscilla*	
Quentin*	
Rachel*	
Ralph	Randolph* Raphael*
Randolph*	
Randy	Brandy* Raymond*
Raphael*	
Ray	Barney* Bradley* Brandy* Brittany* Bryant* Carolyn* Kathryn* Marilyn* Marty* Raymond* Rosemary* Taylor* Tracy*
Raymond*	
Rebecca*	
Regina	Reginald*

(An asterisk indicates names that are secret words. A slash indicates names that can be made with the same letters.)

Name	Lesson(s) Containing That Name
Reginald*	
Rex	Alexander* Alexandra*
Rich	Christy* Richard*
Richard*	
Rick	Derrick* Frederick* Kendrick* Patrick*
Rita	Catherine* Christian/Christina* Harriet* Henrietta* Kristina* Martin* Martina* Patricia* Trisha*
Rob	Brandon* Deborah* Roberta*
Robert	Roberta*
Roberta*	
Rod	Brandon* Deborah* Delores* Dorothy* Fernando* Gordon* Harold* Rudolph* Salvador*
Roland/Ronald*	
Ron	Cameron* Eleanor* Fernando* Gordon* Hermione* Hernando* Leonardo* Morgan* Preston* Randolph* Raymond* Roland/Ronald* Rosalind* Sanford* Tyrone* Veronica*
Roosevelt*	
Rosa	Rosalind* Rosemary*
Rosalind*	
Rose	Roosevelt* Rosemary*
Rosemary*	
Roy	Courtney* Dorothy* Rosemary* Taylor*
Rudolph*	
Ryan	Brittany* Bryant*
Sal	Alisha* Alison* Ashley* Carlos* Isabella* Melissa* Nicholas* Salvador* Samuel* Shaquille* Sheila*
Salvador*	
Sam	Jasmine* Marshall* Melissa* Rosemary* Samantha* Samuel*
Samantha*	
Samuel*	
Sandra	Cassandra* Shandra*
Sanford*	
Sara	Shandra*
Sarah	Shandra*
Scarlet*	
Scott	Prescott*
Seth	Stephen*
Shandra*	
Shane	Deshawn* Stephanie*
Shaquille*	
Shawn	Deshawn*
Sheila*	

(An asterisk indicates names that are secret words. A slash indicates names that can be made with the same letters.)

Making Names • CD-2429 • © Carson-Dellosa

Name	Lesson(s) Containing That Name
Shelley*	
Stacey*	
Stacy	Crystal*
Stan	Austin* Kristina* Langston*
Stephanie*	
Stephen*	Stephanie*
Sterling*	
Steve	Roosevelt* Steven*
Steven*	
Sue	Justine* Samuel*
Taffy	Tiffany*
Tameka*	
Tara	Margaret* Martina* Patricia*
Taylor*	
Ted	Bridget* Destiny* Meredith* Theodore*
Theo	Othello* Theodore*
Theodore*	
Thomas*	
Tiffany*	
Tim	Martin* Meredith* Mitchell*
Tina	Austin* Catherine* Christian/Christina* Henrietta* Juanita* Kristina* Martin* Martina* Natalie*
Tom	Thomas*
Tony	Anthony* Courtney* Tyrone*
Tory	Tyrone*
Tracy*	Crystal*
Trisha*	Christian/Christina*
Troy	Courtney* Dorothy* Taylor* Tyrone*
Tucker*	
Ty	Patsy* Tyrone*
Tyrone*	
Val	Salvador*
Vera	Veronica*
Veronica*	
Victor	Victoria*
Victoria*	
Vincent*	
Ward	Andrew* Willard*
Whitney*	
Will	Willard* William*
Willard*	
William*	

(An asterisk indicates names that are secret words. A slash indicates names that can be made with the same letters.)

Name	Lesson(s) Containing That Name
Wilma	William*
Wolfgang*	
Yolanda*	
Zack	Mackenzie*
Zeb	Elizabeth*

(An asterisk indicates names that are secret words. A slash indicates names that can be made with the same letters.)

Making Names • CD-2429 • © Carson-Dellosa

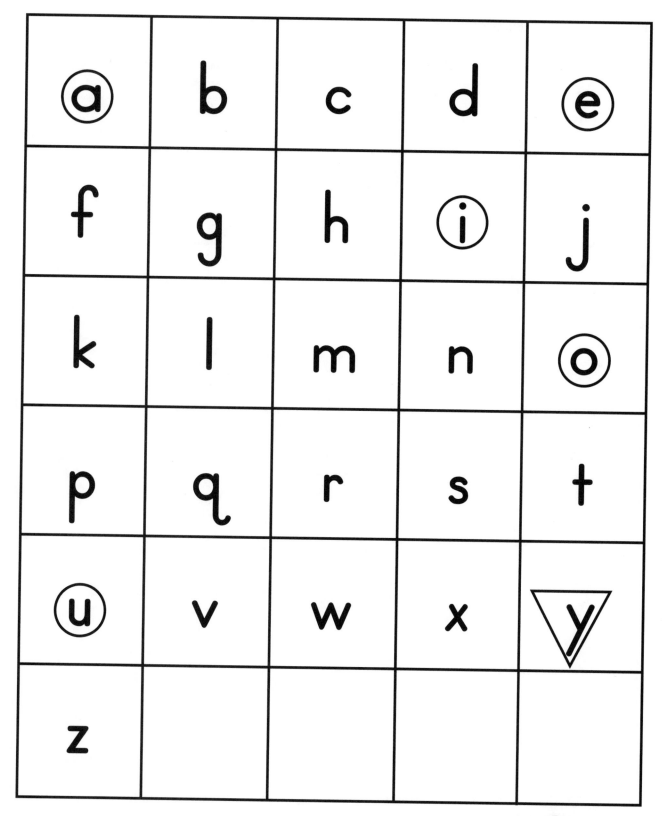

a	b	c	d	e
f	g	h	i	j
k	l	m	n	o
p	q	r	s	t
u	v	w	x	y
z				

E	D	C	B	A
J	I	H	G	F
O	N	M	L	K
T	S	R	Q	P
Y	X	W	V	U
				Z

Making Names • CD-2429 • © Carson-Dellosa

Making Names Take-Home Sheet

Making Words: Lessons for Home or School—Grade 1 by Patricia M. Cunningham and Dorothy P. Hall (Carson-Dellosa, 2001)

Making Words: Lessons for Home or School—Grade 2 by Patricia M. Cunningham and Dorothy P. Hall (Carson-Dellosa, 2001)

Making Words: Lessons for Home or School—Grade 3 by Patricia M. Cunningham and Dorothy P. Hall (Carson-Dellosa, 2001)

Making Words: Lessons for Home or School—Grade 4 by Patricia M. Cunningham and Dorothy P. Hall (Carson-Dellosa, 2001)

Making Words: Multilevel, Hands-On, Developmentally Appropriate Spelling and Phonics Activities by Patricia M. Cunningham and Dorothy P. Hall (Good Apple, 1994)

Michael Jordan: Basketball Superstar by Rob Kirkpatrick (Powerkids Press, 2003)